KU-335-934

CHARMING SMALL HOTEL GUIDES

SPAIN

CHARMING SMALL HOTEL GUIDES

SPAIN

Including the Balearic and Canary Islands

EDITED BY

Tamara Grosvenor

Consultant Editor
Nick Inman

DUNCAN PETERSEN

This new, expanded 2004 edition conceived, designed and produced by
Duncan Petersen Publishing Ltd,
31 Ceylon Road, London W14 OPY

Editorial Director Andrew Duncan
Editor Tamara Grosvenor
Consultant editor Nick Inman
Contributing editors Luke Glass, Helen Varley and Jane Anson
Production Editor Sophie Page
Maps Map Creation
Thanks also to Kate Fortescue

This edition published 2004 by
Duncan Petersen Publishing Ltd,
31 Ceylon Road, London W14 OPY

Visit Duncan Petersen's travel website at:
www.charmingsmallhotels.com

Sales representation and distribution in the U.K. and Ireland by
Portfolio Books Limited
Unit 5, Perivale Industrial Park
Horsenden South Lane
Greenford, UB6 7RL
Tel: 0208 997 9000 Fax: 0208 997 9097
E-mail sales@portfoliobooks.com

A CIP catalogue record for this book is available
from the British Library

ISBN 1-903301-35-1

DTP by Duncan Petersen Publishing Ltd
Printed by E.G. Zure, Spain

Contents

INTRODUCTION

IN THIS INTRODUCTORY SECTION

Welcome to this new, expanded edition of *Charming Small Hotel Guides Spain.* Continuing the pattern we began with our recent new editions of France, Italy, Britain and Germany, we've introduced some big changes:

• *Every hotel now has a colour photograph and a full (or half) page of its own. No more entries without a photograph.*

• *The maps have been upgraded.*

• *The layout has been changed in order to take you more quickly to essential booking information.*

We hope that you will think these real improvements, rather than change for its own sake. In all other respects, the guide remains true to the values and qualities that make it unique (see opposite), and which have won it so many devoted readers. This is its ninth update since it was first published in 1991. It has sold hundreds of thousands of copies in the U.K., U.S.A. and in five European languages.

WHY ARE WE UNIQUE?

This is the only independently-inspected (no hotel pays for an entry) UK-originated accommodation guide that:

- has colour photographs for every entry;

- concentrates on places that have real charm and character;

- is highly selective;

- is particularly fussy about size. Most hotels have fewer than 20 bedrooms; if there are more, the hotel must have the feel of a much smaller place. We have found that a genuinely warm welcome is much more likely to be found in a small hotel;

- gives proper emphasis to the description, and doesn't use irritating symbols;

- is produced by a small, non-bureaucratic company with a dedicated team of like-minded inspectors.

See also *'So what exactly do we look for?'*, page 8.

SO WHAT EXACTLY DO WE LOOK FOR? –
OUR SELECTION CRITERIA

• A peaceful, attractive setting. Obviously, if the entry is in an urban area, we make allowances.

• A building that is handsome, interesting or historic; or at least with real character.

• Adequate space, but on a human scale. We don't go for places that rely too much on grandeur, or with pretensions that could be intimidating.

• Good taste and imagination in the interior decoration. We reject standardized, chain hotel fixtures, fittings and decorations.

• Bedrooms that look like real bedrooms, not hotel rooms, individually decorated.

• Furnishings and other facilities that are comfortable and well maintained. We like to see interesting antique furniture that is there to be used, not simply revered.

• Proprietors and staff who are dedicated and thoughtful, offering a personal welcome, but who aren't intrusive or overly effusive. *The guest needs to feel like an individual.*

• Interesting food. In Spain, it's increasingly the norm for food to be above average. There are few entries in this guide where the food is not of a high standard.

• A sympathetic atmosphere; an absence of loud people showing off their money; or the 'corporate feel'.

Palacio de Bentraces

A FATTER GUIDE, BUT JUST AS SELECTIVE

Our selection criteria are the same in Spain as they are elsewhere. We aim to include only those places that are in some way captivating, with a distinctive personality, and which offer a truly personal service. While being highly selective, we also give as broad a range of recommendations as possible, to suit all budgets; and as hotels are often fully booked, it is useful to have alternatives. For a detailed summary of our selection criteria, see opposite.

In Spain, as elswhere in Europe, we found many hotels which easily satisfied our highly selective approach, but there are a significant number which, though basically recommendable, for one reason or another fall short of our ideal. The description of each hotel makes this distinction clear. However, be assured that all the hotels in the guide are, one way or another, true to the concept of the charming small hotel.

In making our selection, we have been careful to bear in mind the many different requirements of our readers. Some will be backpackers; others will be millionaires; the vast majority will fall between the two.

TYPES OF ACCOMMODATION IN THIS GUIDE

Ideally, our recommendations have fewer than 30 bedrooms, but this is not a rigid requirement. Many hotels with more than 30 bedrooms feel much smaller, and you will find such places in this guide. We attach more importance to size than other guides because we think that unless a hotel is small, it cannot give a genuinely personal welcome, or make you feel like an individual, rather than just a guest. Unlike other guides, we often rule out places that have great qualities, but are nevertheless no more nor less than – hotels. Our hotels are special in some way.

We think that we have a much clearer idea than other guides of what is special and what is not: and we think we apply these criteria more consistently than other guides because we are a small and personally managed company rather than a bureaucracy. We have a small team of like-minded inspectors, thoroughly rehearsed in recognizing what we want. While we very much appreciate readers' reports they are not our main source of information.

Hotel Carmen de Santa Ines

NO FEAR OR FAVOUR

To us, taking a payment for appearing in a guide seems to defeat the object of producing a guide. If money has changed hands, you can't write the whole truth about a hotel, and the selection cannot be nearly so interesting. This self-evident truth seems to us to be proved at least in part by the fact that pay guides are so keen to present the illusion of independence: few admit on the cover that they take payments for an entry, only doing so in small print on the inside. Not many people realize that on bookshop shelves there are many more hotel guides that accept payments for entries than there are independent guides. This guide is one of the few that do not accept any money for an entry.

HOME FROM HOME

Perhaps the most beguiling characteristic of the best places to stay in this guide is the feeling they give of being in a private home – but without the everyday cares and chores of running one. To get this formula right requires a special sort of professionalism: the proprietor has to strike the balance between being relaxed and giving attentive service. Those who experience this 'feel' often turn their backs on all other forms of accommodation – however luxurious.

THE SPANISH HOTEL SCENE

When we first put together this guide in the early 1990's, it was hard to fill 200 pages with recommendable places. Now it is easy to fill 300. Charming old buildings by the hundred have been artfully restored by owners with a flair for design and a talent for creating that omfortable 'home from home' feel which is basic to our selection criteria. Sometimes, however, the welcome and the service falls short of the outward style, and we have tried to reflect this in our selections.

The state-run chain of Paradores are a special feature of Spain and dominate the Spanish hotel scene just as many of the castles the hotels occupy dominate the surrounding landscape. In this guide, we take a highly selective approach to paradores, just as with other places to stay. We give full-page features only to those we like; however we mention many others as useful extra addresses in the area introductions that begin each section. Paradores are not the best hotels in Spain, and few of them are notably good by absolute standards – though in any given locality the Parador is quite likely to be the best in town, for the simple reason that many have been created in areas which private enterprise might not find attractive. But Paradores do have attractions: many are set in wonderfully atmospheric old buildings – mansions, convents, hunting lodges as well as magnificent castles – and many others have spectacular mountain settings. Others are simply very convenient for the traveller on the road, being strategically positioned to fill gaps on the map of Spain.

In terms of their qualities as places to stay, Paradores are much less impressive. Their strong point, usually, is the bedrooms, which are normally very spacious and well furnished. Public rooms may be comfortable and inviting, but may equally be dismally furnished and gloomy. Food, which aims to reflect regional traditions, may be highly satisfactory or extremely ordinary. Service is equally unpredictable, and seems to depend more on individual initiative than any management policy.

CHECK THE PRICE FIRST

In this guide we have adopted the system of price bands, rather than giving actual prices. This is because prices often change after we go to press. The price bands refer to the approximate price of a standard double room (high season rates) with breakfast for two people. They are as follows:

€	less than 50 Euros
€€	50-100 Euros
€€€	100-150 Euros
€€€€	over 150 Euros

To avoid unpleasant surprises, always check what is included in the price (for example, VAT and service, breakfast, afternoon tea, local taxes) when making the booking.

HOW TO FIND AN ENTRY

In this guide, the entries are arranged by province, and the provinces are clustered in convenient regional groups. The regions, and within them the provinces, are arranged in a sequence starting in the extreme north-west (La Coruña) and working west to east and north to south. The Canary Islands come last in the sequence.

Within each regional section the entries follow a set sequence: first comes an **Area Introduction** – an overview of the accommodation scene in that region, together with a few extra addresses of places which didn't quite deserve a full entry, but which might be useful if our main choices are booked up. Next come the full entries themselves, arranged alphabetically by city, town or nearest village. If several occur in or near one town, entries are arranged in alpha order by name of hotel.

To find a hotel in a particular area, use the maps following this introduction to locate the appropriate pages.

To locate a specific hotel, whose name you know, or a hotel in a place you know, use the indexes at the back, which list entries both by name and by nearest place name.

HOW TO READ AN ENTRY

ASTURIAS

EL ALLENDE

LA MONTAÑA MÁGICA
～ MOUNTAIN HOTEL ～

33508 Ouanda, El Allende, Llanes, Asturias
TEL 985 925176 **FAX** 985 925780
WEBSITE www.lamontanamagica.com

ROUGHLY HALF way between San Sebastián and Coruña, there is no danger of confusing this delightful mountain hotel with Thomas Mann's book of the same name. Only 10 km from the best beaches of Llanes, La Montaña Mágica is literally at the end of a mountain road which squeezes past a farm where Asturian mountain ponies are kept for trekking, and then pushes on another half kilometre to a wonderful mountain meadow site. The view, like the air, is brilliant and apart from the mountains you can actually see, there are other peaks and gorges, rivers and five-star caves (decorated and plain) all within a 25 km radius.

Carlos and Pilar started with a broken-down farmstead and have brought sections of it into play as the hotel has prospered – he recently bought himself a bulldozer to move bits of mountain for the next great plan, which is to be a spa with the sort of view that money can scarcely afford. The bedrooms are smooth rustic with plenty of wood everywhere, and the sort of bathrooms most of us are still saving up for. As well as a substantial breakfast, you can order an excellent regional dinner to be ready on your return from the day's activities. There are two living rooms, in separate buildings, so if you don't care for the company in one, you can always migrate to the other.

NEARBY Los Picos de Europa (24 km); Cangas de Onis (23 km); caves of Tito Bustillo, El Pindal, El Buxu and Peña Tú (25 km); beaches (10 km).
LOCATION at end of mountain road high in the Sierra de la Cubeta; ample parking
FOOD breakfast, dinner by arrangement
PRICE €€
ROOMS 14 doubles (5 twin-bedded, 2 suites); all rooms have bath, shower, TV, hair drier
FACILITIES 2 sitting rooms, library, bar, dining room, access to workshop, stables and greenhouse **CREDIT CARDS** AE, DC, MC, V **CHILDREN** welcome
DISABLED one specially adapted room **PETS** not accepted **CLOSED** never
PROPRIETORS Carlos Bueno Sanchez, Pilar Pando Cortes

Name of hotel

Type of establishment

Description – never vetted by the hotel

Places of interest within reach of the hotel

This sets the hotel in its geographical context and should not be taken as precise instructions as to how to get there; always ask the hotel for directions.

Rooms described as having a bath usually also have a shower; rooms described as having a shower only have a shower.

Essential booking information.

This information is only an indication for wheelchair users and the infirm. Always check on suitability with the hotel.

City, town or village, and region, in which the hotel is located.

Some or all the public rooms and bedrooms in an increasing number of hotels are now non-smoking. Smokers should check the hotel's policy when booking.

Telephoning Italy from abroad
To call Spain from the U.K. or U.S.A., dial 00, then the international dialling code 39, then dial the number, including the initial 0.

Postal address and other key information.

Children are almost always accepted, usually welcomed, in Italian hotels. There are often special facilities, such as cots, high chairs, baby listening and early supper. Check first if they may join parents in the dining room.

Breakfast, is normally included in the price of the room. We have not quoted prices for lunch and dinner. Other meals, such as afternoon tea, may also be available. 'Room service' refers to food and drink, either snacks or full meals, which can be served in the room.

We list the following credit cards:
AE American Express
DC Diners Club
MC Mastercard
V   Visa

Always let the hotel know in advance if you want to bring a pet. Even where pets are accepted, certain restrictions may apply, and a small charge may be levied.

In this guide we have used price bands rather than quoting actual prices. They refer to a standard double room (high season rates, if applicable) with breakfast for two people. Other rates – for other room categories, times of the year, weekend breaks, long stays and so on – may well be available. In some hotels, usually out-of-the-way places or restaurants-with-rooms – half-board is obligatory. Always check when booking. The price bands are as follows:

€   less than 50 Euros
€€   50-100 Euros
€€€   100-150 Euros
€€€€   over 150 Euros

REPORTING TO THE GUIDE

Please write and tell us about your experiences of small hotels, guest houses and inns, whether good or bad, whether listed in this edition or not. As well as hotels in Spain, we are interested in hotels in France, Italy, Austria, Germany, Switzerland and the U.S.A. We assume that reporters have no objections to our publishing their views unpaid.

Readers whose reports prove particularly helpful may be invited to join our Travellers' Panel. Members give us notice of their own travel plans; we suggest hotels that they might inspect, and help with the cost of accommodation.

The address to write to us is:

Editor, *Charming Small Hotel Guides*,
Duncan Petersen Publishing Limited,
31 Ceylon Road,
London W14 0PY.

Checklist
Please use a separate sheet of paper for each report; include your name, address and telephone number on each report.

Your reports will be received with particular pleasure if they are typed, and if they are organized under the following headings:

Name of establishment
Town or village it is in, or nearest
Full address, including postcode
Telephone number
Time and duration of visit
The building and setting
The public rooms
The bedrooms and bathrooms
Physical comfort (chairs, beds, heat, light, hot water)
Standards of maintenance and housekeeping
Atmosphere, welcome and service
Food
Value for money

We assume that in writing you have no objections to your views being published unpaid, either verbatim or in an edited version. Names of major outside contributors are acknowledged, at the editor's discretion, in the guide.

HOTEL LOCATION MAPS

16 - 17
18 - 19
20 - 21
26
22 - 23
24 - 25

27 Canary Islands

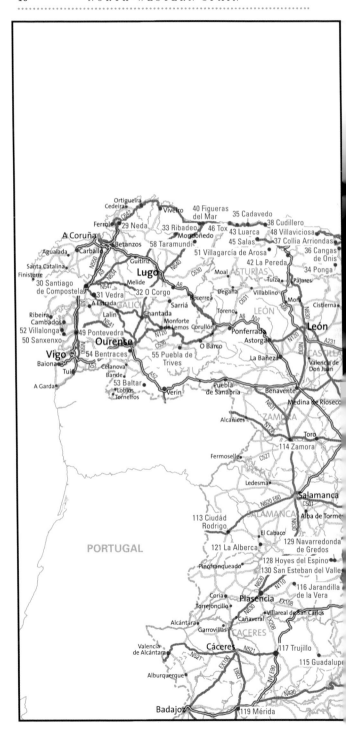

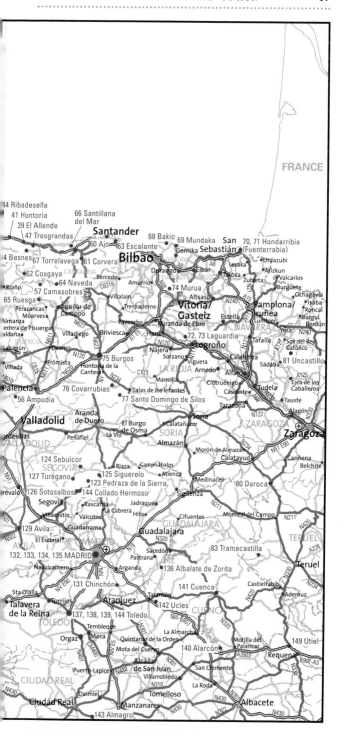

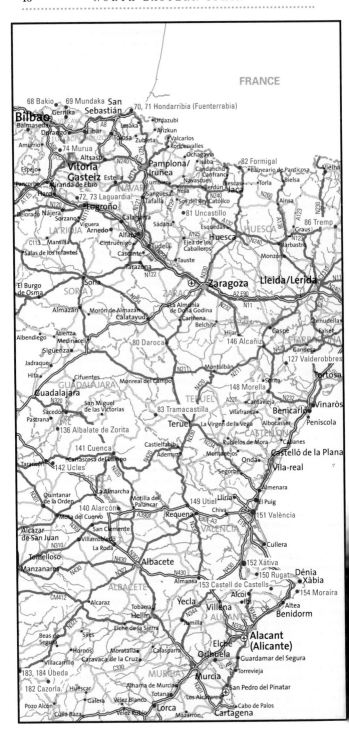

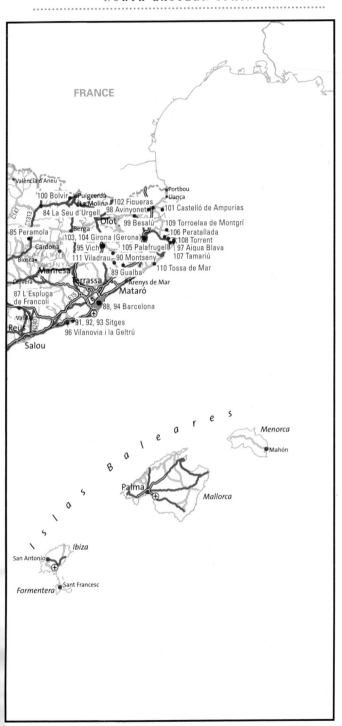

FRANCE

València d'Aneu
'100 Bolvir' Puigcerdà
La Molina 102 Figueras
84 La Seu d'Urgell 98 Avinyonet
Olot
85 Peramola Berga 99 Besalú 109 Torroelaa de Montgrí
103, 104 Girona (Gerona) 106 Peratallada
Cardona 95 Vich 105 Palafrugell 108 Torrent
Bioscaa 111 Viladrau 90 Montseny 97 Aigua Blava
Manresa 107 Tamariú
Cervera Terrassa 89 Gualba 110 Tossa de Mar
87 L'Espluga Arenys de Mar
de Francoli Mataró
Val 88, 94 Barcelona
Reus 91, 92, 93 Sitges
96 Vilanovia i la Geltrú
Salou
Portbou
Llança
101 Castelló de Ampurias

Islas Baleares

Menorca
Mahón

Palma
Mallorca

Ibiza
San Antonio
Formentera Sant Francesc

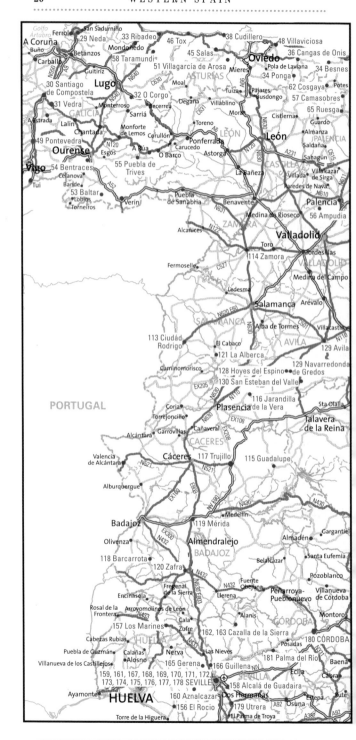

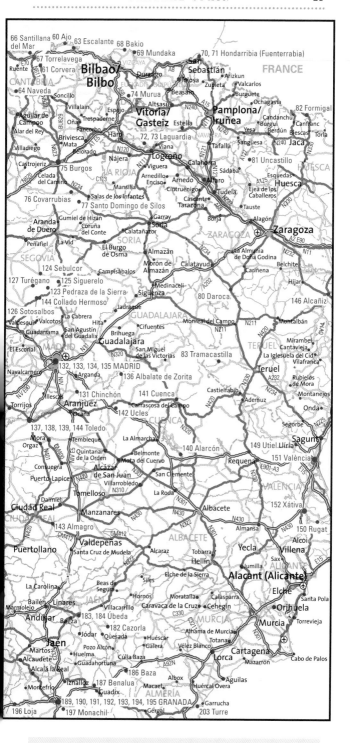

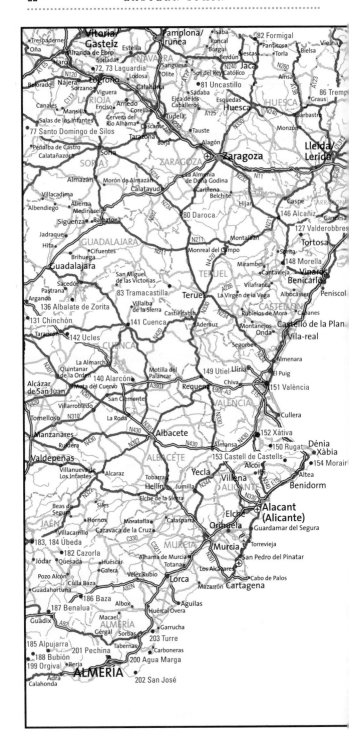

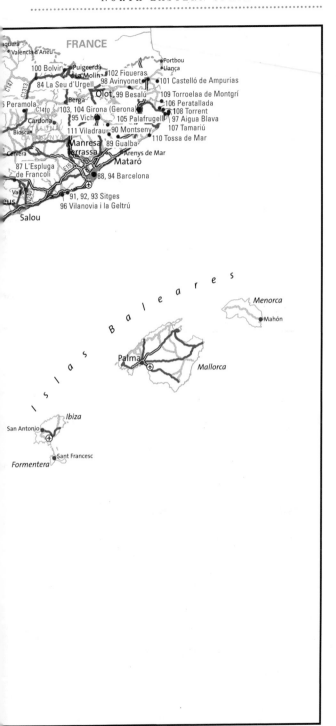

FRANCE

Valencia d'Aneu
100 Bolvir Puigcerdà
La Molina 102 Figueras Portbou
84 La Seu d'Urgell 98 Avinyonet Llança
Peramola Berga 99 Besalú 101 Castelló de Ampurias
C1410 103, 104 Girona (Gerona) 109 Torroelaa de Montgrí
Cardona 95 Vich 105 Palafrugell 106 Peratallada
Biosca 111 Viladrau 90 Montseny 108 Torrent
Cervera 89 Gualba 97 Aigua Blava
Manresa 110 Tossa de Mar 107 Tamariú
Terrassa Arenys de Mar
87 L'Espluga Mataró
de Francoli 88, 94 Barcelona
Vals 91, 92, 93 Sitges
Salou 96 Vilanovia i la Geltrú

Islas Baleares

Menorca
Mahón

Palma Mallorca

Ibiza
San Antonio
Sant Francesc
Formentera

Islas Baleares

Menorca

261 Cala Morell
263 Ferreries
262 Ciutadella
Mahón
264, 265, 266 Sant Lluis

Mallorca

254 Pollença
248 Lluc Agarí
247 Fornalutx
251 Orient
250 Moscari
239 Binissalem
241 Cala Rajada
237 Arta
249 Manacor
258 Son Sureda
246 Felanitx
Santanyi
242, 243 Deia
260 Valldemossa
238 Banyulbufar
245 Estellencs
244 Esporles
259 Son Termes
236 Algaida
255 Porreras
240, 252, 253 Palma
256 Portals Nous
257 Port d'Andratx

Ibiza

272 San Miguel
271 Sant Miguel
273 San Mateo
268, 269 Santa Eulália/Santa Eulária
270 Santa Gertrudis
San Antonio
267, 281 Ibiza
Sant Francesc

Formentera

Islas Canarias

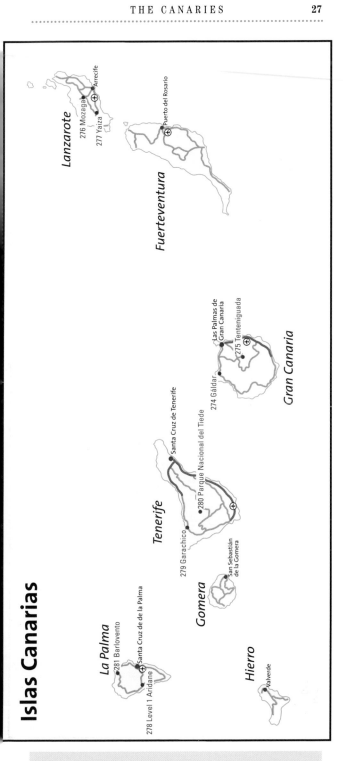

Lanzarote
276 Mozaga
277 Yaiza
Arrecife

Fuerteventura
Puerto del Rosario

Gran Canaria
Las Palmas de Gran Canaria
275 Tenteniguada
274 Gáldar

Tenerife
Santa Cruz de Tenerife
280 Parque Nacional del Tiede
279 Garachico

Gomera
San Sebastián de la Gomera

La Palma
281 Barlovento
Santa Cruz de la Palma
278 Level 1 Aridane

Hierro
Valverde

HOTELS IN THE NORTH-WEST

This section takes in the provinces of La Coruña, Lugo, Asturias, Pontevedra, Orese and Palencia; and it includes the area known as Galicia - the old administrative region and former principality city of Santiago, with its Cathedral of St. James. In this edition we have plenty of new recommendations in the Santiago area, including Casa Grande de Cornide, a beautifully proportioned bed and breakfast, found deep in the countryside, on page 30, **Pazo Cibran**, a traditional 18thC Galician stone building filled with neo-Victorian objects, on page 31 and **Casa Doñano**, a colonial home, on page 33.

Paradors in North-West Spain

NORTH-WEST SPAIN has more than its fair share of Paradores – and some of these are small and charming enough to have earned detailed entries. A number of other paradors in the area are not given entries, but worth a mention: the province of Pontevedra (bordering Portugal on the west coast) is particularly well endowed, with four Paradores within a hundred kilometres of one another. The largest of these (122 rooms), the **Parador de Bayona at Bayona**, is a smart modern hotel built within the walls of an ancient fortress. It has all the classic ingredients – crenellated walls, pillared balconies, an open courtyard, richly decorated rooms, beautifully manicured lawns and spectacular views of the Ría de Vigo (Tel 986 355000). By local standards Bayona is expensive, but it does not even come close to the **Reyes Católicos** in Santiago de Compostela – one of the most expensive Paradores, but also one of the most superior and most historic, built in the 15th century to house pilgrims from all over Europe who came to pay homage at the shrine of St James in Santiago's magnificent cathedral (Tel 981 582200). Beware 25th July: this is the feast day of St James, and the city (and Parador) are packed.

Léon's central 253-room Parador, **San Marcos**, notable for its fabulous *façade* and two-storey cloisters and once a watering-hole on the pilgrim route to Santiago, is now a smart hotel, laden with antiques and surrounded by formal gardens (Tel 987 237300).

LA CORUÑA

NEDA

PAZO DA MERCED

∼ COUNTRY HOTEL ∼

15510, Neda, La Coruña
TEL 981 382200 FAX 981 380104
E-MAIL reservas@pazodamerced.com WEBSITE www.tugalicia.es

NEDA IS A TOWN full of beautiful old mansions, and this hotel, built of dressed stone, and with its own adjacent chapel, dedicated to the *Virgen de la Merced* (Our Lady of Mercy), is housed in one of them.

The *pazo* or country manor house, was built in the 17thC and sits in open countryside on the low-lying green shore at the head of the Ría del Ferrol.

A few years ago, the owners, facing bankruptcy, decided to sell it to an architect specializing in the restoration of old buildings. With patience and skill, he has turned it into a magnificent rural hotel which combines respect for the historic architecture with a certain originality in the use of materials. His wife, Marinela Medina, has taken charge of the management of the hotel.

The *pazo* only has eight rooms, but they are well furnished and equipped with all that you could need. The service is welcoming and diligent: every guest is made to feel at home.

Through the windows you can see Couto monastery. The hotel makes a convenient base from which to visit this and other local examples of Romanesque architecture.

∼

NEARBY San Felipe castle (9 km); La Palma castle (14 km).
LOCATION on the Ría del Ferrol, by the waterside; private car parking
FOOD breakfast, dinner
PRICES €€€
ROOMS 8; 4 double, 4 suites, all with bath; all rooms have central heating, TV, minibar, telephone, hairdrier
FACILITIES garden, swimming pool
CREDIT CARDS AE, MC, V
CHILDREN very welcome
DISABLED limited facilities
PETS not accepted
CLOSED mid-Dec to mid-Jan
PROPRIETOR Marinela Medina

LA CORUÑA

SANTIAGO DE COMPOSTELA

CASA GRANDE DE CORNIDE

~ COUNTRY HOUSE BED AND BREAKFAST ~

Calo, Teo, Santiago, Galicia
TEL 981 805599 **FAX** 981 805751
E-MAIL info@casagrandedecornide.com **WEBSITE** www.casagrandedecornide.com

SANTIAGO DE COMPOSTELA is, like any terminus, a busy place. However, once you've arrived at the end of the Pilgrim's Way there is no rule that says you have to stay there: another ten minutes by car could put you back into deep countryside and a little skilful map reading could put you within striking distance of this laid-back but thoroughly professional hotel. It's all beautifully proportioned. There's a tiny reception area (but what more do you need with only seven bedrooms?); a well-stocked contemporary library; a usefully sized drawing room; and a swimming pool that is quite large but not so big you feel you may never reach the other end. There is no restaurant, but the sunny, glass-walled breakfast room has had as much care taken over it as most people would give to a full-blown eatery. The three bedrooms in the main building are large and smart, with polished wood floors, traditional bedsteads and a well selected mixture of old and modern furniture. The four duplex rooms, ideal for families, are in a separate, much more modern, building but are carefully thought out and comfortable beyond the merely functional. The well-kept walled garden has enough room for everybody to find a quiet corner to themselves. Only breakfast is served, but there are plenty of interesting eating places within a couple of kilometres.

~

NEARBY Santiago de Compostella (10 km); Cape Finisterre (100 km).
LOCATION on a low, wooded ridge, 5 km east of main west coast motorway in large walled garden with ample off-road car parking.
FOOD breakfast
PRICES €€€
ROOMS 10; 4 double, 2 single, 4 duplex for four persons; all rooms have bath or shower, phone, TV, hairdrier, kettle, mini bar **FACILITIES** drawing room, library, breakfast room, internet access, garden, swimming pool, golf course and river swimming all within 20 km **CREDIT CARDS** AE, MC, V **CHILDREN** welcome
DISABLED no specially adapted rooms **PETS** by arrangement **CLOSED** 20 Dec-1 Feb
PROPRIETOR María Jesús Castro, Jose Ramón Pousa Estévez

LA CORUÑA

SAN XULIAN DE SALES

PAZO CIBRAN
~ VILLAGE BED AND BREAKFAST ~

San Xulián de Sales, 15885-Vedra, La Coruña
TEL 981 511515 **FAX** 981 814766
E-MAIL cibran@arrakis.es **WEBSITE** www.pazocibran.com

SEVERAL MILES SOUTH of the bustle of Santiago de Compostella, in a small country village, this traditional 18thC Galician stone building stands on a steep, narrow lane. The cobbled courtyard is a welcome refuge from the busy world outside, and the welcome as warm and friendly as you could wish. The large drawing room is a wonderful neo-Victorian clutter, with chairs, tables, curio cabinets, rugs, books and pictures by Galician artists all vying for space somewhere on the dark wood floor or white-washed walls. A sunny glass-walled breakfast room is the scene of the only meal of the day on offer here, but a brisk 50 m walk brings you to Roberto's, a well-patronised local restaurant. Upstairs, the walls of the corridors and fair-sized bedrooms are also white, with the pale greens and beiges of the soft furnishings bringing a light, peaceful touch of colour to each room. Surprise, surprise, the modern, well-equipped bathrooms are white tiled. Outside is a large garden with more than enough space to lose yourself in, and orchards beyond; close to the house is a small open-front-ed chapel. Impromptu barbecues and tastings of the local Alvariño wines (one of which is made in the house) may punctuate an otherwise supremely relaxed life here. For the more energetic, there are horses to ride, rivers to walk by or canoe down, and a nine-hole golf course nearby.

~

NEARBY Santiago de Compostella (7 km); Ulla valley (4 km); Alto de Candán (45 km); Ria de Muros y Noia (40 km).
LOCATION in small village, surrounded by orchards; ample car parking in courtyard.
FOOD breakfast, dinner by prior arrangement
PRICES €€
ROOMS 11 doubles (5 twin) all with bath and shower
FACILITIES drawing room, breakfast room, terrace, garden
CREDIT CARDS MC, V **CHILDREN** welcome **DISABLED** no specially adapted rooms
PETS small dogs accepted **CLOSED** never **PROPRIETOR** Carmen Iglesias

LUGO

O CORGO

CASA GRANDE A FERVENZA
~ COUNTRY HOTEL ~

Ctra.Lugo-Páramo.Km11, 27163, O Corgo, Lugo
TEL 982 150610 **FAX** 982 151610
E-MAIL info@fervenza.com **WEBSITE** www.fervenza.com

SOUTH OF LUGO, so more or less in the middle of Galicia, this is an idyllic and fascinating retreat in the Terras do Miño nature reserve. At the foot of a long, wooded lane, and guarded by dogs almost as big as donkeys you'll find a collection of buildings. A small, square 19thC manor house contains the bedrooms, while adjacent 17thC farm buildings house a snug bar and a restaurant with picture windows that look across the meadow towards a river and mill. There is an air of complete satisfaction and tradition about this place: the owner has restored the mill to working order, likewise the forge (installing water-powered bellows and grindstones in the process) and now relaxes by making clogs for his friends using tools he made himself in the forge.

The ground floor of the manor is principally occupied by a comfortable sitting area crammed with artefacts of earlier ages. Supremely comfortable and traditionally furnished bedrooms on the galleried first floor have loopholes in the walls, from which occupants in former times could fire a musket at bandits setting about either of the principal entrances. The lace bedspreads are local work. Apart from good local walks, there are kayaks and mountain bikes to help mitigate the effects of the relaxed restaurant, which serves excellent regional food backed up by a well-chosen wine list.

~

NEARBY Lugo (20 km): Roman walls, C12th cathedral, museums; 6thC Samos Monastery (30 km).
LOCATION secluded spot inside La Reserva de la Biosfera, Terras do Miño, in woods by river; in own grounds with ample car parking
FOOD breakfast, lunch, dinner
PRICES €€
ROOMS 9 doubles, all with bath and shower
FACILITIES sitting room, bar, restaurant, terrace, fishing, canoes, mountain bikes
CREDIT CARDS AE, DC, MC, V **CHILDREN** welcome **DISABLED** one specially adapted room
PETS accepted **CLOSED** never **MANAGER** Modesto Seone Pérez

LUGO

RIBADEO

CASA DOÑANO

~ COUNTRY HOTEL ~

Vilela Cubelas 27714, Ribadeo, Lugo
TEL 982 137429 **FAX** 982 134800
E-MAIL turismorural@casadonano.com **WEBSITE** www.casadonano.com

IF YOU APPROACH Ribadeo from the south, the main road from the Sierra de Meira swoops down into the wooded gorge of the River Eo and follows its twists and turns in an almost endless descent to the coast. The pastoral and blissfully quiet setting of Casa Doñano is in sharp contrast to the harsh shapes of the gorge, and was chosen as the site for his house by a Galician expatriate when he first came back in 1907 after making his fortune in Cuba. The name of the house was his nickname, 'Don Año': he came back every year to check on the builders' progress. A row of luxuriant hydrangeas leads you down to the front door and a warm welcome from Mercedes, the present owner. She and her husband found the house as a complete wreck, being used as a stable. Years of painstaking work have brought it back into to apple-pie order, and they have been faithful to Don Año's original colonial Caribbean tastes in their choice of fabrics and bold colours to decorate the handsome, beamed and well-proportioned rooms. The bedrooms have traditional iron bedsteads or hand-carved wooden headboards, and the bathrooms contain proper furniture rather than tile and aluminium confections. In summer the stable doors are opened at both ends of the long hall to let a cooling breeze run through. In winter, log fires warm the drawing room, the sitting room and the dining room. Spanish only spoken.

~

NEARBY Ribadeo.
LOCATION A few minutes drive from the mouth of the River Eo, in small, scattered country village; limited off-road car parking
FOOD breakfast, dinner
PRICES €€ **ROOMS** 8 doubles (three twin), all with bathroom and optional TV
FACILITIES 3 sitting rooms, dining room, garden, astronomical telescopes, archery in own paddock
CREDIT CARDS AE, DC, MC, V **CHILDREN** welcome **DISABLED** one specially adapted room
PETS not accepted **CLOSED** Christmas **PROPRIETOR** Mercedes Pascual Andrés

ASTURIAS

BESNES

LA TAHONA
~ MOUNTAIN HOTEL ~

33578, Besnes-Alles, Asturias
TEL AND FAX 98 5415749
E-MAIL latahona@ctv.es **WEBSITE** www.latahonadebesnes.com

DRIVING FROM Panes up into the Picos de Europa, you follow the course of the Rio Cares, up through a deep and dramatic gorge which winds on towards some of the most stupendous views to be found in these mountains. La Tahona is tucked away behind the tiny village of Besnes, at the end of a cobbled track, beside a stream which runs down through beech woods. It is a peaceful and simple base for walking, horseriding, downriver canoeing or mountain-biking.

The bar by the entrance hall is used by a few local farmers who drop in for a quiet coffee and brandy on their way up and down the valley; beyond is the rustic restaurant, all bare stone, exposed beams, whitewashed rough plaster and red tiles. Bedrooms are similarly simple, but stylish.

The stream runs past the restaurant, the terrace and the windows of the bedrooms – the soothing sound of water and birdsong will be your only distractions while contemplating the choice between salmon with cider, trout from the river or Asturian hotpot. 'A fabulous little place'; 'good value'; 'excellent (huge) packed lunches', says a recent reporter.

NEARBY El Buxu – prehistoric cave paintings (30 km); viewpoint at Las Estazadas (8 km).
LOCATION in quiet wooded valley, off C6312 10 km W of Panes; with garden and car parking
FOOD breakfast, lunch, dinner
PRICES €€-€€€
ROOMS 18 double, 1 appartment for 4 people, all with bath; all rooms have central heating, TV, phone
FACILITIES dining room, sitting room; horse-riding, mountain bikes, fishing, canoeing
CREDIT CARDS MC, V
CHILDREN welcome; play-room; special menus
DISABLED access easy; some ground floor rooms
PETS not accepted
CLOSED mid Jan
MANAGERS Lorenzo and Sarah Nilsson

ASTURIAS

CADAVEDO

TORRE DE VILLADEMOROS
~ COUNTRY HOTEL ~

33788 Cadavedo, Valdès, Asturias
TEL 985 52 64
E-MAIL correo@torredevillademoros.com **WEBSITE** www.torredevillademoros.com

A NEW COAST road now by-passes Cadavedo and it has gratefully reverted to being the sleepy village it once was. Outside the village, heading towards the sea, a small lane ends in open countryside at a ruined tower and a far-from-ruined hotel. (The tower is home to a barn owl who often forsakes his day's sleep to come and catch grasshoppers fleeing the lawn-mower.) Manolo Santullano used contemporary furniture and clean-cut modern materials and fabrics to transform an old, quite small, four-square manor house into a unique and thoroughly comfortable hotel while never allowing his style to jar with the building itself. Total renovation has had other benefits: everything works because everything is new, from the raised hearth in the drawing room to the exposed beams in the ceilings of the top-floor bedrooms. There is a wonderful feeling of space, both inside and outside, all the way to the cliffs and coves of the unspoiled coastline. All the bedrooms are individually decorated in quietly powerful colours, their cool, tiled floors are covered with bold rugs and all have views of a sort. In the glass-walled dining room, which doubles as a breakfast room, there is only one regional menu (with simple alternatives if you don't like what's on offer): it's a matter of pride that the menu is never repeated during any guest's stay. Bicycles and power kites are freely lent.

~

NEARBY fishing villages of Luarca and Cudillero; beaches, gorge of River Esva-Canero (national monument).
LOCATION in open countryside E of Cadavedo, with uninterrupted access to shoreline; ample private car parking
Food breakfast, dinner
PRICES €€€
ROOMS 10 doubles (5 twin-bedded); all rooms have bath, shower, phone, TV, hairdrier **FACILITIES** drawing room, dining room, covered veranda, mountain bikes, kites **CREDIT CARDS** DC, MC, V **CHILDREN** welcome **DISABLED** no **PETS** not accepted
CLOSED 1 Nov-31 Mar open at weekends/bank holidays only
PROPRIETOR Manolo Santullano

ASTURIAS

CANGAS DE ONIS

AULTRE NARAY

~ COUNTRY HOTEL ~

Peruyes, Cangas de Onís, Asturias
TEL 985 840808 **FAX** 985 840848
E-MAIL aultre@aultrenaray.com **WEBSITE** www.aultrenaray.com

IF YOU ARE intending to stay here during the first Sunday in August, and fancy yourself as something of a speed merchant in a kayak, then you could hurry along to Cangas de Onis and enter the race down the River Sella from there to Ribadesella on the coast. On the other hand, you could just sit in the garden of this attractive 19thC stone house on the edge of a pretty village and look at the mountains that seem to have been arranged for the purpose. Inside, old stone floors, soft pale yellow washed walls and pleasing contemporary furniture that doesn't quarrel with the older fabric of the building conspire to produce that fine (and difficult to achieve) balance between comfort and elegance. There is plenty of 'downstairs' to retreat to, including a large drawing room with enormous picture windows giving on to the mountain view. A cosy dining room doubles as the breakfast room and it is a measure of the thought behind the management of the hotel that there is always an extra table laid in case of emergencies. A stone and wrought-iron staircase leads up to comfortable, light, freshly decorated bedrooms, all with respectable bathrooms. Usual and unusual ways of taking exercise are available – riding, trekking, climbing and potholing – but in acknowledgement of the limited number of local marked trails, the hotel can arrange your own personal guide to take walkers safely off the beaten track.

~

NEARBY prehistoric cave paintings in Ribadesella (12 km) and Cangas de Onís (14 km); Los Picos de Europa (40 km); Beyos Gorge (35 km).
LOCATION foothills of Los Picos de Europa, in valley of River Sella; car parking for about six cars by hotel, more space about 150 m away
FOOD breakfast, dinner **PRICE** €€€ **ROOMS** 10 doubles (4 twin, 1 suite), all with bath, shower, phone, TV, safe, hair drier **FACILITIES** drawing room, sitting room, games room, dining room, terrace, garden, guides for mountain walking, riding
CREDIT CARDS AE, DC, MC, V **CHILDREN** welcome **DISABLED** no specially adapted rooms
PETS not accepted **CLOSED** Nov-Easter open weekends and bank holidays only
PROPRIETOR Theresa Barreiro

ASTURIAS

COLLIA ARRIONDAS

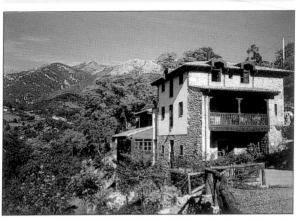

POSADA DEL VALLE
~ MOUNTAIN HOTEL ~

33549 Collia Arriondas, Asturias
TEL 985 841157 **FAX** 985 841559
E-MAIL hotel@posadadelvalle.com **WEBSITE** www.posadadelvalle.com

NIGEL BURCH and his wife Joanne opened in 1997 after a mid-life change of direction: he had had a successful career in horticulture, moving here from a big farm in southern Spain. Out of a late 19th-C 'priest's farmhouse', built on a rock outcrop with a stunning view over the Picos, they have carved a cosy but comfortable family hotel. Its strongest point is the friendly family atmosphere: you'll get a genuinely personal welcome here, together with all the advice you need about exploring the area. It's a great base for the Picos de Europa, the Ponga Mountain Range, the Sueve Reserve, the coastline of Eastern Asturias and the River Sella. Walking, surfing, mountain biking, canoeing, fishing and more, are within reach.

The decoration is relatively simple and pleasing, making the most of the building's original features, including thick walls and exposed stonework. Picture windows give the dining room (good home cooking) a wonderful outlook over a lush green valley rising to a limestone peak. Bedrooms are simple but comfortable, in rustic style, with pretty, well-chosen fabrics. A welcome addition to the guide in an area short of our sort of hotel. No smoking allowed in the house.

~

NEARBY outdoor pursuits, guided and self-guided walking.
LOCATION signposted from the AS-260 on right 1 km (0.5 mile) N out of Arriondas; in own large gardens with car parking
FOOD breakfast, dinner
PRICE ⓔ-ⓔⓔ
ROOMS 12 double, all with bathroom
FACILITIES sitting room, dining room, bar, garden
CREDIT CARDS MC, V
CHILDREN over 8 years
DISABLED not suitable
PETS not accepted
CLOSED 16 Oct-30 Mar
PROPRIETORS Nigel and Joanne Burch

ASTURIAS

CUDILLERO

CASONA DE LA PACA

~ SEASIDE HOTEL ~

El Pito, 33150 Cudillero Asturias
TEL 985 591303 **FAX** 985 591316
E-MAIL addresses hotel@casonadelapaca.com **WEBSITE** www.casonadelapaca.com

IN 1877, A RETURNED 'Indiano', the Spanish equivalent of a colonial grandee, built himself a typically showy house high above the now popular fishing port of Cudillero, whose houses and cobbled streets cling, rather precariously, to the sides of its valley. He was following the established tradition of his kind, and quite a number of these houses still dot the Asturian coast. High ceilings, ornate tiled floors in the public rooms and exotic plants in the formal garden are all standard features of Indianos' houses. Few items of original furniture survive in this one, most being reproduction or contemporary, so it is the building itself that carries the style. A drawing room and a comfortable conservatory provide plenty of space for relaxation indoors, and the surrounding garden offers a peaceful alternative to an expedition to one of the excellent beaches on this stretch of coast. Although breakfast is the only food on offer in the pretty breakfast room, you only need to walk down into Cudillero to have a wide choice of restaurants. With 19 bedrooms, this hotel is getting quite close to the upper limit for this guide, but its friendliness belies its size and the polished wood floors and pastel colour schemes of the bedrooms are a far cry from the standardisation we avoid. The bathrooms are all well-equipped, some actually quite grand rooms in their own right.

~

NEARBY Selgas Palace (100 m) contains a Goya and an El Greco; Artedo beach (5 km); gorge of River Narcea (50 km).
LOCATION above traditional fishing port, 40 km north west of Oviedo, in own grounds with ample car parking.
FOOD breakfast **PRICE** €€
ROOMS 20; 19 doubles, 9 with twin beds, 1 single; all rooms have bathroom and shower, phone, TV, hair drier
FACILITIES drawing room, library, breakfast room, garden, lift
CREDIT CARDS MC, V **CHILDREN** welcome **DISABLED** no specially adapted rooms; lift/elevator **PETS** not accepted **CLOSED** 10 Dec-1 Feb **PROPRIETOR** Juana M.a Fidez

ASTURIAS

EL ALLENDE

LA MONTANA MAGICA
～ MOUNTAIN HOTEL ～

33508 Cuanda, El Allende, Llanes, Asturias
TEL 985 925176 **FAX** 985 925780
WEBSITE www.lamontanamagica.com

R OUGHLY HALF way between San Sebastián and Coruña, there is no dan-ger of confusing this delightful mountain hotel with Thomas Mann's book of the same name. Only 10 km from the best beaches of Llanes, La Montaña Magica is literally at the end of a mountain road which squeezes past a farm where Asturian mountain ponies are kept for trekking, and then pushes on another half kilometre to a wonderful mountain meadow site. The view, like the air, is brilliant and apart from the mountains you can actually see, there are other peaks and gorges, rivers and five-star caves (decorated and plain) all within a 25 km radius.

Carlos and Pilar started with a broken-down farmstead and have brought sections of it into play as the hotel has prospered – he recently bought him-self a bulldozer to move bits of mountain for the next great plan, which is to be a spa with the sort of view that money can scarcely afford. The bedrooms are smooth rustic with plenty of wood everywhere, and the sort of bathrooms most of us are still saving up for. As well as a substantial breakfast, you can order an excellent regional dinner to be ready on your return from the day's activities. There are two living rooms, in separate buildings, so if you don't care for the company in one, you can always migrate to the other.

～

NEARBY Los Picos de Europa (24 km); Cangas de Onis (23 km);
caves of Tito Bustillo, El Pindal, El Buxu and Peña Tú (25 km); beaches (10 km).
LOCATION at end of mountain road high in the Sierra de la Cubeta; ample parking
FOOD breakfast, dinner by arrangement
PRICE €€
ROOMS 14 doubles (5 twin-bedded, 2 suites); all rooms have bath, shower, TV, hair drier
FACILITIES 2 sitting rooms, library, bar, dining room, access to workshop, stables and greenhouse **CREDIT CARDS** AE, DC, MC, V **CHILDREN** welcome
DISABLED one specially adapted room **PETS** not accepted **CLOSED** never
PROPRIETORS Carlos Bueno Sanchez, Pilar Pando Cortes

ASTURIAS

FIGUERAS DEL MAR

PALACETE PEÑALBA

~ TOWN HOTEL ~

El Cotarelo s/n, 33794, Figueras, Asturias
TEL 98 5636125 FAX 98 5636247
E-MAIL info.hotelpalacetepenalba.com WEBSITE www.hotelpalacetepenalba.com

THIS EXTRAORDINARY house was built in 1912 by a disciple of the celebrated Spanish architect Antonio Gaudí. Everything about it – the curved sweep of the entrance steps, the ovals of the balconies, the glazed and tiled atrium, the twin towers with their delicate plasterwork, the arched alcoves in the bedrooms – is redolent of the early Art Nouveau movement which took root in Europe at this time. Much of the original furniture and internal decoration, such as the tapestries, has been preserved, and the whole edifice has been declared a National Artistic Monument. In fact, the atmosphere does rather resemble that of a museum – beware the elegant but delicate chairs in the sitting room. This is not a place to bring unruly children, but if you enjoy the absurdities of this particular era you will come anyway.

The town of Figueras del Mar has been by-passed by the new bridge over the Ria de Ribadeo, but it is busy with fishing and shipbuilding. The hotel's owners also run a restaurant on the waterfront, and both establishments have a reputation in the area for interesting cuisine – specializing, needless to say, in seafood.

~

Nearby Castropol (5 km); beach and lighthouse at Tapia de Casariego (10 km).
LOCATION at top of town above port; with grounds and car parking
FOOD breakfast
PRICES €€-€€€
ROOMS 11; 7 double, 4 suites, all with bath; all rooms have central heating, radio, TV, minibar, phone, safe
FACILITIES dining room, sitting room, bar, restaurant (5min walk)
CREDIT CARDS AE, MC, V
CHILDREN welcome
DISABLED access difficult
PETS not accepted
CLOSED Jan-Feb
PROPRIETOR Avelino Gutierrez Lopez

ASTURIAS

HONTORIA

EL AMA DE LLAVES
~ COUNTRY BED AND BREAKFAST ~

Hontoria s/n, 33593 Llanes, Asturias
TEL 985 407322 **FAX** 985 409760697
E-MAIL asturias@amadellaves.com **WEBSITE** www.amadellaves.com

VIRTUALLY DUE north of Los Picos de Europa, and squeezed between a stretch of new coastal highway and the sea, Hontoria is the kind of sleepy village you could easily find in England's West Country. A couple of turnings away from the centre, down narrow lanes, this 17thC stone farmhouse has been lovingly restored, inside and out, and then populated with antiques and paintings: each looks as if it has been chosen with its exact location in mind. The stone exterior is relieved by boldly coloured stucco, some of which has found its way up the staircase and into the bathrooms. Elsewhere in the house you can guess at some of its history by looking at the traces of long-since moved doors and windows on the bare stone walls. Floors are wood or terracotta, with rugs scattered here and there, and reinforce the comfortable low-tech atmosphere – although this is suspended in the bathrooms, as each has a Jacuzzi bath. In the breakfast room, a dolmen, one of the pointed stone pillars used to support a farmhouse's *horreo*, or granary, was found built into a wall and has been made the centrepiece of the room. The *horreo* in the garden still has its full complement of dolmens, so this one was obviously a spare. Although this is essentially a bed-and-breakfast, it also offers aromatherapy and Justine, the knowledgeable owner, keeps a range of remedies to help you banish the aches and woes of 21stC life. The sea may be out of sight, but it is only 500 m away and some of the best beaches in Asturia are within a short drive. Spanish only spoken as we went to press.

~

Nearby Historic buildings in Llaves (15 km); beaches (ten within 15 km); Los Picos National Park (20 km).
LOCATION on fringe of village with views over coastal farmland; ample car parking
FOOD breakfast **PRICES** ⓔⓔ **ROOMS** 5 doubles, all with hydro-massage bath and shower **FACILITIES** sitting area, breakfast room, terrace, garden, aromatherapy
CREDIT CARDS MC, V **CHILDREN** welcome
DISABLED one specially adapted room **PETS** generally not accepted **CLOSED** never
PROPRIETOR Justine Rodríguez

ASTURIAS

LA PEREDA

EL HABANA

～ COUNTRY HOTEL ～

33509, La Pereda (Llanes), Asturias
TEL 985 402526 **FAX** 985 402075
E-MAIL hotel@elhabana.net **WEBSITE** www.elhabana.net

THERE ARE TWO very different routes to the village of La Pereda: one is a gentle drive south from the coast by Llanes; the other a spectacular (and narrow) mountain road that runs north-east through the foothills of Los Picos from midway between Meré and Vibaño. Whichever way you choose, you'll be pleased to get here. A low, pale gold and light stone building, with shade trees for your car opposite the entrance, stands in a large, lush, informal garden dotted with specimen plants and shrubs and overlooked by the long, high ridge of the Cuesta Caballo. Inside, the drawing room has a lovely feeling of light and space: floor to ceiling windows, tiled floors dotted with rugs and a happy mixture of art deco and ethnic furniture combine in an elegant and uncluttered style. María and Sirio have added some colonial furniture which they picked up when living in New Delhi (also the source of María's excellent English). The restaurant, which also doubles as the breakfast room, is Sirio's department (and as pleasingly unfussy as the drawing room), offering Asturian dishes, salads and grills and a worthy selection of Spanish wines. The bedrooms are all individually decorated, but in keeping with house style. A couple have their own private terraces, and those on the ground floor offer easy access to guests who need, or prefer, to avoid stairs. A well-concealed swimming pool completes the picture.

Nearby Los Picos de Europa (30 km); La Cuesta golf course (2km); caves at Pindal (25 km) and Tito Bustillo (25 km); ethnographic museum at Porrúa (2 km).
LOCATION mid-way beween Santander and Gijon, in scattered hamlet between the Sierra de Cuera and the sea with ample private car parking
Food breakfast, light lunches, dinner
PRICES €€€
ROOMS 12 doubles; 5 twin, 2 family rooms, 3 suites; all rooms have bath, shower, phone, TV, safe, hairdrier **FACILITIES** drawing room, dining room, bar, terrace, garden, plunge-pool **CREDIT CARDS** DC, MC, V **CHILDREN** welcome **DISABLED** 4 ground floor rooms with easy access to outside and public rooms **PETS** accepted
CLOSED mid-Dec-end Feb **PROPRIETORS** María Eugenia Caumel, Sirio Sáinz

ASTURIAS

LUARCA

VILLA LA ARGENTINA
～ SEASIDE HOTEL ～

Villar de Luarca, s/n, 33700 Valdés, Asturias
TEL 985 640102 **FAX** 985 640973
E-MAIL reservas@villalaargentina.com **WEBSITE** www.villalaargentina.com

BUILT BY A retired Spanish colonial in 1899, and set on the heights above the fishing port of Luarca, the exterior of this house is quite an ornate example of what was already established as an ostentatious tradition amongst these wealthy 'returnees'. In common with many similar houses, the original contents have long since been dispersed and the new owners have had to contend with the twin problems of re-furnishing and conversion to hotel use. Here they have been faithful to the original, sometimes startling, colour schemes. But they have been driven, sometimes not wholly successfully, by planning regulations into experimenting with different ways of adding bathrooms. At least, though, they have avoided the wholesale destruction of architectural and period decorative features that often accompanies such work. Some of the original bathrooms are quite spectacular. The furniture is a mixed bag: some contemporary and some antique, but the overall effect gives an impression of how the wonderfully over-dressed original must have looked. A drawing room, an imposing, sunny breakfast room and a billiards room give the guests plenty of opportunity to gather together or to avoid each other as the mood dictates. A separate building houses the restaurant, which offers a range of regional dishes, and a bar with an extended, light and airy seating area for snacks. Outside are formal gardens (with plenty of shade trees), a hard tennis court and a small swimming pool.

～

Nearby Luarca (1.5 km); Viavalez (35 km); Ribadeo (55 km); Navia valley (18 km); Cudillero (35 km).
LOCATION set well back from cliffs above Luarca in own grounds, with ample off-street car parking
FOOD breakfast, dinner **PRICES** €€ **ROOMS** 12 doubles (7 twin-bedded); all rooms have bath, shower, phone, TV, modem point, hair drier, safe **FACILITIES** breakfast room, afternoon tea room, bar, restaurant, billiards room, swimming pool
CREDIT CARDS AE, DC, MC, V **CHILDREN** welcome **DISABLED** no specially adapted rooms
PETS not accepted **CLOSED** Jan-Feb **PROPRIETOR** Carmen Fernandez

ASTURIAS

RIBADESELLA

HOTEL RIBADESELLA PLAYA

∼ SEASIDE HOTEL ∼

Ricardo Cangas, 3, 33560, Ribadesella, Asturias
TEL 985 860715 **FAX** 985 860220
E-MAIL jlgarcia@fade.es **WEBSITE** www.ribadesella-playahotel.com

RIBADESELLA has long been quite a stylish resort, popular with holiday-makers attracted by the port and the estuary of the river Sella, with its sandy beaches and spectacular scenery. The Hotel Ribadesella Playa, converted from one of the many old family villas which line the bay, across the river from the main town, has had a full renovation in 2001 and has been sensitively modernised.

The hotel is right on the beach, beside a grassed promenade, free of traffic, and many of the bedrooms – smartly done up with traditional-style modern furniture – have long windows and balconies with views over the water. The restaurant is in the lower part of the house, cool and airy, with stone floors and sympathetic wooden furniture.

The hotel has no pretensions to luxury, but combines comfortable accommodation with a relaxed and informal atmosphere. A happy choice for a beach holiday, with the added advantage for many visitors of the nearby town and the mountains with their walks, caves and birdlife.

∼

NEARBY Caves of Tito Bustillo (500 mtrs); Mirador de la Reina (45 km).
LOCATION in quiet residential beach area on W side of town; car parking in courtyard
FOOD breakfast, lunch, dinner
PRICES €€€
ROOMS 16 double, 1 single, all with bath; all rooms have central heating, phone, TV
FACILITIES dining room, 2 sitting rooms
CREDIT CARDS AE, DC, MC, V
CHILDREN accepted
DISABLED no special facilities
PETS not accepted
CLOSED never
MANAGER José Luis García

ASTURIAS

SALAS

CASTILLO DE VALDÉS-SALAS

~ Historic town hotel ~

Plaza de la Campa, s/n, 33860, Salas, Asturias
TEL 98 5832222 **FAX** 98 5832299

THE MARKET town of Salas is off the busy and tortuously winding road between Oviedo and the coast, in the foothills of the Cordillera Cantabrica. The town's 16thC castle has been restored and converted into a small and simple hotel, keeping much of the character of the original building intact

The massive doors lead you through the thick walls into the reception area, which also houses the local tourist information desk (both offering good spoken English). The building is constructed around a paved courtyard, with covered cloisters to shelter you from the mountain rain and from the summer sun. On the ground floor, off this patio area, is the cafeteria/restaurant, which is open to the public and serves unfussy dishes with local touches – try their cakes made with rice, milk and sugar, served with freshly brewed coffee. The bedrooms are mostly on the first floor and are very plain but stylish, with shutters at the windows, wooden floors and modern bathrooms tiled in red and white. There are two sitting rooms upstairs; one has a television, games and books, and both have open fires in the winter. All the windows are double-glazed too, so it should be snug.

~

NEARBY Benedictine monastery of San Salvador, Cornellana (10 km); viewpoint at Tineo (24 km).
LOCATION in village just off N634, about 45 km W of Oviedo; with garden and car parking in square
FOOD breakfast, lunch, dinner
PRICES €€
ROOMS 12 double, all with bath; all rooms have central heating, phone
FACILITIES dining room, 2 sitting rooms, bar, terrace
CREDIT CARDS AE, MC, V
CHILDREN accepted
DISABLED access difficult **PETS** not accepted
CLOSED Jan
PROPRIETOR Manuel López

ASTURIAS

Tox

VILLA BORINQUEN

~ COUNTRY HOTEL ~

Tox, Villapedre, Asturias
TEL 98 5648220 **FAX** 98 5648222
E-MAIL villaborinquen@eresmas.com **WEBSITE** www.hoteles.casouasasturiauas.com

THIS DELIGHTFUL hotel could not be more secluded – even the village of Tox does not appear on most maps (look for Villapedre). Between the main coast road and the shore, the Villa Borinquen sits quietly, unsignposted, amid rolling green cultivated land, far from any distractions.

It is a modern building, based on the houses of the wealthy Spaniards who returned from the Americas in the heyday of Spanish colonialism, and everything has been put together with comfort in mind. The bedrooms are enormous, and some have huge balconies overlooking the countryside and the extensive gardens to the sea. They are all carefully and individually furnished with large beds, comfortable armchairs, long drapes at the windows and rugs on the polished wood floors.

The hotel provides breakfast and snack meals, and the same management runs a restaurant down the road at the pretty little village of Puerto Vega, which has something of the atmosphere of a Cornish fishing village. Fish and shellfish are unloaded straight into the kitchen; you can watch the harbour at work as you eat and take a stroll along the sea wall as the sun goes down.

~

NEARBY Barayo beach (5 km); the dramatic Navia valley (10 km).
LOCATION in open fields near village, 1 km N of N634, about 11 km W of Luarca; with grounds and car parking
FOOD breakfast
PRICES €€€
ROOMS 7 double, 1 single, 3 family rooms, all with bath; all rooms have central heating, phone, TV, hairdrier
FACILITIES sitting room, breakfast room, bar
CREDIT CARDS MC, V
CHILDREN welcome; games available
DISABLED access easy; lift/elevator **PETS** not accepted
CLOSED Jan
MANAGER Elisa Méndez

ASTURIAS

TRESGRANDAS

EL MOLINO DE TRESGRANDAS

∼ COUNTRY HOTEL ∼

33598 Tresgrandas, Llanes, Asturias
TEL 985 41 11 91 **FAX** 985 41 11 57
E-MAIL hotel@molinotresgrandas.com **WEBSITE** www.molinotresgrandas.com

THE KEY TO reaching this hotel is to press on down the track that leads to it without succumbing to the less than obvious charms of the two other small hotels you see on the way. The extra few hundred metres are well worth the effort.

Beams and flagstones abound. The furniture may not all be as old as the building, but it is all in keeping. Indoors, there are two sitting rooms as well as a rustic but highly organized dining room. The original mill-stream, where captive trout are penned, is visible through a stout section of glass floor: the fish are destined for owner Luis' kitchen (he is a professional chef), and quite possibly your table. The comfortable bedrooms have a cottagey feel, with old-fashioned bedsteads and wooden furniture. Outside, apart from the river, there are ducks, chickens and a cider press: you can pick your own apples, make your own cider and it will then be barrelled to mature quietly until your next visit. Judging by the number of barrels on the racks, there are quite a few regular visitors.

A 'crime' is committed here almost every other weekend. Luis gives his guests some of the tools of the detective's trade, and asks them to solve it.

∼

NEARBY Los Picos National Park (30 km); La Hermida Gorge (30 km); Cangas de Onís (50 km).
LOCATION by river below village, surrounded by woods and fields; ample car parking
FOOD breakfast, dinner
PRICES €€
ROOMS 12; 8 doubles, 3 triples, one family; all rooms have bath, shower, phone, TV, hairdrier
FACILITIES 2 sitting rooms, bar, dining room, cider press
CREDIT CARDS V, MC
CHILDREN welcome
DISABLED no specially adapted rooms **PETS** not accepted **CLOSED** 1-15 Feb
PROPRIETOR Luis Sanz Hipolito

ASTURIAS

CASTIELLO DE SELORIO
~ COUNTRY HOTEL ~

33312 Villaviciosa, Asturias
TEL 985 996040 **FAX** 985 204359
E-MAIL info@castiellodeselorio.com **WEBSITE** www.castiellodeselorio.com

ONLY A CERTAIN kind of person, when faced with late 17thC doors which don't close properly, would summon the local cabinet maker and ask him to fit all the panels of the old doors into new hand-made doors of the same wood. Marian Fernandez and Antonio Alvarez Apellaniz are two such people, and have lavished this kind of attention to detail on the whole of this hugely attractive late 17thC 'baronial' manor. A section of new highway has drained away the traffic from the old coast road that brings you here from Villaviciosa, so you feel you're well off the beaten track even as you approach. Wrought-iron gates guard the entrance and an ancient bulldog guards the iron-studded front door. Inside, the rooms are of grand proportions and oriental rugs scattered on the stone floor lead the way to a central salon, drawing room and small library all of which lead out on to a veranda which runs virtually the length of the building. A less formal bodega-style bar and smoking room used to be the restaurant, but breakfast now happens in a sunny room that opens on to a small walled garden. The bedrooms are large, with (thankfully) modern beds spiced up with decorative headboards, but the rest of the furniture is very much in keeping with age of the building. The superb bathrooms boast marble or wooden washstands.

~

NEARBY beaches (2 km); Madera III 12-hole golf course (8 km); La Rasa de Berves 9-hole golf course (10 km).
LOCATION off old highway east of Villaviciosa, in hamlet; in own grounds with ample private car parking
FOOD breakfast
PRICES €€€
ROOMS 9 doubles (2 twin-bedded), all with bath, shower, phone, TV, modem point, hair drier
FACILITIES library, drawing room, informal smoking room, breakfast room, veranda, garden, car parking **CREDIT CARDS** AE, DC, MC, V **CHILDREN** welcome
DISABLED no specially adapted rooms **PETS** by arrangement **CLOSED** mid Jan-mid Feb
PROPRIETORS Antonio Alvarez Appelaniz and Marian Fernandez Reposo

PONTEVEDRA

MORANA

LA BUZACA

~ COUNTRY HOTEL ~

Lugar de San Lorenzo 36, 36668 Moraña, Pontevedra
TEL 986 553684 **FAX** 986 552902
E-MAIL info@pazolabuzaca.com **WEBSITE** www.pazolabuzaca.com

A NARROW LANE winds down a wooded hillside to reach this impressive country house hotel. A highly attractive infusion of new wine into old skins, it opened in 2001and took Enrique Varela three years to restore and convert. The result is a pleasing marriage of stone walls, oriental rugs on dark wood floors, antique furniture and period paintings, giving the place a 'baronial' feel without in the least making it oppressive. There are several sitting rooms, including one which is more or less the exclusive preserve of three bedrooms that are semi-detached from the main building and would be perfect for families or friends travelling together. The four bedrooms in the main building are the grandest (and most expensive), although the six rooms in the former stable block are far better than adequate, but much sparser in antique furniture. Outside, there is a small terraced garden, with plenty of shade, from which you can hear a stream gurgling down the hillside. There's plenty of open space around other buildings, which include a chapel and a dovecote, before you reach the woods. Food is taken quite seriously here, with regional dishes well represented on the menus and a thoughtful choice of wines to go with them. A low modern building, just out of sight of the hotel, is used for weddings and conferences, but should have little impact on the residents.

~

NEARBY Menhir de Gargantans (5 km); Alto de Candán (50 km); Campo Lameiro (8 km); Cambados (25 km); Arousa bodegas (20 km).
LOCATION between Santiago de Compostella and Pontevedra, on side of lush valley; ample private car parking
FOOD breakfast, lunch, dinner
PRICES €€€
ROOMS 13, 7 double, 6 twin-bedded; all rooms have bath, shower, hairdrier, telephone, TV **FACILITIES** 2 sitting rooms, dining room, card room, TV, room, terrace, garden, swimming pool, bar service
CREDIT CARDS AE, DC, MC, V **CHILDREN** welcome **DISABLED** no specially adapted rooms **PETS** not accepted **CLOSED** never **PROPRIETOR** Don Enrique Varela

PONTEVEDRA

CASA HOSPEDERIA ALDEA BORDONS

~ VILLAGE HOTEL ~

Outeiro – Bordóns 36960, Sanxenxo, Pontevedra
TEL 986 724374 FAX 986 690738
E-MAIL www.aldeabordons.com WEBSITE hotel@aldeabordons.com

THE NORTH SHORE of the Ría de Pontevedra, with its year-round mild climate, is a popular spot, and Sanxenxo seems to be a focus for much of the crowd. As you climb away from the shoreline, though, up the tiny lanes, the houses thin out and soon you are back in countryside again. This small hotel is perched up on the hillside on one of those lanes so narrow that when you arrive, it's a struggle to open your car door. But no matter: once through the door in the high stone wall surrounding the house you can relax and let the bustle of the coast sink into the background.

There are three distinct buildings, all close together, but at different levels. From the highest you can sit in the shade under a vine and look back up the *ría* towards Pontevedra. At the middle level is a bar that seems to have been carved out of the hill itself. Similarly the modestly sized, but rather spectacular sitting room on the lowest level, with one natural rock wall and one made entirely of glass. At the far end of this room a short spiral staircase leads up to a gallery where there is a sunny dining room/breakfast room. Galician regional dishes (this area is famous for oysters) and local wines are offered at dinner. Outside, a *hórreo* (traditional granary supported on four pointed pillars) has been turned into a playhouse for children. Spanish only spoken here as we went to press.

~

NEARBY Narín and Areas beaches (1 km), and 20 other named beaches in the area; Combarro (10 km); Cambados Island (14 km); Santiago de Compostella (70 km).
LOCATION between the Ría de Pontevedra and the Ría Arousa, on a sunny south facing hillside; car parking on adjacent road
FOOD breakfast, dinner PRICES €€
ROOMS 6 doubles (2 twin), 2 with bath and 4 with shower, one with sitting room and sofa bed, one with balcony; all rooms have central heating, TV, hairdrier
FACILITIES sitting room, dining room, bar, terrace, garden CREDIT CARDS V, MC
CHILDREN welcome DISABLED no specially adapted rooms PETS by agreement in advance CLOSED 6 Jan-6 Feb PROPRIETOR Gerardo Solveiro Otero

PONTEVEDRA

VILLAGARCIA DE AROSA

HOTEL PAZO O'RIAL

COUNTRY HOTEL

El Rial No 1, 36600, Villagarcía de Arosa, Pontevedra
TEL 986 507011 **FAX** 986 501676
E-MAIL reservas@infopazoo'rial.com **WEBSITE** www.pazoo'rial.com

THE ROAD HERE runs along beside the Ría de Arosa as it opens out towards the sea, not quite the open Atlantic, but nevertheless a holiday area for many Spanish visitors as well as northern Europeans.

This lovely old manor house is set back from the coast in its own gardens and has been beautifully converted, making full use of all the usual traditional effects – wooden beams, tiled floors and bare stone walls. The whole effect is softened with deep cushioned sofas, lacy curtains and woollen rugs. The service has been criticised as slack but there is nothing amiss with the housekeeping, the gardening or the cleanliness of the pool, which is surrounded by a protective hedge on one side and lovely views over the countryside on the other.

This is another area famous for its seafood – the bays around here are packed with fish and shellfish farms, and every inlet seems to have its little fleet of fishing boats to win a share of the harvest. The menu of the hotel reflects this, with the ubiquitous grilled prawns coming high on the list along with huge mussels in a thick tomato sauce. We're retaining this hotel for one more edition despite a negative report on the food and the bedrooms ('dull'). Further opinions welcome.

NEARBY Vista Alegre Convent; Mirador de Lobeira (5 km).
LOCATION near sea, set back from road; with car parking
FOOD breakfast, lunch, dinner
PRICES €€€€-€€€€€
ROOMS 60; 55 double and single, 4 suites, 1 apartment, all with bath; all rooms have central heating, phone, TV
FACILITIES dining room, sitting room, bar, swimming pool
CREDIT CARDS AE, DC, MC, V
CHILDREN welcome
DISABLED access easy; ground floor rooms; lift/elevator **PETS** not accepted
CLOSED Christmas till 15 Jan
MANAGER Julio Mondragón

PONTEVEDRA

VILLALONGA

HOTEL PAZO EL REVEL
~ COUNTRY HOTEL ~

Camino de la Iglesia s/n, 36990, Villalonga, Pontevedra
Tel 986 743000 **Fax** 986 743390

Back from the coast road and the small town of Villalonga, up a lane which leads to walks in the hills, a little church and the local cemetery, this lovely 17thC pazo was the family home of Luis Ansorena Garret, an aristocratic gentleman who ran this hotel along his own lines since the 1960s. Since our last inspection we have heard that it has been taken over by OCA Hotels, which is a shame - but we have been reassured that the charm of the hotel hasn't been diminshed.

The creeper-covered façade has no noticeboard or sign to give the hotel away. You park across the lane and help will be at hand to carry your bags through the archway to the courtyard and your neat, tiled room. Swallows nest in the age-old beams and eaves of the house and verandas, while quiet men rake the gravel and tend the beautiful formal gardens and lawns.

In the heat of summer, nothing could be more calming than to take your iced fino to the colonnaded terrace overlooking the trees and flowers and to sit in a padded wicker armchair for an hour or so before dinner. The dining room is quite informal and – please note – is open only at the height of the season; but lazy breakfasts can be enjoyed into the late morning, making the most of the excellent fresh coffee and newly baked rolls, croissants and sweet cakes.

~

Nearby Cambados – pazos and restaurants (10 km); beaches at San Vicente do Mar (5 km).
Location a short way up hill overlooking town; with gardens and car parking
Food breakfast
Prices €€-€€€€
Rooms 20 double, 2 single, all with bath; all rooms have central heating, phone
Facilities dining room, sitting room, bar, terrace; tennis court, swimming pool
Credit cards MC, V
Children tolerated
Disabled access difficult **Pets** not accepted **Closed** Oct to May
Proprietor OCA Hotels S.L

ORENSE

BALTAR

CASA A ROUSIA
~ COUNTRY HOTEL ~

Aldea de Abaixo 12, Baltar, Xinzo de Limia, Orense
TEL 988 466905 **Fax** 988 460381
E-MAIL arousia@arousia.com **WEBSITE** www.arousia.com

BALTAR, 45 KM SOUTH of Orense, is separated from the Portugese border by a high ridge which, at its eastern end, is 'decorated' by a line of wind-turbines. Comfortably out of sight of the wind farm, this hotel is hidden behind a high wall on the outskirts of the village, looking out across its own large garden and swimming pool towards open countryside. It is housed in a collection of former farm buildings, beautifully rehabilitated and reorganized so that there is no feeling of crowding: each room you visit is a little like going into your own house. Behind each rustic exterior is a new, cool and uncluttered interior with modern services discretely tucked away out of sight. The drawing room, white and cream with modern designer furniture has one wall made entirely of glass, giving an unconventional view of the rustic wall of the neighbouring building. The bedrooms have tiled or polished wooden floors, pale walls and (mostly) high ceilings. There is more period furniture here, but the emphasis is again on simplicity, with each piece given room to be admired. There is a bungalow in the garden that is ideal for families travelling with small children (the swimming pool is fenced). The restaurant is housed in yet another building and offers a wide range of regional dishes: the menus are largely driven by what looks good in the market that day, and local wines are offered as well as the ubiquitous Riojas. Spanish only spoken here as we went to press.

~

NEARBY Portugal (7 km); Monasterio de Trandeiras (16 km); Castillo de Monterrei (28 km); Ribadavía - Jewish Quarter and museum of ethnology; *bodegas* for Ribeiro wines (80 km).
LOCATION on outskirts of border village, on high plain (about 1,000 m); ample secure off-street parking
FOOD breakfast, lunch, dinner **PRICES** €€
ROOMS 7 doubles (3 twin, 1 suite) all with bath, shower, telephone and hairdrier
FACILITIES drawing room, self-service bar, dining room, garden, swimming pool
CREDIT CARDS AE, V **CHILDREN** welcome **DISABLED** no specially adapted rooms
PETS not accepted **CLOSED** Jan **PROPRIETORS** Luis y Marisa

ORENSE

BENTRACES

PALACIO DE BENTRACES
~ COUNTRY HOTEL ~

32890 Bentraces - Barbadás, Orense
TEL 988 383381 **FAX** 988 383035
EMAIL info@pazobentraces.com **WEBSITE** www.pazobentraces.com

SPACIOUS, ELEGANT, and yet, with just seven rooms, the Palacio de Bentraces has warmth and intimacy. The hotel occupies a fine old *pazo* – a stonebuilt Galician country house whose walls still display the escutcheon of former noble owners. It was built in the 1400s as a bishop's palace, but by the 1700s had been converted into a manorial seat by a family of Portuguese descent. Its present owners have taken pride in its sensitive restoration using only natural materials. They decorated each bedroom differently and furnished the rooms with antiques and bold colours.

The house, in a hamlet on Galicia's southern edge close to the Portuguese border, is supremely peaceful. There are no balconies, but one suite has a private terrace overlooking the flower gardens, and every bedroom window has a view across the hotel grounds and woods to the country-side beyond. Couples and families with older children predominate among the guests, who love to tour the ancient towns and villages of southern Galicia. This is essentially a guesthouse offering bed and breakfast but the owners have a restaurant in the village (about 100 m away), where the cooking is up to date and international, and based on good local produce.

~

NEARBY On the Ruta de los Monasterios – medieval monasteries along the pilgrim route to Santiago de Compostela – which is an hour's drive away.
LOCATION in Bentraces village on minor road off N540, 7km NW of Orense; 5km SW of autopista N1/A5 to port of Vigo and Portuguese border; 7 min in taxi from Orense station; free parking
FOOD breakfast; separate restaurant serving lunch, dinner
PRICE €-€€€
ROOMS 5 double, 2 suites, all with shower, bath, phone, PC jack, TV, hairdrier, safe
FACILITIES reception, lounge, breakfast room, separate restaurant 100 metres away, lift/elevator, function room, meeting room, gardens, car park
CREDIT CARDS AE, DC, MC, V **CHILDREN** welcome **DISABLED** unsuitable
PETS not accepted **CLOSED** Christmas to New Year
DIRECTOR Angeles Peñamaría

ORENSE

PUEBLA DE TRIVES

PAZO CASA GRANDE
~ TOWN HOTEL ~

Marqués de Trives 17, 32780, Poboa de Trives, Orense
TEL AND FAX 988 332066
E-MAIL informacion@casagrandetrives.com **WEBSITE** www.casagrandetrives.com

PAZO CASA GRANDE is a noble 18thC stone mansion clustered around a solid central tower, crowned by a coat of arms showing a knight on horseback killing a dragon. For many years the house lay in a state of disrepair until the Alvarez family decided to renovate it in the late 1980s and open it as a pousada, or little hotel.

From the outside, the Casa Grande appears to be an imposing, aristocratic residence; but inside its thick walls all is elegant, cosy and welcoming. It is furnished and decorated with antiques: and Limoges ceramics, and original watercolours adorn the walls. The 18thC piano is a decoration: Doña Adelaida now prefers a modern instrument. Like any self-respecting big house, Pazo Casa Grande has its own chapel which every year, on the feast of Corpus Christi, is decorated with a carpet of flowers.

Outside, there is a delightful garden with fruit trees and a copse of chestnuts. This is a popular base from which to follow the Route of the Monasteries (*Ribera Sagrada*), also the Romanesque Route, and in winter for skiing.

~

NEARBY Montefurado reservoir (6 km); Montaña Manzaneda ski resort (16 km); San Esteban de Ribas de Sil Monastery and gorges of the River Sil (60 km).
LOCATION in a main street of the town; garden and car parking
FOOD breakfast
PRICES ⊕-⊕⊕
ROOMS 9; 8 double,1 suite with bath; all rooms have central heating, TV
FACILITIES dining room, TV room, chapel
CREDIT CARDS AE, DC, MC, V
CHILDREN welcome; play area
DISABLED access difficult
PETS accepted by arrangement
CLOSED never
PROPRIETOR Adelaida Alvarez

PALENCIA

AMPUDIA

POSADA DE LA CASA DEL ABAD
~ TOWN HOTEL ~

Plaza Francisco Martin Gromaz 12, 34160 Ampudía, Palencia
TEL 979 768008 **FAX** 979 768308
EMAIL hotel@casadelabad.com **WEBSITE** www.casadelabad.com

HIGH ON THE *MESETA*, Spain's fertile central plain, this historic inn overlooks the central square of Ampudía town. The house was built in the 1600s for the abbots of the town's collegiate church – and guests can use the former abbots' private chapel. The present owners have taken immense pride in its restoration, using only local materials and preserving the adobe walls, wrought-iron balconies and other original features. The 17 bedrooms and public rooms are furnished traditionally and rather grandly with the paintings and other possessions of the Castillian family who owned the house from the 18th century. The atmosphere verges on the formal and some visitors may find this hotel a bit of a museum piece.

But look around, and you find subtle 21st-century updates, not just the works by contemporary artists secreted among the Old Masters, but also two digital telephone lines and PC Internet connections in each bedroom, an all-weather swimming pool (heated by solar panels, with environmentally friendly salt purification) and hi-tech, low-energy cleaning and lighting.

The abbots' old wine cellar has become a fine restaurant, with two Michelin stars and a selection of international and fine local wines produced in the surrounding vineyards of fertile Castile's Tierra de Campos.

NEARBY Medina de Rioseco with medieval churches decorated Valladolid style (30 km).
LOCATION Ampudía town centre, 30 km W of Dueñas and autopista N620/E80 Burgos– Valladolid); 20 min in taxi from Venta de Baños station; free garage parking
FOOD breakfast, lunch, dinner, snacks
PRICE €€€€-€€€€€
ROOMS 13 doubles, 5 suites, all with bath, shower, TV, clock/radio, PC jack, air-conditioning, minibar, safe; 1 suite with Jacuzzi
FACILITIES reception, lounge, bar/restaurant, business suite, sauna, heated swimming pool, fitness centre, spa, sauna, tennis court, garage
CREDIT CARDS AE, MC, V
CHILDREN welcome **DISABLED** no special facilities **PETS** accepted, small charge
CLOSED never **DIRECTOR** Begoña Mindes

PALENCIA

CAMASOBRES

POSADA DE LA PERNIA
～ COUNTRY HOUSE HOTEL ～

Calle Real s/n, 34849 Camasobres, Palencia
TEL 979 184099 **FAX** 979 184283
WEBSITE www.posadalapernia.galeon.com

THE PARQUE NATURAL de Fuentes Carrionas y Fuente Cobre surrounds this old inn. Like many of Spain's protected 'natural parks', access is restricted, but not to guests of La Pernía, whose owners provide a 4x4 for those who want to explore. The hotel, in a country house built in the 1700s, takes its name from the valley in which it lies, surrounded by hills.

María Carmen, the hotel's engaging proprietress, has taken pains to maintain its historic style and atmosphere. There are bedrooms with four-posters, antiques in the old hall, and a fine former library. The cooking in the hotel restaurant (guests only) is as traditional as the hotel's furnishings, reflecting the abundance of game (wild boar and venison in season) and trout and other river fish in this mountainous region.

This is a house for active guests. In a building adjoining the *casona* – the old hall – is a newer building housing a heated swimming pool. There is a golf course nearby, skiing in winter around Aguilar de Campoo, and skiing, walking and climbing in the magnificent Picos de Europa mountain range, a half-hour's drive away. The staff speak mainly Spanish, but know enough English to help their foreign guests with information about the area.

NEARBY Medieval fortified town of Aguilar do Campoo (41 km).
LOCATION in Camasobres village on C627, 33 km S of Potes; half hour by taxi to Aguilar de Campoo station; free car parking
FOOD breakfast, lunch, dinner, snacks
PRICE €€€-€€€€
ROOMS 14 double, 3 suites, all with bath and shower, 1 suite with whirlpool bath; all rooms have phone, PC jack, TV, clock/radio, hairdrier, minibar, air conditioning
FACILITIES reception, lounge, bar, café, restaurant, breakfast room, meeting room, lift, Jacuzzi, sauna, solarium, heated swimming pool, terrace, garden
CREDIT CARDS DC, MC, V
CHILDREN welcome **DISABLED** one special room **PETS** accepted, small charge
CLOSED never
PROPRIETOR María Carmen Gómez

ASTURIAS

PONGA

LA CASONA DE MESTAS

MOUNTAIN HOTEL

Las Mestas 33557, Ponga, Asturias
TEL 98 5843055 FAX 98 5843092
WEBSITE www.casonademetas.com
FOOD breakfast, lunch, dinner
PRICES €€
CLOSED 20 Jan to 1 March
MANAGER Georges Gonzalez

T O REACH THIS mountain hideaway you follow the sinuous course of the Ponga river to the regional capital of San Juan de Beleño, passing below sheer rocky hillsides and climbing over beautiful passes. The hotel – another Rural Tourism Centre – is at the heart of some of the most spectacular walking country you could hope to find anywhere, with several well known routes starting at the Casona itself. The main building has been converted from an old house with overhanging, Alpine-style roofs, and the restaurant area is a sympathetic modern, wooden glass-sided extension looking out on to fabulous views of the surrounding peaks.

TARAMUNDI

LA RECTORAL

MOUNTAIN HOTEL

33775, Taramundi, Asturias
TEL 98 5646767 FAX 98 5646777
E-MAIL larectoral@intonegocio.com
WEBSITE www.larectoral.com
FOOD breakfast, lunch, dinner
PRICES €€€€
CLOSED never
MANAGER Jesus Manuel Mier

T HIS WAS THE first of the Rural Tourism hotels to be encouraged by the government of Asturias – a lovely old 18thC stone house converted into simple but comfortable accommodation reflecting the architectural, decorative and gastronomic traditions of the region. It is on the westernside of Asturias, on the border with Lugo, in the remote hilly country of Los Oscos. The Rectoral looks out over unspoiled countryside which is still quietly tilled using locally made tools. Six of the bedrooms have their own lounge and private terrace, sharing the peaceful view with the hotel's patio.

BASQUE COUNTRY/NAVARRA

This section covers the provinces of Cantabria, Vizcaya, Guipuzcoa, Alava and Burgos, and includes the 'Basque Country' next to the border with France, a distinctive region with its own strong Celtic heritage, language and customs.

Visitors tend to overlook the Basque country in their hurry to explore the Picos or the coastline of Galicia to the west. Yet it has much to offer. Not least of the attractions is the smart seaside resort of San Sebastián (or Donostia – duplicate names are a constant reminder here of the Basque separatist movement). In a region noted for fine food, this is probably the gastronomic headquarters; sadly, none of the best restaurants has rooms. Two places to stay stand out, neither of them cheap: the big and charmless **Monte Igueldo**, which enjoys a heart-stopping view (especially at night) from the peak of the same name at one side of the sweeping Bahía de la Concha (Tel 943 210211); and the lovely old seafront **Hotel de Londres y de Inglaterra** (Tel 943 426989), as gracious a seaside hotel as you could wish for.

Thanks largely to Hemingway's novels, Pamplona is world-famous for its July fiesta. The bulls run under the windows of the centrally-located and old-fashioned **La Perla** (Tel 948 227706). Upper rooms in the more peaceful, 28-room **Eslava** (Tel 948 222270) look out on the countryside beyond the city walls.

Paradors in North Central Spain

Those who arrive in Spain on the Santander ferry are in reach of three Paradores. The **PT Gil Blas at Santillana del Mar** (Tel 942 818000) is one of the best of the chain. The others are modern, but enjoy enviable positions in the mountains of the Picos de Europa. The otherwise dreary **PT Río Deva at Fuente Dé** is spectacularly set high up in a natural amphitheatre, close to a cable-car giving access to wonderful views and walks (Tel 942 736651). **PT Fuentes Carrionas** is further south at Cervera de Pisuerga in the less spectacular foothills of the Picos, but is a rather more stylish hotel (Tel 979 870075).

East and south-east of Santander are some wonderfully historic Paradores. The **PT de Argómaniz**, east of Vitoria, has 54 rooms in wings built on to a mellow 300-year-old mansion (Tel 945 293200). South of Pamplona is the **PT Príncipe de Viana** at Olite (medieval capital of Navarra), a fairy-tale castle of turrets and towers, with some splendid rooms within (Tel 948 740000). The **PT Marco Fabio Quintiliano** at nearby Calahorra in La Rioja is a modern building of five floors with 62 rooms (Tel 941 130358).

CANTABRIA

AJO

CASONA DE LA PEÑA

~ RESTAURANT WITH ROOMS ~

Barrio de La Peña, 39170 Ajo, Cantabria
TEL 942 670567 **MOBILE** 00 34 629516234
E-MAIL lacaona@infosystems.com **WEBSITE** www.cantabria.com/casonadelapena

A LMOST AT THE tip of Cape Ajo, and standing alone on a hillside above the small seaside town and river that share the same name, this is essentially the sleeping quarters of a restaurant that has created a very high reputation for itself in a short space of time, despite, or quite possibly because of being squeezed between the fleshpots of Santander and Bilbao. Housed in a 17thC manor – whitewashed outside and cool honey-coloured stone on the inside – and standing in several acres of grass, the entire establishment has been renovated to a very high standard. Given the size of the restaurant and the small number of bedrooms, it is clear that most of the diners go after eating. But there is a treat in store for those who stay: the gloss on the antique furniture is that little bit brighter, the pile of the rugs beneath the beamed ceilings is that little bit deeper, the sheets on the bed a little bit crisper and the standard of service that little bit more attentive than they might have hoped for. By the same token, the bill may be a little larger than normal - but a brisk half-mile walk down to Cuberris beach should put everything back into perspective, and set you up for your next meal.

~

NEARBY Cuberris beach (800 m); Santander and airport (25 km); Pedreña Golf Course (10 km); Bilbao and airport (50 km).
LOCATION on outskirts of Ajo, looking out over sea; ample off-street parking
FOOD breakfast, lunch, dinner
PRICES €€€€
ROOMS 4 doubles (2 twins, 1 suite); all rooms have water-jet bath, shower, radio, TV, VCR, minibar, hair drier, modem point, air conditioning
FACILITIES two drawing rooms, breakfast room, restaurant, terrace, garden, putting green, laundry, parking
CREDIT CARDS AE, DC, MC, V
CHILDREN welcome
DISABLED one specially adapted room **PETS** not accepted **CLOSED** never
PROPRIETOR Marian El Heverria

CANTABRIA

CORVERA

LA CASONA AZUL DE CORVERA
~ TOWN HOTEL ~

Gral. Díaz de Villegas 5, 39697 Corvera
TEL 942 596400 **FAX** 942 596400
WEBSITE www.casonazul.com

THE HOTEL IS AS blue as its name, and can be recognized from quite a distance, especially if you are making the descent from Lake Ebro towards Santander. It's a town house on a main road in the valley, which carries much of the commercial traffic travelling to and from the port at Santander. That said, it is a handsome house built at the end of the 19thC by a returned Indiano, one of the many Cantabrians who returned home after making a fortune in the West Indies and built themselves large, often ostentatious houses. This one is not in the least flashy, and is tucked into a corner of the property. There's a large garden, edged with apple, pear and walnut trees, with plenty of room for children to undo the kinks of a long car journey. The building needed extensive restoration before opening as a hotel, and the architect, Luis Castillo, stayed fairly faithful to the house's original form, both in use of materials and of colours. The small sitting room is dotted with items from the appropriate era, and the breakfast room has the traditional black-and-white, diagonally tiled floor. The wood-floored bedrooms are light and comfortable, with well-equipped bathrooms, and those that look over the garden also have a view of the surrounding hills. One particularly welcome rarity is a lockable garage, available to guests. Spanish only spoken here as we went to press.

~

NEARBY Lake Ebro (32 km); Saja-Besaya Nature Park (30 km); Santander (32 km); Santillana (20 km).
LOCATION in small town in the Pas valley, S of Puente Viesgo, as it descends from the Cordillera Cantábrica; street car parking and own garage
FOOD breakfast, dinner by arrangement
PRICES €€
ROOMS 9 doubles (5 twin-bedded); all rooms have bath, telephone
FACILITIES sitting room, dining room, garden
CREDIT CARDS MC,V **CHILDREN** welcome **DISABLED** no specially adapted rooms
PETS by arrangement **CLOSED** during winter only open for fiestas, weekends and bank holiday weekends **PROPRIETOR** Beatriz Vallejo Martínez

CANTABRIA

COSGAYA

HOTEL DEL OSO
~ MOUNTAIN HOTEL ~

39539, Cosgaya, Cantabria
TEL 942 733018 **FAX** 942 733036
E-MAIL hoteldeloso@mundivia.es **WEBSITE** www.hoteldeloso.com

YOU WILL ALREADY have come through some exceptional scenery to reach Cosgaya, climbing steadily all the way from the coast, and once you arrive you are surrounded by peaks, many snow- covered until early summer.

A small bridge over a clear mountain stream takes you into the forecourt of this stone-built hotel, with its wooden balconies, arched veranda and overflowing flowerpots. The public rooms are cool and dark in the summer heat, but cosy and welcoming in the winter, with log fires in the sitting room. Although the hotel has only recently been built, it is traditional in style with plenty of workmanship to admire, in wood, terracotta tiling and bare stonework. The restaurant, too, makes use of regional specialities – fresh river trout, interesting local cheeses and regional spirits.

There is always the chance of getting snowed in when staying in this area, so bring plenty of books – it has been known to happen in June, though at that time of year you are more likely to be lazing around their pool, playing tennis or off hiking in the hills. They are used to British visitors here, and good English is spoken at the desk.

~

NEARBY Cable-car at Fuente De (10 km) to 1800 m.
LOCATION by stream in mountains; with garden and car parking
FOOD breakfast, lunch, dinner
PRICES €€€-€€€€
ROOMS 50; 46 double, 4 single, all with bath; all rooms have central heating, phone, TV
FACILITIES dining room, 3 sitting rooms, bar; swimming pool, tennis court, garden
CREDIT CARDS DC, MC, V
CHILDREN welcome
DISABLED access difficult
PETS not accepted
CLOSED 7 Jan to 15 Feb
PROPRIETOR Severo Rivas

CANTABRIA

ESCALANTE

SAN ROMAIN DE ESCALANTE
~ COUNTRY HOTEL ~

Carretera de Escalante a Castillo km 2, 39795 Escalante, Cantabria
TEL 942 677728 **FAX** 942 677643
E-MAIL escalante@relaischateaux.com **WEBSITE** www.relaischateaux.fr/escalante

IF YOU WERE TO merge an enthusiastic *restaurateur* with a dedicated hotelier, and to offer them a generous budget, they might well come up with something like this hotel, perched on a hill above the salt marshes which isolate Santoña and sweep past Escalante to the Asón estuary and Laredo. It stands in manicured gardens, dotted with palms, statues and enough pillars to start a Roman builder's yard: this is definitely an up-market establishment. Some of the bedrooms are in the main building (a stout, honey-coloured stone building that used to be a manor) and there is also a small library equipped with chintz covered armchairs for those who want to escape the peace of the garden or the brilliant white paving and walls which border the swimming pool. The rest of the bedrooms are in a newly-built block next door, all on the ground floor and all with their own front doors. These are high, cool rooms with acres of space, good 'baronial' furniture interspersed with thoughtfully selected modern pieces, and the sort of bathrooms you'd like to pack and take home with you. On the other side of the main building stands the restaurant, a galleried half-timbered building, which is something of a magnet for local, and not-so-local, people - proof of the quality of its food and wine list.

~

NEARBY Bilbāo (60 km); Santander (35 km); Santoña (10 km).
LOCATION 2 km up hill from village, with open views; large gated private car park
FOOD breakfast, lunch, dinner
PRICES €€€€
ROOMS 16; 13 doubles, 3 suites; all rooms have bath, shower, phone, TV, modem point, air conditioning, minibar, hairdryer
FACILITIES drawing room, restaurant, terrace, garden, swimming pool
CREDIT CARDS AE, DC, MC, V
CHILDREN welcome
DISABLED 6 ground floor bedrooms **PETS** allowed in standard rooms only
CLOSED 21 Dec-21 Jan
MANAGERS/PROPRIETORS Juan Meli, Juan A. Iribarnegaray, Victoria Rey

CANTABRIA

NAVEDA

CASONA DE NAVEDA
~ MOUNTAIN HOTEL ~

Plaza del Medio Lugar, nº37, 39210 Naveda,-Cantabria
TEL 942 779515/77966 **FAX** 942 779681
E-MAIL *info@casonadenaveda.com*

IF YOU WANT TO wake up on top of the world, or at least a comfortable distance above sea-level, then head up the River Ebro to its source west of Reinosa. Then choose the tallest mountain you can see and continue west towards that. Soon you will arrive in Naveda, a tiny village on the flat, broad floor of this high valley, guarded by the Pico de Tres Mares and Alto Campóo (which, at higher than 2,000 m, has skiing in winter). Your arrival will arouse little interest from the village dog, but will trigger a warm welcome from Paloma López. She took this low, stone-built 17thC farmhouse and rebuilt the interior using wood everywhere, opened out some of the windows to let in more light and the stunning views of the peaks at the head of the valley. She furnished it with light, elegant antiques instead of the dark and massive 'baronial' furniture favoured by so many. In the drawing room she has added comfortable sofas, rugs on the highly polished wooden floors, and an open fire. In the glass-walled dining room, crisp white tablecloths cover darker blue ones on each of the tables, and at dinner tall-stemmed wineglasses stand guard over ranks of gleaming cutlery. The beamed bedrooms are of fair size with pale walls, wrought-iron or wooden bedheads and thoughtfully equipped bathrooms with grey and white chequered tile floors. A gem.

Within 20 km are golf, fishing, shooting, rafting, windsurfing, pot-holing, skiing and watersports. Spanish only spoken.

~

NEARBY Reinosa (8 km); winter sports resort of Alto Campoo (15 km); Nestares Golf Course (6 km); Juliobriga Roman ruins (8 km).
LOCATION in village; parking in quiet square
FOOD breakfast, dinner **PRICES** €€
ROOMS 7; I single, 6 doubles (all of which are 'suites', four with twin beds); all rooms have bath, shower, phone, TV, VCR, hair drier
FACILITIES drawing room, bar, dining room, garden **CREDIT CARDS** AE, DC, MC, V
CHILDREN welcome **DISABLED** no specially adapted rooms **PETS** not accepted
CLOSED never **PROPRIETORS** Paloma Lopez Sarasa and Jesus Mantilla Blanco

CANTABRIA

RUESGA

TORRE DE RUESGA
~ CONVERTED PALACE ~

Bº de la Bárcena s/n, 39810 Valle de Ruesga, Cantabria
TEL 942.641060 **FAX** 942.641172
E-MAIL reservas@t-ruesga.com **WEBSITE** www.t-ruesga.com

CARMEN CAPRILE STUCCHI's family told her she had taken leave of her senses when she decided to buy a wrecked 17thC palace in the Alto Asón. It had been left empty for 40 years because of a disputed will. Forgotten frescos by the Catalan painter Leon de Criach emerged during the course of the restoration and are just one of the many features of this unique building. Inside, the furniture and wall-hangings are a fair substitute for the original, long-since dispersed, contents, and 21stC technology has been carefully threaded through the old building to deliver modern services as unobtrusively as possible. The bedrooms in the main building have all the beams and bare stone you could wish for – but they also have air conditioning, telephones, artfully placed lighting and excellent bathrooms. Five newly-built rooms, arranged as a line of cottage-suites in the garden, are ideal for families. The stone-flagged restaurant serves a well-prepared and presented selection of regional dishes with a well chosen wine list. A small, comfortable bar, a sunny breakfast–room and a richly gilded salon with a grand piano in it complete the list. An amiable combination of history and hands-on hotel-keeping in a wonderful area of woods, waterfalls, mountains and caves.

~

NEARBY Cuevas de Covalanas (12 km); Santa Marina de Udalla (14 km); Cabárceno safari park (50 km); beaches: Laredo (25 km), Berria (30 km), Liendo (32 km).
LOCATION an hour from Bilbão, overlooked by Mount Mortillano in the narrow Asón valley, on edge of village; ample private car parking
FOOD breakfast, lunch, dinner
PRICES €€€
ROOMS 15; 6 doubles, 4 suites, 5 garden-suites; all rooms have bath, shower, TV, VCR, minibar, air conditioning, hair drier
FACILITIES restaurant, bar, breakfast room, card and billiards room, library, gardens, swimming pool, gym, sauna, fishing on River Asón
CREDIT CARDS AE, DC, MC, V **CHILDREN** welcome **DISABLED** easy access to garden-suites and public rooms **PETS** not accepted **CLOSED** mid-Jan-1 Feb
PROPRIETOR Carmen Caprile Stucchi

CANTABRIA

SANTILLANA DEL MAR

LOS INFANTES
~ VILLAGE HOTEL ~

Avenida Le Dorat 1, 39330, Santillana del Mar, Cantabria
TEL 942 818100 **FAX** 942 840103
E-MAIL informacion@grupolosinfantes.com **WEBSITE** www.grupolosinfantes.com

THE HOTEL LOS INFANTES, set slightly back from the main road, just outside the village of Santillana del Mar, has been built around a lovely old 18thC stone country house. Entering the hall from the terrace through a decorated stone archway you can sense the grandeur of the old ways of life. There are huge carved chests on stone floors, wrought iron chandeliers hanging from high ceilings with massive wooden beams, and an impressive collection of antique clocks. The bar is in the lobby area, and you can sink into a deep leather armchair and soak up the atmosphere here or take your drink out into the sheltered garden. The upstairs sitting room also has leather armchairs, as well as more formal reproduction furniture.

The restaurant is modern and unfussy, in café style. Some of the bedrooms are rather undistinguished, with small bathrooms; others are individually furnished with antique bed-heads, paintings on the walls, white handwoven bedspreads, comfortable chairs, carpets, balconies and large, immaculate bathrooms. A few metres from the hotel is a recent annexe offering 20 more bedrooms.

~

NEARBY sights of Santillana del Mar; Altamira cave exhibition (1.5 km).
LOCATION on main road past village, near Diocesano Museum; parking for 20 cars
FOOD breakfast, lunch, dinner
PRICES rooms €€-€€€
ROOMS 25 double, 3 single, 2 suites, all with bath; all rooms have central heating, phone, TV
FACILITIES dining room, sitting room
CREDIT CARDS AE, DC, MC, V
CHILDREN accepted
DISABLED ground floor rooms
PETS by arrangement only
CLOSED Oct to Apr
PROPRIETOR Mesones Gómez

CANTABRIA

QUIJAS, TORRELAVEGA

HOSTERIA DE QUIJAS
~ COUNTRY HOUSE HOTEL ~

Barrio Vinuesa s/n, 39590, Quijas, Reocín, Cantabria
TEL 942 820833 **FAX** 942 838050
E-MAIL quijas@telelineb.es **WEBSITE** www.lanzadera.com/hosteriaquijas

AFTER SEVERAL YEARS living abroad, the Castañeda family returned home to transform this palatial 18thC house near Torrelavega into an exemplary rural hotel.

The house, with its stone walls, spreading eaves, bay windows and timbered ceilings, has been restored with great care, especially noticeable in the former library (now the reception area) and the private oratory of a former owner (approved by a bull of Pope Leon XIII).

The hotel's most outstanding feature is the 4,000 square metre garden which surrounds it on three sides with hydrangeas, climbers, and a magnolia several hundred years old, under which you can sit. The terrace is covered by a shady grapevine.

Demetrio Castañeda and his daughter Sonia serve their guests in person. The restaurant enjoys a reputation of its own: Javier Sobrón, a local chef who once cooked for the King of Spain, supervises the excellent cooking which includes too many specialities, all exquisitely presented, to list in full.

It is a shame that the main Oviedo to Santander road, with its heavy traffic, runs so close to the hotel. When booking, make sure you ask for a room on the other side.

~

NEARBY Santillana del Mar (4 km); Altamira caves (5 km).
LOCATION on the main road from Oviedo to Santander; car parking and garden
FOOD breakfast, lunch, dinner
PRICES €€-€€€€€
ROOMS 12 double, one single, 6 suites, all with bath; all rooms have central heating, telephone, TV (satellite), hairdrier, minibar
FACILITIES sitting room, 2 dining rooms, bar, terrace; garden, swimming pool
CREDIT CARDS AE, DC, MC, V
CHILDREN welcome
DISABLED access difficult **PETS** not accepted
CLOSED 23 Dec to 4 Jan
PROPRIETOR Demetrio Castañeda

VIZCAYA

BAKIO

HOSTERIA DEL SEÑORIO DE BIZKAIA

~ TOWN HOTEL ~

José M.ª Cirarda 4, 48130 Bakio, Vizcaya
TEL 946 19 4725 **FAX** 946 19 4725
E-MAIL hostbizkaia@hosteriasreales.com **WEBSITE** www.hosteriasreales.com

ONE OF THE BEST points of this cheerfully reasonable hotel north-east of Bilbao is that you don't have to drive through the city to get here from the airport. Bakio is a popular spot for the city dwellers, quite a number of whom have weekend flats here, so although the beach is large, you will be sharing it. The hotel, a 19thC Basque farmhouse, is tucked away behind the sea front in a peaceful woody spot by one of the two rivers that flow down to the bay – even more peaceful than normal as we went to press since the nearest bridge had been washed away by a flash flood. The only public rooms are the dining room and bar (although in summer there is plenty of space outside), but the bar is a very family-friendly spot, with doors straight out on to the garden. The fair-sized bedrooms are squeaky clean, freshly decorated and well-equipped and there are additional beds available for families. The stone-walled dining room offers a good breakfast and a range of Basque dishes in the evening. Apart from the beach, the fairytale Castle Butrón is a short drive away and looks like the original inspiration for every Walt Disney castle ever drawn. Another worthwhile expedition, not far to the north-east, is a marine conservation area presided over by the tiny church of San Juan de Gaztelugatxe, perched on its own rocky peninsula and reached by a spectacular pedestrian causeway.

~

NEARBY Bilbão (30 km); Bakio beach (0.5 km); cave paintings at Santimamiñe (30 km).
LOCATION on coast north of Bilbão and west of Urdaibai Nature Park 600 m from beach; ample private car parking
FOOD breakfast, dinner
PRICES €€
ROOMS 16 doubles (12 twin-bedded); all rooms have bath, TV, telephone, hair drier, safe
FACILITIES bar/café, dining room, garden
CREDIT CARDS AE, DC, MC, V
CHILDREN welcome
DISABLED no specially adapted rooms **PETS** accepted **CLOSED** Jan
PROPRIETOR Jorge Laustalet Santos

VIZCAYA

MUNDAKA

ATALAYA

~ TOWN HOTEL ~

Paseo de Txorrokopunta, 2, 48360, Mundaka, Vizcaya
TEL 946 177000 **FAX** 946 876899
E-MAIL reservas@hotel-atalaya-mundaka.com **WEBSITE** www.hotel-atalaya-mundaka.com

THERE ARE NO major changes to report at this turn-of-the-century house, with its bright white façade dominated by bay windows, which stands close to the fishing port of Mundaka at the mouth of the Ría de Guernica. It has been decorated in an English style and transformed into a small family hotel. Extremely well kept and run, it undoubtedly provides the best accommodation on this stretch of coast.

To enter, you have to use the intercom. You will be received by the owner, Mari Carmen Alonso, or her husband. Both exude Basque honesty and hospitality. An air-conditioned conservatory (without plants) serves as a breakfast room and bar, and for meals there is a new cafeteria and terrace. Bedrooms have been very carefully put together, with every detail attended to: the magazine racks, for instance, may well contain up-to-date foreign publications. They are, however, a little small, even if the beds themselves are large.

Through the bay windows there are views of the church, the adjacent beach and the Bay of Biscay where it meets the estuary. This is a place for anyone who appreciates silence and a seemingly home-like atmosphere.

~

NEARBY Santa María church; Guernica, Basque capital (14 km).
LOCATION in front of the port, on the Ría de Guernica; garden and car parking
FOOD breakfast
PRICES €€€-€€€€
ROOMS 10 double, 1 single, one suite, all with bath; all rooms have central heating, telephone, radio, TV (satellite), minibar
FACILITIES dining room, sitting room, bar, garden
CREDIT CARDS AE, DC, MC, V
CHILDREN welcome; baby-sitting service
DISABLED obliging staff to help
PETS accepted
CLOSED never
PROPRIETOR Mari Carmen Alonso

GUIPUZCOA

HONDARRIBIA (FUENTERRABIA)

PAMPINOT

~ HISTORIC PALACE ~

Mayor, 3, 20280 Hondarribia (Fuenterrabía), Guipúzcoa
TEL 943 640600 **FAX** 943 645128

OLGA ALVAREZ bought this palatial house in the oldest part of historic Hondarribia with the intention of living in it herself. Only after renovating it did she have the idea to convert it into a small and uniquely personal hotel with eight cosy rooms.

The building has almost as long a history as the town, whose steep streets and ramparts are a reminder of its former importance. Before becoming a hotel, the house served variously as a warehouse, cider brewery and aristocratic residence. With such a distinguished pedigree, it is, as you would expect, filled with antique furniture, chandeliers, plastered lintels, carpeted floors and other fine ornaments.

The bedrooms are spacious, comfortable and softly lit. The TV seems out of place, however, and the bathrooms are rather sparingly decorated. But the core of this place's appeal lies in the feminine touch, the sensitivity, and the good manners of Olga Alvarez and her team. Caution: streetside rooms can suffer from noise, and with no air-conditioning to allow windows to be closed, or ceiling fan, this has given a sleepless night to at least one visitor of whom we know. Reports welcome.

~

NEARBY Castle of Carlos V, now a Parador; Jaizkíbel golf course (5 km); San Sebastian (21 km).
LOCATION in the main street, in the historic city centre; no car parking
FOOD breakfast
PRICES €€€€-€€€€€
ROOMS 3 double, one single, 3 family rooms, one suite, all with bath; all rooms have central heating, telephone, TV, minibar, safe
FACILITIES sitting room, bar, breakfast room
CREDIT CARDS AE, DC, MC, V
CHILDREN very welcome; games and stories available
DISABLED access difficult
PETS accepted **CLOSED** Nov
PROPRIETOR Olga Alvarez

GUIPUZCOA

HONDARRIBIA (FUENTERRABIA)

PARADOR DE HONDARRIBIA
∽ TOWN HOTEL ∽

Plaza de Armas 14, 20280 Hondarribia, Guipuzcoa
TEL 943 645 500 **FAX** 943 642 153
E-MAIL hondarribia@parador.es **WEBSITE** www.parador.es

A 12THC FORTRESS with walls ten feet (3 m) thick, originally built to protect Spain from French incursions, this is the oldest of northern Spain's paradors. (It is also known as PT el Emperador.) On a recent visit we immediately noticed the friendliness of the welcome and a feeling of warmth and elegance: quite a contrast to its bygone military grimness. Guests clearly find it easy to respond to this appeal.

In fact, our inspector described it as 'simply stunning'. There are some beautifully furnished public rooms, a bar, a cafe and 'the most wonderful inner courtyard'. There are impressive antiques throughout, and the conversion from castle to hotel has been done in 'the most pleasing way'. Bedrooms are attractive and individual.

The lack of a restaurant is no drawback: there's an excellent local selection. Our inspector recommends Sebastian, a short walk from the parador, with innovative Basque/French dishes.

∽

NEARBY Jaizkibel golf course; San Sebastian.
LOCATION centre of old city, close to church, singposted; own car parking
FOOD breakfast
PRICE €€
ROOMS 36, all with bath, heating
FACILITIES two drawing rooms, cafe, breakfast room
CREDIT CARDS AE, DC, MC, V
CHILDREN welcome
DISABLED special facilities in some rooms
PETS small ones accepted
CLOSED never
MANAGER Jose Carlos Campos Regalado

ALAVA

LAGUARDIA

CASTILLO EL COLLARDO

~ TOWN HOTEL ~

Paseo El Collado, 01300 Laguardia, Alava
TEL 941 121200 **FAX** 941 600878
E-MAIL castillocollado@euskalnet.net

BY REPUTE, THIS is one of northern Spain's most interesting new hotels of the 1990s, but before putting it in the guide we decided to take a close look.

Castillo means a fortified manor house, but the building, with its distinctive tower, was originally a cosmectics factory. Later, under church ownership, it became a residence for priests. In 1981, Sr Javier, the current proprietor, fulfilled a long-standing ambition by buying it to convert into a hotel. It took ten years, and the result really is different from anywhere else you may have stayed: 'somewhat eccentric, but utterly charming'. It is furnished in a highly individual style, with beautiful woodwork and many art nouveau features, particularly tiles and glass. The eight bedrooms are all different, with contrasting colour schemes, ornate turn-of-the 20th century embossed radiators and oval baths. They offer luxury with an appealing hint of decadence.

There is a small bar and an enormous wine cellar, as befits the hotel's location in the heart of Rioja wine country. The restaurant 'has a personality of its own' and an extensive wine list. Climb the tower for views over vineyards and mountains. If you feel jaded by standardised hotels, this will freshen you up. ~

NEARBY Vitoria (Gasteiz), Logrono, Soria.
LOCATION signposted in town, no private car parking; public parking nearby
FOOD breakfast, lunch, dinner
PRICE ©©
ROOMS 8, all with bath, air-conditioning
FACILITIES sitting room, dining room, garden
CREDIT CARDS AE, DC, MC, V
CHILDREN welcome
DISABLED not especially suitable **PETS** accepted by prior arrangement
CLOSED never
PROPRIETORS Sgr Javier

ALAVA

LAGUARDIA

POSADA MAYOR DE MIGUELOA

~ TOWN HOTEL ~

Mayor de Migueloa Nº 2001300, Laguardia (Basque Country/Rioja)
TEL 945 621175 **FAX** 945 621022
E-MAIL reservas@mayordemigueloa.com **WEBSITE** www.mayordemigueloa.com

LAGUARDIA IS a lovely cobble-stoned town, once a fortified stronghold of the Navarrese kings. Tucked among the streets is this former palace, known in its day as the Viana, built in 1619 by Don Martin Sánchez Samaniego. The wine cellar (worth a tour: it's as old as the building itself) is stuffed with the hotel's own reputable Rioja, and the restaurant keeps up ably under the direction of Miguel Arrabe and the well-loved Luis Irízar. Don't forget you are in Basque country here, so the Spanish (both spoken and written) is slightly different. The staff are more than happy to help with the menu and offer suggestions. We enjoyed local dishes such as *chorizo* soup, served with a plate of hot green peppers. Bedrooms are good value – large, individually decorated, with exposed stone walls, oriental rugs, rich colours, antique furniture. Be careful though: any savings made on the accommodation can be spent in the dining room with little difficulty.

~

NEARBY Rioja, Cantabrina mountains.
LOCATION in town centre; limited car parking in hotel's own grounds – phone ahead to be sure of a space
FOOD breakfast, lunch, dinner
PRICE €€€–€€€€
ROOMS 8; 7 doubles, one suite; all rooms have bath, phone, TV
FACILITIES restaurant, bar, wine cellar, swimming pool, children's pool
CREDIT CARDS AE, DC, MC, V
CHILDREN welcome
PETS accepted
DISABLED no specially adapted rooms
CLOSED late Dec to early Feb
PROPRIETORS Meri G. Huergo and Jaime Gutierrez

ALAVA

MORUA

GUIKURI

~ COUNTRY BED AND BREAKFAST ~

Carerío Guikuri, 01138 Murua, Alava
TEL 945-464084 **FAX** 945-464084
E-MAIL guikuri@euskalnet.net **WEBSITE** www.guikuri.com

ON THE SOUTHERN edge of the Gorbeia Nature Park, at no great distance south-west of Bilbao, this old farmhouse in its sizeable garden is the last stop on the smallest, highest lane in the village. Javier Puyo and his wife started their renovation programme in 1984, and, doing all the work themselves, opened their first two rooms eight years later. They now have five rooms and two family apartments, each sleeping four people. The 1850s building has been rehabilitated rather than renovated: the timbers are just as original as the walls but have been carefully oiled and waxed, and the rough plaster which covers some of the interior stonework has been painted in strong but natural shades. The double height, galleried living room has a fully equipped kitchen off it, available for guests' use, so although this is strictly speaking a bed-and-breakfast hotel, guests can choose not to go out to one of the local restaurants for dinner. The fair-sized bedrooms are decorated in a simple, comfortable country style and all have excellent bathrooms. Fresh bread is baked every day for breakfast, and very often a sponge cake too.

~

NEARBY Gorbeia Nature Park (0.5 km); Otxandio (15 km); Vitoria-Gasteiz (15 km); Puerto de Cruceta (15 km); Museum of Basque Pottery (3 km); Guggenheim Museum (63 km).
LOCATION an hour S of Bilbão, virtually inside one nature park and close to another, on hillside backed by woods; off road car parking
FOOD breakfast
PRICE €€
ROOMS 5 doubles (2 twin-bedded), two apartments for 4; all with bathroom
FACILITIES sitting room, kitchen for self catering, garden
CREDIT CARDS V
CHILDREN welcome
DISABLED no **PETS** by arrangement
CLOSED never
PROPRIETOR Javier Puyo

BURGOS

BURGOS

HOTEL LANDA PALACE

~ ROADSIDE HOTEL ~

Carretera Madrid km 235, 09000, Burgos
TEL 947 206343 **FAX** 947 264676
E-MAIL landapal.es **WEBSITE** www.landapalace.es

FORGET REAL PALACES for a moment; this is the eccentric dream of one Señora Landa. Some consider it luxurious, charmingly over-the-top or supremely pretentious; we see it as great fun. A sense of excess is aroused by the prodigious collection of old horse carts outside; but inside you are positively whisked away from reality into a Gothic fantasy. The tower you step into, transported to this convenient roadside location from a neighbouring village, is the only genuinely old part of the hotel. All the rest – including the Gothic vaults over the larger dining-room and the swimming pool, and the carved spiral staircases – was built in the 60s.

The bedrooms are no less excessive. The grand suite has doors of polished walnut and a brass bedstead surmounted by a crown. Its sitting room – containing a massive antique desk and five-seater settee – could house a numerous family. But don't look out of the romantic, *ajimez* window or the spell will be broken by the sight of the main Burgos-Madrid road.

There are antiques and greenery everywhere, and surprises at every turn. The corridor outside the dining rooms ticks to the rhythm of umpteen wall clocks.

~

NEARBY Burgos; Miraflores Carthusian Monastery (5 km).
LOCATION on main road to Madrid; with garden and car parking
FOOD breakfast, lunch, dinner
PRICES €€€€
ROOMS 40; 14 double, 3, single, 23 suites, all with bath; all rooms have central heating, air conditioning, phone, TV; most rooms have hairdrier
FACILITIES dining room, 4 sitting rooms, bar, swimming pool
CREDIT CARDS MC, V
CHILDREN welcome; baby-sitting available
DISABLED access difficult; lift
PETS not accepted
CLOSED never
MANAGER Francisco Javier Revuelta

BURGOS

COVARRUBIAS

HOTEL ARLANZA

~ VILLAGE HOTEL ~

Plaza de Doña Urraca, 09346, Covarrubias, Burgos
TEL 947 406441 **FAX** 947 400502
E-MAIL reservas@hotelarlanza.com **WEBSITE** www.hotelarlanza.com

THE ARLANZA takes up one side of an attractive cobbled square (closed to traffic) in a clean, prettily restored village full of half-timbered houses, shady porticoes and flowery balconies.

It is not one of those hotels brimming over with space and facilities, and is all the more refreshing for this. But, with black beams overhead and a handsome, wide, tiled staircase, it has some character. The sitting-room ('smokey', notes a recent visitor), is combined with the bar, and there is nowhere else pleasant to sit. You'll eat adequately in the dining room, which is dimly lit by one small window. The Castilian soup is served so hot that it has to be eaten with a wooden spoon. Wild boar – plentiful in these parts, and a nocturnal traffic hazard until the start of the hunting season – is served in rich savoury slices.

The bedrooms, leading off dark corridors paved with squeaky red tiles, are very simply furnished. There is an occasional clash of striped and stippled marbles and the bathrooms are in need of improvement. But you get no more or less than you need for a comfortable night.

~

NEARBY Santo Domingo de Silos and Yecla Gorge (20 km), Quintanilla de las Viñas (25 km).
LOCATION on main square; no car parking in square
FOOD breakfast, lunch, dinner
PRICES €€€-€€€€
ROOMS 32 double, 2 single, 2 suites, one family room, all with bath; all rooms have central heating, phone, TV
FACILITIES 2 dining rooms, sitting room, bar, terrace
CREDIT CARDS AE, DC, V
CHILDREN welcome
DISABLED access difficult
PETS accepted
CLOSED 12 Dec to 1 Mar
PROPRIETOR Juan José Ortiz

BURGOS

SANTO DOMINGO DE SILOS

HOTEL TRES CORONAS DE SILOS

~ VILLAGE HOTEL ~

Plaza Mayor 6, 09610, Santo Domingo de Silos, Burgos
TEL 947 390047 **FAX** 947 390065
E-MAIL nieves.martin@amena.es

A CHARMING, peaceful establishment, so unpretentious that it doubles as the village newsagents, this is the place to come if you want to be undisturbed. You can hear the birds singing – though in high season you must wait until the coach parties go home.

The hotel is the dominant house on the village square, with a semi-circular arched doorway and a proud coat of arms over its central balcony (which belongs to room number 9, by the way). Inside, there is an overwhelming effect of renovated stone and ancient, seasoned wood (all of it skilful reproduction). Each of the rooms has at least one bare stone wall, an ample ration of solid furniture and a large, tinted mirror. Those at the front of the building look out on to the square through leaded lights fringed with stained glass.

The bar is small, frequently dominated by the TV and insufficently lit to write in, and the only sitting area is on the second floor landing. The dining room includes its own wood-fired roasting oven. (But for half the price of a menu here you can get a good, although more casual, meal in the Hostal Santo Domingo de Silos, a minute's walk away, prepared and served by a delightfully jolly landlady.)

~

NEARBY Monastery and cloister; Yecla Gorge (5 km).
LOCATION near monastery, in main square; car parking on square
FOOD breakfast, lunch, dinner
PRICES €€€
ROOMS 16; 14 double, 2 single, all with bath; all rooms have central heating, phone
FACILITIES dining room, bar
CREDIT CARDS AE, MC, V
CHILDREN welcome
DISABLED access impossible
PETS not accepted
CLOSED 4 days over Christmas
PROPRIETOR Emeterio Martín

HOTELS IN NORTH-EAST SPAIN

AREA INTRODUCTION

In this section we look at the provinces of Huesca, Lerida and Barcelona. Huesca and Lerida are somewhat off the beaten track for most foreign tourists, but this is not to say that they have nothing to offer the visitor, but the major attractions are the outdoor activities and scenery of the Pyrenees, the mountains forming the border with France, and rightly or wrongly these are not the usual target of non-Spanish holiday-makers. Not surprisingly, the best hotels are concentrated here; access is not easy – even by Alpine standards, the Pyrenean roads can be tortuous and slow.

Simple but satisfactory accommodation can be found in and around Torla; the 70-room **Ordesa** is beautifully situated (Tel 974 486125). Lérida does not attract many visitors and is not notably well prepared to receive them, but Huesca is a pleasant place with some interesting sights. Best-in-town (it does not face much opposition) is the smooth 120-room **Pedro I de Aragón**, just outside the centre (Tel 974 220300).

Hotels in Barcelona

Most of the hotels in the much visited city of Barcelona are in the centre, in two areas – around the Plaça Catalunya and Las Ramblas (the broad, leafy avenue that leads to the sea), and around the cathedral and the medieval quarter (Barrio Gótico). They are mostly conventional city hotels, of no real interest for this guide, so to compensate we have increased our coverage of hotels within an easy drive of the city - see, for example pages 86 and 87, for a couple of delightful new recommendations within half and hour's drive of the city.

Back inside the city, the Placa de Catalunya has the more traditional grand hotels, such as the **Ritz** (Tel 93 318 5200), an imposing building of 1919 with an abundance of gold-leaf and marble, and recently refurbished palatial rooms making it one of Barcelona's best. The **Gran Vía** (described on page 88) is another old charmer, as is the **Avenida Palace** (Tel 93 301 9600), dignified and extremely popular, with excellent service and welcome. **The Regente** (Tel 93 487 5989) has the added bonus of a roof-top swimming pool. Further out, near the Francescá Macià Plaza, is a very British establishment, the **Derby** (Tel 93 322 3215) which is smart and subdued, and, should you be in need, has Guinness on tap.

Of the Barrio Gótico hotels, the **Colón** (Tel 93 301 1404) is an old favourite with tourists. It stands opposite the magnificent Gothic cathedral (ask for a front room with a balcony or a sixth-floor room with a terrace) and a stone's throw from many of the city's sights. Rooms have elegant high ceilings and comfortable furniture.

Barcelona was described by the Catalan poet Joan Maragall as '*La gran encisera*' - the great enchantress. And so it is. This is a vibrant city, industrious, cultured and pace-setting. You can immerse yourself in art and music, indulge gourmet dreams, or live it up all night. No coincidence that this is one of the most popular short break destinations in Europe.

Hotels on the Costa Brava

The 'Spanish Riviera' has emerged over the past 30 years as the Costa del Sol's major competitor for Spain's holiday trade. But, unlike the Costa del Sol, it is a naturally rugged coastline of rocky coves, sandy beaches, pine-clad cliffs and Roman remains.

Thoughtless development has blighted many of the once delightful fishing villages, but much charm remains, in fact the Costa Brava's rep-

HOTELS IN NORTH-EAST SPAIN

AREA INTRODUCTION

utation does not do it justice. It can be difficult to find a room in high season, but by October the crowds have gone. Bear in mind, though, that many of the hotels and restaurants then shut for the winter, turning resorts into ghost towns.

Blanes, the 'official' starting point of the Costa Brava, has many inexpensive hotels, pensions and campsites along one of the Costa's longest beaches. Lloret de Mar boasts an even longer beach and a even greater concentration of hotels, restaurants and nightclubs. If you want some solitude, try the 80-room family-owned **Santa Marta** (Tel 972 364904), down a winding driveway in an area of private villas and botanical gardens. Tossa de Mar has several smart little hotels, including one which merits a detailed description (page 110). The 74-room **S'Agaró Hotel** (Tel 972 325200) is a good choice in S'Agaró.

Paradors in North-East Spain

The Pyrenees have a handful of remote modern Paradores. The most remote is the **PT del Monte Perdido** near Bielsa, hidden in a beautiful valley of bubbling mountain streams; the 24 rooms are appropriately rustic and the fireplace is the focal point (Tel 974 501011). The **PT Valle de Arán** at Viella and the **PT Don Gaspar de Portolá** at Arties are separated only by 6 km of bumpy mountain road. Both come into their own in winter, serving the smart ski resort of Baqueira-Beret. The **Viella Parador** (135 rooms) has a semi-circular glass lounge to allow panoramic views (Tel 973 640100), and the **Arties Parador** (40 rooms) is stuffed with hunting trophies and easy chairs (Tel 973 640801). Just south of Andorra is the **PT Seo de Urgel**; the modern hotel incorporates an ancient cloister, now filled with plants and functional sofas (Tel 973 352000).

Further south are two impressive hilltop Paradores, at Cardona and Vich (see page 95). And to the west, out of the mountains, the 66-room **PT Fernando de Aragón** in the captivating hilltop village of Sos del Rey Catolicó (the famous Fernando's birthplace) – one of the best modern Paradores (Tel 948 888011). The modern 87-room **PT de la Costa Brava** at Aiguablava is chiefly remarkable for its splendid cliff-top setting (Tel 972 622162). Further south and a little way inland is the **PT Castillo de la Zuda** at Tortosa (Tel 977 444450).

ZARAGOZA

DAROCA

POSADA DEL ALMUDI
~ TOWN HOTEL ~

Grajera, 7 50360 Daroca, Zaragoza
TEL 976 800606 **FAX** 976 801141
EMAIL posadadelalmudi@teleline.es **WEB** www.staragon.com/posadadelalmudi

Daroca, a former moorish stronghold, is the historic setting for this hotel. The Posada del Almudí was begun in the 1400s in Moorish style, and finished in the 1500s as a building of the Renaissance. Just a short walk from the town's celebrated Renaissance fountain, the Posada is cheerfully yellow-painted, outside as well as in, so easy to spot.

All 13 bedrooms look out onto Daroca's ancient, well-preserved streets. They are large and well-proportioned, many with original ceiling beams, decorated with elegance in period colours, and furnished in keeping with the style of the building. The duplexes are especially spacious and atmospheric. The sense of space is everywhere, from the vaulted hall (marvellously cool in summer) to the well-stocked library, to the restaurant, where the tables are so well separated that there is little danger of a conversation being overheard, to the patio garden where guests can sit with drinks on hot days. For cooler seasons there is the first-floor café, or the *bodega*, with a respectable wine list. The Restaurant Catalayud specializes in traditional Aragonese cooking based on lamb and other local produce.

But drivers should note that the Posada's hospitality does not extend to cars – parking is free but the car park is a short walk away, in a town square close by.

~

NEARBY Medieval walls and towers, Romanesque and Mudéjar buildings of Daroca.
LOCATION Centre of Daroca, 50 m from the casino and fountain; off N234 (Daroca exit) 86 km SW of Zaragoza; 45 min in taxi from Catalayud station; free parking in public square beside hotel
FOOD breakfast, lunch, dinner, coffee and drinks
PRICE €€
ROOMS 9 double, 2 duplex, 1 suite, all with shower and bath, phone, TV.
FACILITIES reception, lounge, bar/*bodega*, restaurant, café, lift, patio garden
CREDIT CARDS MC, V **CHILDREN** welcome **DISABLED** no special facilities
PETS not accepted **CLOSED** 24/25 Dec **PROPRIETOR** Carmen León

ZARAGOZA

UNCASTILLO

POSADA LA PASTORA
~ TOWN HOTEL ~

Roncesvalles, 1 - 50678 Uncastillo, Zaragoza
TEL 976 679499 **FAX** 976 679211
EMAIL lapastora@lapastora.net **WEB** www.lapastora.net

THERE IS AN appealing informality about this diminutive B&B hidden in one of the medieval alleys of a little one-castle town in Aragón. Inma and Miguel dote on their 1850 town house with its flagstone floors and ceiling beams – which they've restored themselves and furnished very simply, in rustic style.

La Pastora is basic. From their basement kitchen, Inma and Miguel serve breakfast only – and you can ask to be served drinks in the lounge. There are two bars in the town, and, for lunch and dinner, two restaurants. The bedrooms are individually decorated, tasteful and colourful, and four have a balcony – but only with views of the winding, medieval street below. All offer an escape from urban communications technology: you get a TV – but no phone, PC jack, or broadband internet connector. There's nowhere to work out, no Jacuzzi, no spa. Bring a book and comfortable shoes in which to explore the town, tour its five Romanesque churches, climb the hill for the view from the 11thC castle's two remaining towers, or stroll along the river.

To speak of the hospitality of hotel owners is something of a cliché, but visitors heap tributes on owners Inma and Miguel for their informal friendliness. Perhaps they deserve just one minus mark for piping music to the bedrooms – but it always seems discreet and no one complains.

~

NEARBY Sos del Rey Católico medieval town (16 km); Javier Castle (32 km).
LOCATION S side of Uncastillo, opposite the Church and Plaza of Santa María. Uncastillo is on a minor road that leaves the C124 at Sádaba; car park close by
FOOD breakfast, drinks
PRICES €
ROOMS 8 doubles, 2 with shower, 6 with bath and shower; all with TV, hairdrier, safe;
FACILITIES reception, lounge, breakfast room
CREDIT CARDS DC, MC, V **CHILDREN** welcome
DISABLED unsuitable **PETS** not accepted
CLOSED two days over Christmas **PROPRIETORS** Inma and Miguel

HUESCA

FORMIGAL

VILLA DE SALLENT
～ MOUNTAIN HOTEL ～

Urbanización Formigal, 22640, Sallent de Gállego, Huesca
TEL 974 490223 FAX 974 490150
E-MAIL hotelvillasallent@lospirineos.com WEBSITE www.hotelvillasallent.com

FIDEL TEJERO and his family, owners of a well-known restaurant, invested all their savings in this stone and slate hotel situated at the foot of the ski slopes of Formigal, the ski resort in the Tena Valley of the Pyrenees. As you enter the hall you almost feel that you are in Switzerland or Scandinavia, rather than Spain. The wood panelling, pine furniture, the indirect lighting and the linen curtains are restful and charming.

The rooms are perfectly sealed to resist the cold. Watching the snow fall past your window while you are under a hot shower is not the least of the pleasures of this place. The bathrooms are small, however, and the bedroom walls thin.

Villa de Sallent is as comfortable for a snowed-in winter week, spent by the fireplace in the sitting room, as for a month in summer, spent walking – walking is good not only from here but from other centres in the valley, particularly Sallent, off the C136.

There is a convenient lift to take you directly from the garage-cum-ski store to your bedroom at the end of an exhausting day's skiing. As you ascend, there is also the happy thought that Fidel is in the kitchen preparing supper.

～

NEARBY France (6 km); Panticosa spa (21 km); Jaca (49 km).
LOCATION on the hill of the estate, near the church and the ski office; garage with ski store
FOOD breakfast, lunch, dinner
PRICES ©©©
ROOMS 36 double, 4 single, one suite, all with bath; all rooms have central heating, telephone, TV
FACILITIES sitting room, bar, dining room
CREDIT CARDS AE, DC, MC, V
CHILDREN welcome; 20% discount
DISABLED lift/elevator, obliging staff PETS not accepted
CLOSED never PROPRIETOR Fidel Tejero

HUESCA

TRAMACASTILLA

EL PRIVILEGIO DE TENA
~ MOUNTAIN HOTEL ~

Zacalera, 1 - 22663 Tramacastilla de Tena, Huesca
TEL 974 487206 **FAX** 974 487270
EMAIL info@hoteltramacastilla.com **WEB** www.hoteltramacastilla.com

ISOLATED THOUGH it is in the tiny Aragonese hamlet of Tramacastilla on a mountainside 1,244 m above the River Tena, this hotel can find plenty for its guests to do. In winter there are ski slopes just up the road; and in summer, rafting and canoeing on the river, swimming and other water sports on nearby lakes, climbing, potholing and horse-riding – and Aragón province is scattered with unmissable early medieval churches. But it can be hard to drag yourself away from this hotel, with its amazing views of the Pyrenean peaks and plunging valleys, its peaceful gardens, and the quiet.

The hotel has two buildings: a former abbey, built in the 1500s in chalet style; and a new annexe, where most of the guests are housed. All the rooms have individuality and atmosphere – those in the old building have exposed stone walls; those in the new have strong colours and subtle lighting. Book an upper room for the best views (both buildings have a lift). Juan Ignacio and Anabél, the owners, like to look after their guests and are always in evidence – at reception, in the restaurant. The restaurant serves very reasonably priced regional and international dishes, all based on produce from the locality. Well-chosen Spanish regional wines dominate the wine list.

~

NEARBY Fourteen 1,000-year-old Mozarab churches of the Serrablo; medieval churches along the pilgrimage routes (details from hotel).
LOCATION in Tramacastilla de Tena village off the C136 between Formigal and Biescas; 20 min in taxi from Sabañiego station; garage parking, small charge
FOOD breakfast, lunch, dinner, snacks
PRICE €€€–€€€€€
ROOMS 18 double, 4 suites, all with shower and whirlpool bath, phone, PC jack, TV, clock/radio, professional hairdrier, safe, minibar, air conditioning, garage
FACILITIES reception, lounge, bar/café, restaurant, function room, 2 lifts, Jacuzzi, terrace, garden, garage
CREDIT CARDS AE, DC, MC, V **CHILDREN** welcome **DISABLED** 2 rooms with wide doors and easily accessible shower – 1 double, 1 junior suite with Jacuzzi
PETS not accepted **CLOSED** never **PROPRIETORS** Juan Ignacio and Anabél Perez

LÉRIDA

LA SEU D'URGELL

EL CASTELL DE CIUTAT

~ MOUNTAIN HOTEL ~

Ctra. de Lérida a Puigcerdà, km 129, 25700, La Seu d'Urgell, Lérida
TEL 973 350704 **FAX** 973 351574
E-MAIL elcastell@relaischateaux.com **WEBSITE** www.hotelcastell.com

THIS HOTEL IS 10 kilometres from the border with Andorra, in the Urgellet Valley. A low-lying modern building of wood and slate, it sits snugly and unobtrusively under the castle of Seu d'Urgell. Its long line of balconies gives impressive views of the Cadí mountains.

The interior is intimate and sumptuous, but not affected. Owners Jaume Tàpies and his wife Ludi have managed to create one of the most welcoming atmospheres in the Catalan Pyrenees. They pay more than due attention to the kitchen, of which they feel especially proud and which has had some outstanding reviews. The menu includes Catalan mountain dishes (wild boar and pigs' trotters) but is also influenced by the proximity of France, evident in the exquisite foie gras and the interesting wine list. The dining room has large windows opening on to the River Segre and the town of La Seu, which has a magnificent Romanesque cathedral.

A distinguished clientèle, more used to grand city hotels, comes here at weekends and holidays for the peace of the mountains and the rich living. It's an excellent base for skiing or hiking in the mountains, or for shopping in Andorra. Enthusiastic reports keep coming in. Only problem: the need to book well ahead.

~

NEARBY castle; La Seu d'Urgell cathedral; Andorra (10 km); Sant Joan de l'Erm ski resort (30 km).
LOCATION on top of a hill with views of the valley of Urgellet; car parking and garden
FOOD breakfast, lunch, dinner
PRICES ©©©©
ROOMS 34 double, 4 suites, all with bath; all rooms have air conditioning, telephone, minibar, radio, TV (satellite), safe
FACILITIES dining room, cafeteria, meeting room, terrace; swimming pool
CREDIT CARDS AE, DC, MC, V
CHILDREN welcome **DISABLED** no special facilities
PETS accepted **CLOSED** never
PROPRIETOR Jaume Tàpies i Travé

LÉRIDA

PERAMOLA

HOTEL CAN BOX DE PERAMOLA
~ COUNTRY HOTEL ~

Afueras, s/n – 25790 Peramola, Lleida
TEL 973 470266 **FAX** 973 470281
EMAIL hotel@canboix.com **WEB** www.canboix.com

A PALLARÉS FAMILY MEMBER published a book telling the story of this house, which one of his forebears bought for a song in 1763, another converted into a hotel in 1931, and which, through family faith, perseverence and hard work, is now known and loved far beyond the borders of Catalonia. The mountain views are one major reason to stay at this hotel. You reach it via the attractive C1313 through the Pyrenean foothills. From its vantage point on a wooded hillside, the hotel looks down toward the pretty valley of the River Segres – all 41 rooms have views across wild landscapes and most have a balcony. The cuisine is another reason for a visit: in recent years the kitchen has won international recognition for original interpretations of Catalan cooking – innovative, yet based on local, organic ingredients. Guests book here from all over Europe and for many, the supreme peacefulness is the third major attraction. The Can Boix, though little more than an hour's drive or so from Andorra, is remote and isolated. Yet with tennis and petanque in the gardens, horse-riding and golf nearby, excursions arranged by the family, and the delightful prospect of walking in the surrounding hills and valleys, there is little danger of boredom.

~

NEARBY Ancient Pyrenean town of Seu d'Urgell with Romanesque buildings.
LOCATION On a minor road off the C1313 (Lleida–La Seu d'Urgell), just north of Oliana; buses from Lleida and Barcelona railway stations to Oliana bus station, where hotel will collect guests; free parking
FOOD breakfast, lunch, dinner, snacks
PRICE ⓔ ⓔ ⓔ **ROOMS** 3 single with shower, 41 double, all with bath, shower, Jacuzzi, phone, PC jack, TV, clock/radio, hairdrier, minibar, air conditioning
FACILITIES main building with reception, lounge, bar, 2 dining rooms, restaurant; annexe with steam room, sauna, solarium; separate chapel with business/conference facilities; café-terrace, garden; unheated swimming pool
CREDIT CARDS D, MC, V **CHILDREN** welcome **DISABLED** 2 specially adapted bedrooms, ramps and toilets on ground floor **PETS** accepted in bedrooms only, small charge
CLOSED Jan-Feb **PROPRIETORS** Señor Joán Pallarès and family

LÉRIDA

TREMP

CASA GUILLA

~ VILLAGE GUEST HOUSE ~

Santa Engràcia, Tremp 25636, Lérida
TEL AND FAX 973 252080
E-MAIL info@casaguilla.com **WEBSITE** www.casaguilla.com

BRITONS **RICHARD** AND **SANDRA** LODER opened this ancient, labyrinthine stone farmhouse on the edge of a rock as a guest-house in 1986.

The former granaries and animal pens have become bedrooms, part of the stables a bar, the hayloft a sitting room-cum-library and the farmyard a terrace overlooking the two lakes of the Tremp valley from a height of 1000m.

This is still the Loders' home and although the house will take 10-15 people they prefer to keep the numbers down 'so that our guests can feel the house is theirs to come and go freely from.' On the edge of a nature reserve, Casa Guilla is popular with naturalists.

Guests pay for half-board with discounts for meals not taken. Everyone eats together around the same table shipboard style. 'When you have the right mix of people,' says Sandra Loder, 'everything goes fine.' If after-dinner conversation is not for you there are a TV, video and board games in the sitting room.

The village of Santa Engràcia can be hard to find and you'd be wise to ask the Loders to send you directions in advance.

NEARBY hang gliding centre (43 km); Aigues Torres National Park (72km); ski resorts (59 km); Andorra (102 km), Lake Sant Antoni (10km).
LOCATION from Tremp take C13 towards Pobla de Segur. After 2 km turn left at sign to Santa Engràcia. Follow road 10 km to Santa Engràcia (house is near church); with ample private car parking
FOOD breakfast, dinner
PRICES €€
ROOMS 3 double, 1 family room, all with shower
FACILITIES sitting room, dining room, bar, library; terrace, swimming pool
CREDIT CARDS not accepted
CHILDREN no children under 12 years in Jun, Jul and Aug
DISABLED access difficult **PETS** accepted
CLOSED 1 Nov to end Feb
PROPRIETOR Richard and Sandra Loder

TARRAGONA

ESPLUGA DE FRANCOLI

HOSTAL DEL SENGLAR
~ COUNTRY HOTEL ~

Pl Montserrat Canals, 143440, Espluga de Francoli, Tarragona
TEL 977 870121 **FAX** 977 870127
E-MAIL recepcio@hostaldelsenglar.com **WEBSITE** www.hostaldelsenglar.com

BUILT IN 1965, this three-storey whitewashed and terracotta-roofed hostal is now almost completely obscured by the evergreen trees of its own garden, together with those of the neighbouring civic park.

It is a white-walled and wooden-beamed labyrinth inside. The many-chambered dining hall, with its wooden balconies, nooks, crannies and murals of country scenes, is highly festive when full, and pleasantly intimate when not. The five-course Menu de Calcotada is an appropriately medieval feast – a traditional celebration of the vine and onion crops specific to the area (calcots is Catalan for shallots).

There is yet more timber and pottery in the salon, together with well-upholstered reproduction furniture from which the garden can comfortably be viewed. On Saturday evenings in August there is a splendid barbecue under the trees.

The bright bedrooms have stout wood and leather chairs, and decent-sized tables in addition to good, solid beds. Generous rugs add warmth to the red-tiled floors, and plants, pots and original oil-paintings are dotted around.

~

NEARBY Poblet Monastery, (2 km); Museum of Rural Life in L'Espluga.
LOCATION up hill from main square in civic gardens; with garden and car parking
FOOD breakfast, lunch, dinner
PRICES €€€-€€€€
ROOMS 30 double, 10 single, 2 suites, all with bath; all rooms have central heating, phone, radio; some have TV
FACILITIES dining room, sitting room, TV room, disco; swimming pool, tennis court
CREDIT CARDS AE, DC, MC, V
CHILDREN welcome; special menus; play area in garden
DISABLED access easy; lift/elevator; ground floor rooms
PETS not accepted
CLOSED never
MANAGER Albert Lopez

BARCELONA

HOTEL GRAN VIA

~ CITY HOTEL ~

Gran Vía 642, 08007, Barcelona
TEL 933 181900 **FAX** 933 189997
E-MAIL hgranvia@nnhotels.es **WEBSITE** www.nnhotels.es

IN THE HELL OF BARCELONA'S traffic, the Gran Vía could not be easier to find: entering the city from the airport, on the main street of the same name, you pass it on the right.

A large town house, it does not look much from the outside, but once through the double-doored entrance, it is very grand. An impressive staircase sweeps up to the mezzanine, with its palatial dining room in burgundy and grey and co-ordinating regency chairs. Here, English-speaking guests can have fun explaining to the Spanish-speaking matron who serves the extensive international breakfast how they want their bacon and eggs.

Above is another fine room – a salon with stucco ceiling and many antiques – and, true to Spanish form, there is a huge television stuck in the middle of the room. Beyond is a gorgeous roof terrace.

The bedrooms, set around the gallery, have all been renovated and refurbished. The air-conditioning is effective, if a bit noisy, and the Gran Vía displays the kind of ageing grandeur that is hard to resist. The staff remember you and you remember them. An American reader tells us that the fairly recent change of management has been for the good.

~

NEARBY Las Ramblas; cathedral, museums.
LOCATION set back from Gran Vía, near Plaza Cataluña; with garden and car parking
FOOD breakfast only
PRICES €€€-€€€€
ROOMS 37 double, 11 single, all with bath; all rooms have central heating, air conditioning, phone, minibar
FACILITIES breakfast room, sitting/TV room, terrace
CREDIT CARDS AE, DC, MC, V
CHILDREN accepted
DISABLED no special facilities; lift/elevator
PETS not accepted
CLOSED never
MANAGER José Luis García

BARCELONA

GUALBA

HOTEL MASFERRER

~ COUNTRY HOTEL ~

Carretera C-35, desvío a Gualba 08474
Tel 938 487705 **Fax** 938 487084
E-mail hm@hotelmasferrer.com

IF YOU LIKE THE idea of contrasting the vibrant bustle of Barcelona with silence and a slower pace of life, this could be a great choice. A few km north-east of the city, off the A71/E15 near Gualba on the edge of the Montseny national park, is this a solid old farmhouse, parts dating from the 12thC. We like the chunky walls, especially impressive in the reception area with its Romanesque arcade, simple desk and sparse furnishings. There's a feeling of space in all the public rooms, with original features artfully preserved (see the splendid beamed ceiling in the sitting room), but not at the expense of comfort. Some of the bedrooms have been forced out of available space, with somewhat boxy results, but others are pleasing and uncluttered. Bathrooms are gleaming and modern. The owner doubles as the chef, and his Spanish regional dishes attract diners from outside the neighbourhood. If the sights of Barcelona aren't enough to keep you busy, the national park offers cycling, fishing, riding and walking.

~

Nearby Gualba's 'black gorge'; Riells; Santa Fé; beaches and golf 20 km.
Location exit 11 from the A7 motorway on the C35. In 4km look for signs; in own grounds with ample private car parking
Food breakfast, lunch, dinner
Prices €€€-€€€€
Rooms 11 rooms, 8 doubles, 1 single, 2 suites; all rooms have phone, TV, air conditioning,
Facilities bar, restaurant, swimming pool, riding,
Credit cards AE, MC, V
Children accepted
Disabled please enquire
Pets by arrangement
Closed Feb
Manager Montse Guinovart

BARCELONA

MONTSENY

HOTEL SANT BERNAT

∽ COUNTRY HOTEL ∽

Finca El Cot 08460, Montseny, Barcelona
TEL 938 473011 **FAX** 938 473220
E-MAIL hsantbernat@husa.es **WEBSITE** www.santbernat.com

HIDDEN AWAY up a tiny track off the winding Tona road, amid the dense low forest of the lush Montseny Sierra, this large, attractive terracotta-roofed villa, built in the 50s and now covered in vines, is a sleepy delight. The grounds are glorious, with a willow tree, pond and fountain to the front, and a stone terrace, and the charming little chapel of Sant Bernat behind. You can stand peacefully admiring the view, or listen to the water trickling down the mountainside.

Inside, it is equally serene, though at times the TV in reception is liable to intrude. A series of restful sitting rooms with fireplaces, leather chairs and rugs lead past the bar to the comfortable dining room, prettily decorated with floral upholstery, wooden panelled pillars and fresh flowers. The spotless bedrooms are equally attractive, and contain all the extras, from full-length mirrors down to a free comb.

Lunch and dinner involve a three-course fixed menu which changes every day, supplemented by a short but interesting *carte*. There are regular services in the chapel on Sundays and holidays, and recitals on the Feast of St Bernard in June. A regular thought that food and welcome might have been 'down' since his last visit.

∽

NEARBY Montseny (8 km); Montseny Sierra.
LOCATION in mountains, up tiny road from Montseny to Tona; with garden and car parking
FOOD breakfast, lunch, dinner
PRICES €€€€-€€€€€
ROOMS 18 double, 2 family rooms, all with bath; all rooms have central heating, phone, TV, hairdrier
FACILITIES dining room, 2 sitting rooms, bar
CREDIT CARDS AE, DC, MC, V
CHILDREN accepted
DISABLED no special facilities **PETS** not accepted
CLOSED never **MANAGER** Jordi Riera

BARCELONA

SITGES

HOTEL ROMÀNTIC
～ SEASIDE HOTEL ～

Sant Isidre 33, 08870, Sitges, Barcelona
TEL 938 948375
E-MAIL romantic@hotelromantic.com **WEBSITE** www.hotelromantic.com

THE MANAGEMENT ARE passionately in love with their careful restoration of three 19thC town villas, originally built by Catalan rum barons returning from Cuba. They have good cause. This is a real rarity, and, considering it merits, very modestly priced. With its airy halls, blue and white tiles, sculptures, marble bays and ceramics, it could easily be the setting for a novel by García Marquez – or perhaps Graham Greene. In the club-style bar (the bar itself being an original imported from Cuba) you half-expect to spot Our Man From Havana sipping a rum while ensconced in one of the creaking wicker chairs.

Even the old stone washing troughs are preserved (though no longer in use). All the bedrooms are individually furnished with genuine antiques from the period, with original paintings and ceramics. The management is proud that they contain not a single 'mod con' (save, of course, en suite bathrooms), and there are few comfortable sofas; but this is the nineteenth century, after all. Sadly, only breakfast is served in the palmed, patio-garden these days: a shame, since it would be a most 'romantic' setting for a longer, leisurely meal. We can only apologize for not mentioning in earlier editions that this is a gay hotel – though none the less charming for that.

～

NEARBY Old Sitges, museums, main beach.
LOCATION in side-street in heart of old city; with large garden, no car parking
FOOD breakfast
PRICES €€€-€€€€
ROOMS 34 double, 30 with shower, 4 with bath; 18 single, 3 with wash-basin, 15 with shower; all rooms have phone, fans
FACILITIES 3 sitting rooms, bar
CREDIT CARDS AE, V
CHILDREN welcome
DISABLED no special facilities **PETS** accepted
CLOSED 1 Nov to 15 Mar
PROPRIETOR Josep Manuel Venorell, S.L

BARCELONA

HOTEL MASIA SUMIDORS
~ COUNTRY HOTEL ~

Carretera de Villafranca km 2.4, 08810 Sant Pere de Ribes, Sitges
TEL AND FAX 093 8962061
E-MAIL info@sumidors.com **WEBSITE** www.sumidors.com

THE PLEASING PATINATION on the stone front of this 400-year-old Catalan *masia* 25 km from Barcelona could set the tone for a delightful experience. It's run on an intimate scale by a Dutch-speaking Belgian couple with high housekeeping standards. The accommodation is in six rooms of varying size (some rather small, but still charming) two suites and a bungalow sleeping five. All the rooms are different - reflecting the themes suggested by their sometimes surprising names - 'African', 'Music Room', 'Marine' and so on. Guests remark on the peace, and warmth of the welcome. It is 25 minutes by car from Barcelona in the mountains of Sant Pere de Ribes, and, like our recommendation on page 89, would make an interesting alternative to staying in Barcelona itself, where to be honest, the hotels don't really offer much of what we look for in this guide. Airport shuttle.

~

NEARBY Sitges (10m); Barcelona; 18-hole golf course (3 km).
LOCATION close to coastal motorway SW of Barcelona; take exit 28 off the A16 (from Barcelona to Tarragona) then take C15B, direction Vilafranca Del Pénedes, after 5km take turn on right. Or from A7 take exit 29 and follow C15 direction Sitges and Sant Pere de Ribes, in own grounds with private car parking
FOOD breakfast, lunch, dinner
PRICES €€-€€€€
ROOMS 9, 6 doubles, 1 double with twin beds, 1 suite, 1 bungalow max 5 people; all rooms have bath or shower and central heating
FACILITIES bar, restaurant, garden, swimming pool, solarium, sauna
CREDIT CARDS MC, V
CHILDREN welcome, babybeds, special menus and games provided
DISABLED not suitable
PETS not accepted
CLOSED Nov-March, but open for groups of eight or more
MANAGER Manfred Bogaert and Wenke Claus

BARCELONA

SITGES

LA SANTA MARIA

~ SEASIDE HOTEL ~

Passeig de la Ribera 52, 08870, Sitges, Barcelona
TEL 938 940999 **FAX** 938 947871
E-MAIL info@lasantamaria.com **WEBSITE** www.lasantamaria.com

So successful is La Santa María in the centre of smart Sitges, that it expanded to having two restaurants – both on the seafront – and almost doubled the number of bedrooms. It is still refreshingly unpretentious and invariably packed, with all kinds of customers enjoying local seafood and wines. From inside the atmospheric restaurants, glimpses can be caught of the kitchens. Giant wooden fans in the ceiling waft in the smells. Señora Uti – amazingly fluent in English, Spanish, French and German – reserves special treatment for her hotel guests, and is generally to be found behind the bar.

The hotel itself is modern, behind an older five-storey moulded plaster frontage, the chief advantage being that inside it is clean and bright rather than notably well equipped. In the bedrooms you will find pleasant wooden furniture, firm beds, good views and plenty of space. Here there is no hint of the restaurant bustle. In addition, a small TV room with leather armchairs, dotted with antiques, ceramics and magazines, provides a quiet backwater, as does the small sun terrace, where you can be alone with the geraniums.

~

NEARBY Main promenade and beach.
LOCATION on seafront in centre of promenade; car parking (1,350 pesetas per 24 hours)
FOOD breakfast, lunch, dinner
PRICES €€€€
ROOMS 67 double, 3 family rooms, all with bath; all rooms have phone, minibar, safe, TV, air conditioning, central heating
FACILITIES dining room, sitting room, bar
CREDIT CARDS AE, DC, MC, V
CHILDREN accepted
DISABLED lift/elevator **PETS** small dogs accepted
CLOSED 15 Dec-1 Feb
PROPRIETOR Antonìo Arcas

BARCELONA

RELAIS D'ORSA
~ CITY HOTEL ~

Mont d'Orsa, 35 Vallvidrera, 08017
TEL 934 069411 **FAX** 934 069471
E-MAIL info@relaisdorsa.com **WEBSITE** www.relaisdorsa.com

THE VIEWS OF Barcelona from the terrace of this sophisticated small hotel are worth a visit in their own right. Built in 1900 high above the city, it is now run with charm by husband and wife Rosa and Paco, who masterminded its recent renovation. Don't come here if you are looking for traditional Spanish atmosphere: this is an elegantly international operation, stylish, but thankfully not too polished, with the exception of the marble floors. Chinese tea chests stand besides antique chairs; modern bathroom fittings shine next to Victorian roll-top baths.

The chef, on the other hand, steers clear of internationalism and produces plenty of excellent Spanish dishes – he does a great *arroz a la cazuela*, the local version of *paella*, and just as delicious. It's hard not to be drawn to the round window in the dining room, with its wonderful view of the city spread out below, especially romantic at night. The pool and gardens are a delight, too: plenty of hidden stone benches and shady nooks.

~

NEARBY Barcelona.
LOCATION Mont d'Orsa, Vallvidrera; in own grounds with ample private car parking
ROOMS 7; 6 double (some twin bedded), 1 suite; all rooms have bath, phone, TV
FOOD breakfast, lunch, dinner
PRICES €€€€
CREDIT CARDS AE, DC, MC, V
FACILITIES dining room, bar, gardens, swimming pool
CHILDREN welcome
PETS not accepted
DISABLED no specially adapted rooms
CLOSED never
PROPRIETORS Rosa Maria Escofet and Paco Gomez

BARCELONA

VICH

PT DE VIC
~ MODERN PARADOR ~

Paraje el Bach de Sau, 08500, Vich, Barcelona
TEL 938 122323 **FAX** 938 122368
E-MAIL vic@parador.es **WEBSITE** www.parador.es

ISOLATED ON A steep mountainside overlooking the expansive Sau reservoir, this Parador de Turismo is an imposing grey stone edifice. Completed in 1972 to mimic a Catalan farmhouse, it is quite wrong in scale, but it is nevertheless not without beauty. The conservatory-style entrance gives way to a vast galleried hall with murals, polished wooden pillars and a stained glass ceiling worthy of Chartres.

The sons and daughters from the *masías* dotted throughout the surrounding sierra have their wedding receptions here. Walkers and cyclists with sufficient energy come in search of a little luxury and a comfortable bed to rest their limbs. They are rarely disappointed. Rooms are furnished in classical Castilian or Catalan style. Those with larger bathrooms have the unusual luxury of double basins.

The dining room is another large hall with mock-medieval chandeliers, marble pillars, and more murals. The three-course menu of international, Spanish and Catalan dishes is enhanced by the magnificent view, and as night falls the sounds of the wilderness outside add atmosphere to the occasion. The staff serve with appropriate hushed efficiency.

~

NEARBY Vich (15 km); walks to nearby sights.
LOCATION 14 km E of Vich, clearly signed from Vich; with gardens and parking for 30 cars
FOOD breakfast, lunch, dinner
PRICES €€€-€€€€
ROOMS 29 double, 4 single, all with bath; all rooms have central heating, air conditioning, phone, TV, minibar, safe
FACILITIES 2 sitting rooms, bar, dining room; tennis, swimming pool
CREDIT CARDS AE, DC, MC, V
CHILDREN welcome
DISABLED access easy; lift **PETS** accepted
CLOSED never
MANAGER Arturo Gutierrez

BARCELONA

HOTEL CÉSAR
~ RESORT HOTEL ~

Isaac Peral 4-8, 08800 Vilanova i la Geltrú, Barcelona
TEL 938 151125 **FAX** 938 156719
E-MAIL reservas@hotelcesar.net **WEBSITE** www.hotelcesar.net

A FOUR-STOREY WHITE building with mediterraean blue paintwork around the windows, the César has been built up by the same family over four generations and more than 100 years.

Although from the outside it seems like just another block-shaped resort hotel, inside this one has a touch of taste without pretension. Classical music plays downstairs and the bar houses a small library.

The rooms are decorated simply but with interest using a variety of carefully chosen modern fabrics. All of them look onto the patio below and from the higher floors you can see the sea. The choice is the Albéniz suite on the first floor in which a fine china tea service and packet of Earl Grey awaits you in a homely sitting room with cane furniture and a pine desk.

Much of the hotel's trade is from business groups and the public rooms reflect this with a conference room on the ground floor squeezing the sitting room/library into a minimal area in front of reception. In good weather, however, the patio will meet most needs.

The restaurant, La Fitorra, is adjacent to the hotel in an old fisherman's cottage with a pleasant patio of its own at the back.

~

NEARBY Casa Papiol, castle and Balaguer Museum; Sitges (7km); Vilafranca del Penedès palace and wine museum (20km).
LOCATION behind Ribes Roges beach; car parking on street
FOOD breakfast, lunch, dinner
PRICES €€€-€€€€€
ROOMS 28 double, 2 suites, all with bath; all rooms have air conditioning, central heating, TV, minibar, phone, safe, free internet access in rooms
FACILITIES dining room, bar, 2 conference rooms, sauna/ solarium, hydromassage pool **CREDIT CARDS** AE, DC, MC, V
CHILDREN accepted
DISABLED lift **PETS** accepted
CLOSED restaurant only Sun dinner, Mon and Jan
PROPRIETOR Esther Nolla

GERONA

AIGUA BLAVA

HOTEL AIGUA BLAVA
~ SEASIDE HOTEL ~

Playa de Fornells, 17255, Aigua Blava, Gerona
TEL 972 622058 FAX 972 622112
E-MAIL hotelaiguablava@aiguablava.com WEBSITE www.aiguablava.com

TOO BIG TO INCLUDE in the guide but too distinctive to leave out, the Aigua Blava is a holiday village with a difference – a collection of delightful annexes among shady, pine-covered cliffs and flowered terraces, set round a tiny fishing harbour and beach, the whole arrangement is the opus of multi-lingual ex-swimming champion, Xiquet Sabater – a man whose life history would defy belief if it were not confirmed in the Spanish Who's Who?

The complex provides everything you need, even a boutique complete with genuine French assistance. Each room has individual style, ranging from summerhouse brightness in some annexes to the more formal bedrooms in the main hotel. Even the least inspiring are immaculate, and the sea views are out of this world. Guests who reserve a table in the pleasant restaurant are rewarded with a feast of a four-course meal, with plenty of choice and desserts ranging from the holy to the sinful.

This area has always been Xiquet's home, and he wants his guests to feel the same warmth as if it were theirs, too. If the four generations who come back to this Mediterranean idyll year after year (making early booking essential) are any guide, he succeeds – with abundant help from his cheerful staff.

~

NEARBY Begur (4 km); beach.
LOCATION in quiet spot near beach; with gardens and ample private car parking
FOOD breakfast, lunch, dinner
PRICES €€€-€€€€
ROOMS 60 double (some with terrace), 3 special junior suite, 17 junior suites, 5 singles, all with bath; all rooms have central heating, phone; most rooms have air conditioning
FACILITIES 4 dining rooms, 4 sitting rooms, 3 bars; swimming pool, tennis courts, volley ball, hairdresser
CREDIT CARDS AE, DC, MC, V
CHILDREN welcome; play area
DISABLED no special facilities **PETS** not accepted **CLOSED** Nov to end Feb
MANAGER Juan Gispert

GERONA

AVINYONET

MAS FALGARONA

∾ COUNTRY HOTEL ∾

Avinyonet de Puigventós, Girona, 17742
TEL 972 546628 **FAX** 972 547071
E-MAIL email@masfalgarona.com **WEBSITE** www.masfalgarona.com

PULL UP OUTSIDE this lovely 17thC honeyed-stone building in the Pyrenean foothills and, most likely, either the mother and son team who run this peaceful country hotel will be at the door to greet you. The ten rooms are all beautifully decorated with pale woods, stone arches and fresh white bed-linen. Some can be a little small, so it may be worth splashing out on one of the suites. Room 9 has a lovely balcony and a connecting door to another bedroom - good for a family; or try room 1, still larger-than-average, but fairly priced.

Brigitta buys all the food daily and prepares the menu according to what's best at the market; Jallas turns these fresh ingredients into light and inventive Spanish dishes. There is no *a la carte* menu: they cook enough for two if there are two guests, 20 if there are 20… nothing goes to waste, and nothing is kept behind for the next day.

∾

NEARBY Figueres.
LOCATION exit 4 on the A7 motorway; in countryside close to French/Spanish border; car parking outside hotel
FOOD breakfast, lunch, dinner
PRICE €€€€
ROOMS 10; 8 doubles, 2 junior suites; all rooms have bath, telephone, TV, hairdrier
FACILITIES dining room, swimming pool, golf nearby
CREDIT CARDS AE, DC, MC, V
CHILDREN accepted
DISABLED 3 ground floor rooms
PETS not accepted
CLOSED 1 week Jan, 1 week Jul, 1 week Sep – can vary
PROPRIETORS Severino Jallas Gandara and Brigitta Schmidt

GERONA

BESALU

MAS SALVANERA

~ COUNTRY HOTEL ~

Residencia Casas de Pages 17850 Beuda, Girona (Cataluyna, Pyrenees)
TEL 972 590975 **FAX** 972 590863
E-MAIL Salvanera@salvanera.com **WEBSITE** www.salvanera.com

THE SETTING, APPROACH and environment of this hotel are hard to fault. An attractive 17thC fortified farmhouse, it is set high up in a national park close to the medieval town of Besalu, with stone and wood dominant inside and out. Our only hesitation would be over some of the furniture, bedspreads and rugs: the current owners took over in 1994 and perhaps could do well to update some of the fittings. The bedrooms, however, are spaced out over several floors, all a fair size, carved out of irregular spaces, with plenty of attractive exposed beams; we like the rooms up in the eaves, with their sloping roofs and dark oak furniture and fittings. Other pleasing touches include the comfortable seating areas on each floor, so you can always find a quiet corner in which to read or chat. More and more places to stay are opening up in this area between coast and mountains, but we favour this one because of the welcome, and the hosts' local knowledge: you would find plenty to do for a stay of several days.

~

NEARBY Besalu, Seguero, Girona.
LOCATION exit 6 from the A7 motorway; in countryside of the Olot National Park; own grounds with ample car parking
ROOMS 8; 6 doubles, 2 singles; all rooms have bath, phone, internet connection
PRICE €€€
FOOD breakfast; no lunch or dinner July, Aug or Sept – but available rest of the year
FACILITIES sitting room, dining room, library, swimming pool, garden
CREDIT CARDS AE, DC, MC, V
CHILDREN welcome
PETS accepted
DISABLED no specially adapted rooms
CLOSED mid Dec to mid Jan, one week June, one week Sept
PROPRIETORS Rocío Niño and Ramón Ruscalleda

GERONA

BOLVIR

TORRE DEL REMEI

~ TOWN HOTEL ~

Camí Reial s/n, 17463, Bolvir de Cerdanya, Gerona
TEL 972 140182
E-MAIL info@torredelremei.com **WEBSITE** www.torredelremei.com

WITH CONSIDERABLE EFFORT and impeccable taste, José María Boix and his wife, Loles Vidal, turned the Boix in Martinet into one of the most renowned restaurant-cum-hotels in the Catalan Pyrenees, and one of the top ten restaurants in Spain. Now they are repeating their success with this sumptuous mansion a short way from Puigcerdá.

The house, a colonial caprice of the *belle époque*, was built in 1910 and has been equipped as a luxury hotel by some of the most imaginative designers in Catalonia. The marble is from Greece; the furniture from Italy; the carpets from Tibet. Outside there is a 20,000 square metre garden planted with firs, towering redwoods, a swimming pool and a putting green.

The Boix have created an oasis of elegance: expensive details abound – Bang & Olufsen video and TV, the selection of Loewe perfumes served by a valet. You will not lack creature comforts: the bathroom floors are heated and the king-size baths have hydromassage.

As you would expect, the cooking is also imaginative and appetizing. But the core of the appeal is most appreciated is the personal service that José María and Loles offer their guests.

~

NEARBY S Domingo church; walls, town hall of Puigcerdá (3 km).
LOCATION in the outskirts of Puigcerdá; garden and car parking
FOOD breakfast, lunch, dinner
PRICES €€€€€
ROOMS 21, 4 double, 7 suites all with bath; all rooms have hydromassage, central heating, telephone, video, TV (satellite)
FACILITIES dining room, video library, private meeting room; swimming pool, putting green
CREDIT CARDS AE, DC, MC, V
CHILDREN welcome **DISABLED** no special facilities; lift/elevator
PETS accepted in bedrooms **CLOSED** never
PROPRIETOR Josép María Boix and Loles Boix

GERONA

CASTELLO DE AMPURIAS

HOTEL ALLIOLI
~ COUNTRY INN ~

Urbanización Castellonou 17486, Castelló de Ampurias, Gerona
TEL 972 250320 **FAX** 972 250300
E-MAIL h.r.allioli@turinet.net **WEBSITE** http//es.turinet.net/empresa/h.rallioli

THE SETTING FOR this country inn, in a dusty basin below the main Roses-Figueras road, could be better. But it could also be much worse: the neighbouring blue and white-washed Danone plant is almost picturesque as factories go. And the building itself more than makes up for its surroundings: a two-hundred-year-old Catalan farmhouse of considerable character.

Inside, the Peig Callol family have sympathetically fitted it out with antiques, lamps and benches, spiced up with fresh and dried flowers. Huge, whole dried Jamon Jabugos hams hang over the intimate bar to dry. The bedrooms display pure rural simplicity with linen counterpanes, exposed beams and whitewashed walls. But there are creature comforts too: clean en suite bathrooms, plenty of gadgets, and well-placed electric lights. The beamed four-chambered restaurant is well suited to the vast feasts local Spanish families come to devour on a Sunday. During the week Maria Callol will serve you a quieter, but no less sumptious Catalan meal, or even paella. Breakfast on the patio can be a very pleasant experience, provided the seasonal winds don't blow away your croissant. On such occasions, the bar is a safer alternative. Visitors to Allioli wrote that they were 'charmed'.

NEARBY Figueras (10 km); Rosas (8 km).
LOCATION in grounds set back from main Figueras/Roses road; with private car parking
FOOD breakfast, lunch, dinner
PRICES €€€
ROOMS 31 double, 8 single, 1 suite, all with bath; all rooms have central heating, air conditioning, phone, TV
FACILITIES 2 dining rooms, 2 sitting rooms, bar
CREDIT CARDS AE, MC, V
CHILDREN accepted
DISABLED access difficult **PETS** accepted in rooms
CLOSED 20/23 Dec to 10 Feb
PROPRIETOR José Peig Rions and Maria Callol

GERONA

MAS PAU
~ COUNTRY HOTEL ~

Avinyonet de Puigventós, 17742, Figueras, Gerona
TEL 972 546154

THIS CREEPER-COVERED family-run hotel is a converted 17thC *masia* (a large, well-to-do farmhouse) standing by itself in wooded and farmed countryside near the village of Figueras (made famous by Salvador Dali). It has been run by Nuria Serrat and her family since the 70s and, wedding parties permitting, you can be certain of friendly personal service.

The public rooms are essentially rustic, but decorated in modernista style, the Spanish equivalent of art nouveau. They include an arched bar (with painted mirrors, vases of ferns, wicker chairs around tables made from old sewing machines), and three interconnecting dining rooms. The largest of these, the banqueting room, has a beamed ceiling and stone walls covered in old photos of Figueras. The seven suites look out on to tranquil gardens and cypress trees. They are decorated entirely in pink and grey; grey carpets, pink marble bath-rooms and – according to Señora Serrat – curtains and bedspreads that change with the seasons: warm pink in winter, cool grey in summer.

In the well established gardens is a modest but attractive pool, with a shaded terrace on hand.

~

NEARBY Figueras – Dali museum; Gerona (40 km).
LOCATION in countryside, 4 km SW of village of Figueras; with garden and car parking
FOOD breakfast, lunch, dinner
PRICES €€€-€€€€
ROOMS 12 suites, all with bath; all rooms have central heating, phone, TV, air conditioning, minibar
FACILITIES dining room, sitting room, bar, banquet/conference room, terrace; swimming pool
CREDIT CARDS AE, DC, MC, V
CHILDREN welcome; playground
DISABLED easy access; some ground floor rooms **PETS** dogs accepted
CLOSED never; restaurant only, Sun in winter
PROPRIETOR Nuria Serrat

GERONA

GERONA

HOSTAL BELLMIRALL
~ TOWN GUEST-HOUSE ~

Calle Bellmirall 3, 17000, Gerona
TEL 972 204009
E-MAIL carme.quintana@pas.udg.es **WEBSITE** www.grn.es/bellmirall

ISABEL AND CHRISTINA run this diminutive guest-house, hidden away just to the right of the cathedral steps. The house is a 14thC historic monument of ancient stone, which the previous proprietors Anna and Isidre started converting to take guests in the 60s. Isidre was supposedly the artist of the family, and his paintings, and those of Catalan colleagues, line the walls, and are displayed in a small gallery; his studio was on the top floor. The interior design was highly individual (the brightly decorated breakfast room and hand-made bedspreads were a joy), which gave the hotel something special. However Christina and Isabel have re-decorated the bedrooms, still keeping the individuality, but with their personal touch and adorned them with some charming antique furniture.

Isabel and Christina serve no other meals, though they offer the occasional beer, and advise (at length) on where to eat in the town. Breakfast is served on the pretty patio. Service is highly personal, but this is not a hotel. Rooms have few en suite facilities but this is no real hardship. The atmosphere is friendly and relaxed, with a memorable breakfast served on the patio in the summer.

~

NEARBY Cathedral; museums; old Gerona.
LOCATION in tiny street next to cathedral; no private parking
FOOD breakfast
PRICES €€-€€€
ROOMS 3 double, 2 with shower; 2 single, one with shower; 2 family rooms, both with shower
FACILITIES sitting room, breakfast room, patio
CREDIT CARDS not accepted
CHILDREN welcome
DISABLED no special facilities
PETS not accepted
CLOSED 4 Jan to 28 Feb
PROPRIETOR Isabel and Christina

GERONA

GERONA

EL FAR DE SANT SEBASTIAN

~ SEASIDE HOTEL ~

Playa de Llafranc, s/n 17211
TEL 972 301639 **FAX** 972 304328
E-MAIL hotelfss@intercom.es **WEBSITE** www.elfar.net

WONDERFULLY LOCATED by the lighthouse of Saint Sebastian, with far-reaching views over the Mediterranean, this intimate, well-restored hotel has a typical Spanish feel – plenty of sun-warmed tiles, and splashes of yellows, ochres, whites and blues – and a relaxed elegance that makes it worth seeking out if you don't mind about the cost – it seemed relatively expensive.

Housed in a recently-restored 15thC building with an impressive vaulted entrance hall, the spacious bedrooms are simply and traditionally decorated (most of the rooms have terraces looking out on to rocky outcrops and coves, with the main suite opening directly on to the sea). The balconies between the bedrooms are somewhat close together and don't offer privacy. But we love the bathrooms, which are often startlingly bright, with cheerful curtains and refreshingly powerful showers.

The restaurant is renowned for its seafood, as you would expect, which really is exceptional. We couldn't resist having the calarmari every night, but other guests raved about the swordfish, and the enormous local mussels. No swimming pool, but the beach is a two-minute walk, and you can take a boat out to the little bays that are dotted along the Catalan coastline.

~

NEARBY Llafranc, Palafrugell, Girona.
LOCATION exit 6 from the A7 motorway (Girona), a few km S of Pals; close to rocky sea shore in own grounds with ample private car parking
FOOD breakfast, lunch, dinner
PRICES €€€€
ROOMS 9; 8 doubles, 1 suite; all rooms have bath, phone, TV, hairdrier
FACILITIES parking, garden, golf, beach and watersports nearby
CREDIT CARDS AE, DC, MC, V
CHILDREN yes
PETS no **DISABLED** no access
CLOSED never
PROPRIETOR Isabel Villena

GERONA

PALAFRUGELL

HOTEL SANT ROC

~ SEASIDE HOTEL ~

Pl del Atlántico, 2, Calella de Palafrugell, 17210, Palafrugell, Gerona
TEL 972 614250/615286 **FAX** 972 614068/617012
WEBSITE www.santroc.com

HIGH ON THE CLIFFS of Calella de Palafrugell, with magnificent views from the leafy terrace over the bay and steps down to the shore, the Sant Roc started life as a family home in the 1950s but was soon converted to an hotel, and has been expanded since. It is an appealing building, in style somewhere between a grand Catalan country house and a mini-monastery, featuring a terracotta roofed tower.

It aims to be a family-run hotel run for families; guests are treated like old friends, and some return to the Sant Roc year after year. The interior is stylish, but pleasantly lived in. The wicker rocking chairs and antiques are there to be used, as is the more utilitarian furniture. You might find the wallpaper peeling in those rooms that are next on the list for re-furbishment, and not all of them have sea views, but they are clean, with original oil paintings on the walls and traditional Catalan wooden furniture painted in red, green or blue, known as polycromodo.

The three-course dinner and lunch menu has excellent choices for starter and main-course (especially the fish), and there is a good range of fairly priced wines.

~

NEARBY Calella (0.3 km); Palafrugell (4 km); beach.
LOCATION on cliffs, set back from road amid trees; with garden and public car parking
FOOD breakfast, lunch, dinner
PRICES ©©-©©©
ROOMS 40 double, 1 single, 5 suites, 1 family room, all with bath; all have central heating, some with air conditioning, phone, TV, safe
FACILITIES dining room, sitting room, bar, terrace
CREDIT CARDS AE, DC, MC, V
CHILDREN welcome; baby-sitting available
DISABLED lift/elevator
PETS by arrangement
CLOSED 8 Dec to 15 Mar
MANAGER Teresa Boix

GERONA

PERATALLADA

EL PATI

~ VILLAGE HOTEL ~

C. Hospital, 13 C. la Roca, s/n 17113 Peratallada
TEL 972 634069 **FAX** 972 634702
E-MAIL peratallada@hotelelpati.net **WEBSITE** www.hotelelpati.net

THE STONE WALLS that surround this 18thC Catalan house help foster a sense of escape and isolation, despite its location in the middle of Peretallada village. The layout inside is unusual – open doorframes, half walls, large communal areas... expect to know your fellow guests well by the end of your visit. Earthenware pots and urns are artfully dotted around, and the usual Spanish whites and blues are offset by rich, deep colours that give the whole place a feeling of elegance. The cherubs that adorn the bathroom walls can get a little too *faux*-Renaissance for our liking, but the beds are very comfortable, and we would have found it difficult to rouse ourselves were it not for the enormous breakfasts of patisseries and fruits. Food is one of the main draws here: the restaurant is popular with locals as well as residents, and in summer you will be eating outside in the large courtyard, surrounded by walnut, lemon and orange trees. Peratallada itself is well known for gastronomic restaurants: you will be spoilt for choice and we would recommend a stay of more than one night.

~

LOCATION in village centre; car parking outside hotel.
NEARBY Girona
PRICES €€€
ROOMS 5 doubles; all rooms have bath, phone, TV, internet access
FOOD breakfast, lunch, dinner
FACILITIES dining room, garden, beach and golf nearby
CHILDREN welcome
PETS not accepted
DISABLED no specially adapted rooms
CLOSED mid Jan to mid Feb
PROPRIETOR Yolanda Coll

GERONA

TAMARIU

HOTEL HOSTALILLO
～ SEASIDE HOTEL ～

Bellavista 22, 17212, Tamariú, Gerona
TEL 972 620228 **FAX** 972 620184

THIS MODERN HOTEL is lifted out of the Costa rut by attention to detail and its tranquil location. Staff are friendly, efficient and helpful, the atmosphere welcoming – the hotel feels much smaller than its rule-breaking number of rooms would at first suggest.

Even from the outside, the Hostalillo is more than usually appealing: the five storeys are set into the steep hillside and pitched terracotta roofs help to break up the lines of the concrete.

The white walls inside give a cool, airy feel. The large split-level dining-room is flexible enough not to seem bare, even in low season. Here the four-course menu (constantly varied, with plenty of choice) can be struggled through, overlooking the inviting sun terrace full of geraniums and simple, comfortable chairs. Below is the once-picturesque fishing village of Tamariú, where the boats on the beach still out-number the frying bodies except in July and August. Steps lead through the garden, down the cliffs to the beach.

Bedrooms have all you can expect from a sound, basic beach hotel, including a view of the bay or the mountains.

～

NEARBY Palafrugell (4 km); coastal walks; beach.
LOCATION on cliffs above village, overlooking Tamariú; with garden and parking for 13 cars
FOOD breakfast, dinner
PRICES ©©©-©©©©
ROOMS 59 double, 2 single, 3 family rooms, 6 suites, all with bath; all rooms have phone; most rooms have central heating
FACILITIES dining room, sitting/TV room, bar
CREDIT CARDS AE, MC, V
CHILDREN accepted
DISABLED access difficult **PETS** accepted
CLOSED 20 Sep to 1 May
MANAGER José M Biarge

GERONA

TORRENT

HOTEL MAS DE TORRENT
~ COUNTRY HOUSE HOTEL ~

Afores s/n, 17123, Torrent, Gerona
TEL 972 303292 **FAX** 972 303293
E-MAIL mastorrent@relaischateaux.com **WEBSITE** www.mastorrent.com

THE SETTING OF THIS stunning conversion of a 1751 Catalan *masia* is truly superb: in lush grounds concealing extensive terraces, pelota, paddle-ball and tennis courts, and the inevitable swimming pool, amid open countryside, with views over Pals to the castle at Bagur beyond.

Just when you have come to terms with the exterior, you are confronted by further splendour inside. The style of the original interior is faithfully reproduced, but with a layer of luxury applied with impeccable taste. A series of arched salons with bright sofas and a fireplace gives way to the bar and terraces. Upstairs there are further spacious salons, with huge sofas and antiques, around which the individually named and styled rooms are set. 'Las Hortensias' is all antiques and lace, for example, while 'Las Dacias' is pure Barcelona chic. The 20 rooms in the garden bungalows have private, hedged terraces and more of a summerhouse feel. All are faultless in terms of facilities.

The dining room which adjoins the main building is an impressive reproduction, with the exposed roof beams and slates typical of the region. There is an extravagant four-course menu and seasonal carte of Catalan, Basque and French cuisine. The year 2000 saw the building of seven new rooms with their own private swimming pool. We are sure that they will be to the high standard of the rest of the hotel, but reports would be welcome.

~

NEARBY Pals (4 km); Costa Brava beaches (14 km).
LOCATION near tiny village; with garden, car parking
FOOD breakfast, lunch, dinner **PRICES** €€€€
ROOMS 39 double, all with bath; all rooms have central heating, air conditioning, phone, TV, minibar, radio, hairdrier, safe
FACILITIES dining room, 4 sitting rooms, games room; swimming pool, tennis court
CREDIT CARDS AE, DC, MC, V
CHILDREN accepted;
DISABLED access easy; specially adapted room and other ground floor rooms
PETS accepted (extra charge) **CLOSED** never **MANAGER** Oriol Casas

GERONA

TORROELAA DE MONTGRI

PALAU LO MIRADOR
∽ VILLAGE HOTEL ∽

Passeig de l'Esglesia, 1, 17257 Torroelaa De Montgri (Girona, Costa Brava)
TEL 972 758063 **FAX** 972 758246
E-MAIL palaulomirador@teleline.es **WEBSITE** www.palaulomirador.com

L O MIRADOR MEANS 'vantage point' in Spanish, no doubt why the feudal castle of the village of Torroella de Montgrí once stood on this spot. In the 13th century, the building became a royal castle, and remains an important historical monument, now turned into this interesting hotel. The kitchen produces Mediterranean food, which means plenty of fish (you are only 6 km from the coast here, and the village itself feels like a fishing port in many corners) but also North African dishes from Morocco and Tunisia. We found the dining room slightly imposing – an enormous chandelier hangs over your head, and oil paintings look down on you on all sides. More intimate are the bedrooms, each named after an illustrious former guest, and filled with an assortment of antique beds, chests and mirrors. Ask for a room on the second floor with their views over the village – we especially like Guillem de Montgrí. The hotel, no doubt due to its grand stature, is often given over to weddings and conferences, so check when booking.

∽

NEARBY The Medieval city of Pals, L'Escala, Girona.
LOCATION In the middle of Torroella de Montgri village, near the church. Take exit 65 on A7 motorway, direction L'Escala, then road towards Bellcaire (ample parking within the hotel grounds)
FOOD breakfast, lunch, dinner
PRICES €€€€
ROOMS 10 (6 doubles, 3 triples, 1 suite, all have telephone, Internet access, ensuite bathroom, minibar, cd player, hairdryer)
FACILITIES sitting room, dining room, bar, garden, swimming pool,
CREDIT CARDS AE, DC, MC, V
CHILDREN welcome
DISABLED no access
PETS accepted (no extra charge)
CLOSED mid Dec to mid Jan, one week in June, one week in Sept
PROPRIETOR Alfonso de Robert

GERONA

TOSSA DE MAR

HOTEL DIANA
~ SEASIDE HOTEL ~

Plaza d'España 6, 17320, Tossa de Mar, Gerona
TEL 972 341886 **FAX** 972 341103

AFTER THE CASTLE, the Hotel Diana is architecturally one of the most important buildings in Tossa. A family town house built on the central Plaza d'Espana in the 1850s, and backing on to the main promenade, it became a hotel a hundred years later. Today, when it opens for the summer season, it attracts an international clientele of art-nouveau-lovers.

The entire building is a tribute to the period, with a Gaudi roof faced with characteristic broken turquoise tiles, stained glass windows, a sweeping marble staircase and original Gaudi fireplace. The central salon contains art-nouveau frescoes, which have recently been restored, and a bronze fountain in naked female form by the Catalan sculptor Mares; light streams in through the glass roof three storeys above. The bedrooms are set in the surrounding gallery. With their high arched ceilings, marble floors and grand wooden shutters, they have plenty to offer in terms of style. Breakfast is taken either on the sea-front terrace or in the inner courtyard.

In 1989, after a period on lease, the Diana was returned to its original owners, a local hotel-owning family, who are continuing to carry out extensive refurbishment.

~

NEARBY Castle; promenade; central beach.
LOCATION entrance on Plaza d'España, rear entrance on beach promenade; private car parking 800 mtrs from hotel
FOOD breakfast
PRICES €€-€€€
ROOMS 20 double, one suite, all with bath; all rooms have satellite TV, air conditioning, phone, minibar; some with sea views
FACILITIES sitting room, TV room, bar, bar/cafeteria in front of the beach
CREDIT CARDS AE, MC, V
CHILDREN welcome
DISABLED access easy; lift/elevator **PETS** no
CLOSED Oct to May
MANAGER Fernando Osorio

GERONA

VILADRAU

HOSTAL DE LA GLORIA
~ COUNTRY HOTEL ~

Torreventosa 12, 08553, Viladrau, Gerona
TEL 938 849034 **FAX** 938 849465
E-MAIL informacio@hostaldelagloria.com **WEBSITE** www.gourmethotel.org

THIS COSY COUNTRY lodge was built over 50 years ago in simple Catalan style. Set just above the pleasant mountain village of Viladrau, with a pretty, peaceful garden terrace in front and the Sierra rising behind, it is a favourite with ageing Spanish card-players, who fill the inter-connecting small salons and leatherette armchairs at weekends throughout the year.

The Formatje family have decked the place out with copper pots, brass lamps, paintings and some fine old Spanish chairs, and keep the whole spotlessly clean. They are proud of their hostal, always eager to please, and genuinely apologetic when their rooms are full.

Rooms are simple and old-fashioned, with modern bathrooms. The four-course lunch and dinner menus are different each day, and are highly recommended. They are served in an attractive arched dining room with a pretty tiled floor, wooden beams, green lace curtains and white walls hand-painted with birds and decorated with plates.

Overall, the result is an unpretentious home from home, where relaxation comes naturally – aided by the knowledge that rooms and meals are notably cheap.

~

NEARBY Gerona (60 km); Vich (25 km); Montseny Sierra.
LOCATION above mountain village in Sierra de Montseny; with covered car park
FOOD breakfast, lunch, dinner
PRICES €€€-€€€€
ROOMS 20 double, 3 single, one suite, 2 family rooms, all with bath; all rooms have central heating, phone, TV
FACILITIES dining room, sitting room, bar, swimming pool
CREDIT CARDS MC, V
CHILDREN accepted
DISABLED no special facilities
PETS not accepted
CLOSED 22 Dec to 7 Jan
PROPRIETORS Eudald Formatje

HOTELS IN WESTERN SPAIN

THIS SECTION COVERS the provinces of Salamanca, Zamora, Carceres and Badajoz. Our new recommendations for this edition include **Monasterio de Rocamador**, a monastery that has been adapted into a hotel, with the atmosphere of a retreat, by the opera singer Lucia Dominguín (page 118). If you fancy staying in a monastery, then we can also highly recommend the **Hospederia del Real Monasterio** (page 115) which is still a working monastery.

PARADORS IN WESTERN SPAIN

The provinces of Zamora and Salamanca (around the NE corner of Portugal) have several pleasant Paradores which are described in detail in this section. In addition, Salamanca's modern white Parador sits on a hill above the town, traditionally the site of one of Castille's biggest cattle fairs. The best we can say about the hotel is that every guest room has a superb view of the town at night. Rooms are adequate and have sliding doors leading to small 'galleries' furnished with cane chairs (Tel 923 192082).

The further south you travel, the fewer and further between Paradores become. The harsh terrain of Extremadura has kept the developers out from Roman times onwards, and only recently (and with a lot of funding from the EC, drawn to your attention on huge billboards at regular intervals) has the area been opened up by an extensive network of new roads. The existing Paradores, now more accessible, are all in ancient buildings – converted monasteries (Trujillo, Guadalupe, Mérida), hilltop castles (Oropesa, Jarandilla, Zafra) and a 14thC town house at Cáceres. Most have detailed entries. Two Paradores in splendid castles have recently undergone extensive renovation – one in an imposing 15thC fortress in the middle of Zafra (Tel 924 554540) and the **PT Virrey de Toledo**, perched above the little town of Oropesa (Tel 925 430000).

SALAMANCA

CIUDAD RODRIGO

PT ENRIQUE II

~ CASTLE PARADOR ~

Plaza del Castillo 1, 37500, Ciudad Rodrigo, Salamanca
TEL 923 460150 **FAX** 923 460404
E-MAIL ciudadrodrigo@parador.es **WEBSITE** www.parador.es

DON'T BE DISAPPOINTED if what you thought was the hotel – a stout tower with battlements – turns out to be only a warehouse. The hotel itself is the low-lying, attractively ivy-clad building beneath it. This was the second Parador to be opened, and the first to occupy a historic building. Fortunately, the present manager has paid more personal attention to it than many of those running other castles in the state hotel chain, and is still continuing to make improvements.

The rooms are spread out along two wings – one ancient, one modern. The former are reached by an arched curving white corridor; the 'star' is Room 10, a suite in which the bedroom is circular with a domed roof. Four of the rooms abut the old city walls and have views over the hotel's formal gardens. The public areas are decorated with occasional antiques, some suits of armour and plenty of green pot plants. The dining room and sitting room are both attractive, with partially sloping ceilings and wide basket-handle stone arches.

For pure history and a great view, don't forget to climb the tower. It is reached through the castle's original gate (ask for the key from reception), now in a splendid, crumbling state.

~

NEARBY Plaza Mayor; Portugal (30 km); La Alberca (50 km).
LOCATION on a quiet open square near centre of town; with garden and car parking
FOOD breakfast, lunch, dinner
PRICES €€€€
ROOMS 31 double, 2 suite, 2 single all with bath; all rooms have central heating, phone, TV, minibar
FACILITIES dining room, 2 sitting rooms, bar, patio
CREDIT CARDS AE, DC, MC, V
CHILDREN welcome; 20% discount for children under 10
DISABLED access to public rooms easy **PETS** not accepted
CLOSED never
MANAGER Pilar de Miguel

ZAMORA

PT CONDES DE ALBA Y ALISTE
~ PALACE PARADOR ~

Plaza Viriato 5, 49001, Zamora
TEL 980 514497 **FAX** 980 530063
E-MAIL zamora@parador.es **WEBSITE** www.paradores.es

ZAMORA MAY seem out of the way for most visitors, but here is a hotel worth the detour. Much less interfered with than other Paradors occupying historic buildings, this palace surrounds a photogenic Renaissance courtyard fringed with carved stone pillars. The sunny enclosed halls and balconies along the four sides of the courtyard are decorated with antiques and pot plants (there are even plants sprouting out of an antique chest).

Many of the furnishings are original, or at least apt; the tarnished-green dining room chandeliers have stags fleeing from their hubs. And at the foot of the stairs a complete suit of armour for a knight and his horse is on display. Most of the bedrooms have an old-fashioned feel; that is, they don't feel anonymously modern, but the number of rooms has doubled since our last edition. Some of them have double-doored windows opening on to the swimming pool, others have canopied double beds, while the six suites available are as large as apartments.

The swimming pool is open to the public, making this Parador feel less privileged than most others, particularly at weekends, when the pool can be busy (and noisy).

~

NEARBY Romanesque churches; Gothic altarpiece, Arcenillas (6 km); 7thC Visigothic church, near El Campillo (20 km).
LOCATION in main square; with garden and car parking
FOOD breakfast, lunch, dinner
PRICES €€€€
ROOMS 46 doubles, 6 suites, all with bath; all rooms have central heating, air conditioning, phone, TV, minibar
FACILITIES dining room, 3 sitting rooms, bar, garden, terrace; swimming pool (public)
CREDIT CARDS AE, DC, MC, V
CHILDREN welcome
DISABLED easy access; lift/elevator **PETS** No
CLOSED never
MANAGER Miguel Angel Chica

CACERES

GUADALUPE

HOSPEDERIA DEL REAL MONASTERIO
∽ CONVERTED MONASTERY ∽

Plaza Juan Carlos 1, 10140, Guadalupe, Cáceres
TEL 927 367000 **FAX** 927 367177
E-MAIL rmsmguadalupe@planalfa.es **WEBSITE** www.monasterioguadalupe.com

THE HOSPEDERIA is part of a 16thC monastery, which dominates the Guadalupe skyline. It is still a working monastery; Franciscan brothers live in one half of the building, guests in the other.

The bedrooms are set around a magnificent stone-arcaded courtyard. Many of them are the original monks' cells – long narrow rooms with high ceilings and low stone doorways. They are all different; some very elaborate, some very basic. On one side there is an exquisite suite full of ornate antiques, on the other, simple single rooms. The public rooms downstairs are equally original; the sombre sitting room contrasts with a cheerful white dining room, with fresh flowers on every table. There is also a TV room arranged like a cinema, and an inviting bar with an arched roof and marble floor. Tables are set out in the charming courtyard.

Although we arrived in the middle of a wedding reception for two hundred guests, the staff were not remotely put out and could not have been more helpful – the monks even gave us a guided tour of the monastery. 'Wow' says an American reader who recently stayed in 15 hotels in the guide: 'the nicest place we stayed in and probably the best bargain in the book.'

∽

NEARBY 14thC Franciscan monastery (Zurbarán's paintings); mountain passes and surrounding countryside.
LOCATION within monastery, entrance up a flight of steps from main road; parking for 30 cars
FOOD breakfast, lunch, dinner
PRICES €€
ROOMS 40 double, one single, 5 family rooms, one suite, all with bath; all rooms have central heating, phone; some rooms have air conditioning
FACILITIES dining room, sitting room, TV room, bar
CREDIT CARDS MC, V
CHILDREN welcome
DISABLED ground floor rooms, lift/elevator **PETS** not accepted
CLOSED mid-Jan to mid-Feb **MANAGER** Javier Cordoba

CACERES

JARANDILLA DE LA VERA

PT CARLOS V
~ CONVERTED CASTLE ~

Avda García, Prieto 1, 10450, Jarandilla de la Vera, Cáceres
Tel 927 560117 **Fax** 927 560088
E-MAIL jarandilla@parador.es **Website** www.parador.es

AN IMPOSING 15THC castle on the edge of a little white town makes a perfect setting for a Parador – which is why the Carlos V is often fully booked. The Parador architects have modernized it without losing any of its medieval flavour; it is difficult to tell that the new extension is not part of the original building. An arched doorway between round towers leads into a cobbled courtyard. Small shuttered windows peep out of cold grey walls and an arcaded balcony looks down from solid square towers.

Most of the public rooms are simply furnished in a modern style. Sombre oil paintings hang on the walls of the upstairs sitting room, which opens on to the balcony set with yellow and white chairs. The bar and dining room are bright and comfortable, and look on to the Parador gardens. The original bedrooms lead off tall, narrow, beamed corridors and have all the usual facilities. Rooms in the extension are light and spacious.

There is plenty to do outside; for the energetic, a swimming pool and tennis court; for children, a play area with swings and slides; and for those who just want to relax, lovely rose gardens surrounding this historic castle.

~

NEARBY Yuste monastery (10 km); Trujillo, Cáceres, Avila, within driving distance.
LOCATION at top of town, on a rock with gardens around it; with car parking
FOOD breakfast, lunch, dinner
PRICES ⓔⓔⓔ-ⓔⓔⓔⓔ
ROOMS 43 double, 10 single, all with bath; all rooms have central heating, air conditioning, phone, TV, minibar
FACILITIES 2 dining rooms, 3 sitting rooms, bar; swimming pool, tennis court
CREDIT CARDS AE, DC, MC, V
CHILDREN welcome
DISABLED ground floor rooms
PETS not accepted
CLOSED never
MANAGER Tomas Cardo Arenas

CACERES

TRUJILLO

MESON LA CADENA
~ TOWN HOUSE ~

Plaza Mayor 5, 10200, Trujillo, Cáceres
TEL 927 321463 **FAX** 927 323116

A SMALLER, CHEAPER alternative to the Trujillo Parador is the Mesón La Cadena, on the main square. Situated in a rambling 16thC palace, it is really a restaurant (and noisy bar) with rooms, rather than a hotel, but it merits inclusion because of its central location and views over the square – a great place for watching the world go by from tables set out on the cobbled street.

The bedrooms are all on the third floor of this attractive granite house, far enough away from the noisy bar to be assured of a good night's sleep. They are simple and charming, with dark wooden furniture and brightly coloured rugs, woven locally. Rooms at the back have sloping ceilings, and look out on to the hill leading up to the castle.

One floor below is the restaurant, on three sides of a tiny internal courtyard, decorated with wrought iron lamps and local pottery plates on white walls. It is a lively place in the evenings, offering an interesting daily menu at a very reasonable price. The food is simple and good, and the waiters are friendly. The bar on the ground floor is also a popular spot and a good place to meet the locals.

~

NEARBY Castle, palaces of the Conquistadors, old city walls.
LOCATION on main square in middle of town; car parking in square
FOOD lunch, dinner
PRICES €€
ROOMS 8 double, all with bath; all rooms have central heating, air conditioning, TV
FACILITIES dining room, sitting room, bar
CREDIT CARDS AE, MC, V
CHILDREN welcome
DISABLED access difficult
PETS not accepted
CLOSED never
MANAGER Juan Vicente Mariscal

BADAJOZ

BARCARROTA

MONASTERIO DE ROCAMADOR

~ COUNTRY HOTEL ~

Carretera Badojoz-Huelva, 06142 Barcarrota (Andalucia)
TEL 924 489000 **FAX** 924 489001
E-MAIL mail@rocamador.com **WEBSITE** www.rocamador.com

OPERA SINGER Lucia Dominguín, practically a European treasure in her own right, bought and renovated this 15thC Franciscan monastery with her theatre director husband Carlos Tristancho in 1990. You can see why it appealed to them: it's full of drama and romance - you can choose to stay in the monk's old cells, their praying rooms, their library, even their cattle sheds. The monastery itself is like a small village – it's a series of low stone buildings spread out over some distance, making it tricky to find your room after dinner. The drama extends to the Michelin-starred restaurant, set in the former chapel with delicious, if expensive food – far more international than the majority of Spanish hotels. Expectations can be high when staying somewhere like this, and we found the hotel, on occasion, cloying – colours in the main areas can be garish and the size makes it slightly impersonal. Thankfully, they have resisted over developing, leaving the walls crumbling and rundown in some areas, the gardens wild and the furniture eclectic, so the atmosphere of a retreat can still be found, if you look hard enough.

~

NEARBY Monsalud mountains, Badajoz, Jerez de los Ccaballeros .
LOCATION in the Sierra Aracena National Park; ample car parking in own grounds
FOOD breakfast, lunch, dinner
PRICES €€€-€€€€
ROOMS 26; 23 doubles or twin-bedded, 3 suites; all rooms have bath, phone, TV, hairdryer, air conditioning
FACILITIES dining room, garden, swimming pool, tennis, riding
CREDIT CARDS AE, DC, MC, V
CHILDREN welcome
DISABLED no specially adapted rooms
PETS accepted
CLOSED Christmas Day
PROPRIETOR Lucia Dominguín and Carlos Tristancho

BADAJOZ

MÉRIDA

HOTEL EMPERATRIZ

~ TOWN MANSION HOTEL ~

Plaza de España 19, 06800, Mérida, Badajoz
TEL 924 313111 **FAX** 924 313305
E-MAIL comercial@hotel-emperatriz.com **WEBSITE** www.hotel-emperatriz.com

MÉRIDA IS A LIVELY historic town, although now (thanks to Moorish plundering of its stone) no more than half the size that it was in Roman times. The Emperatriz stands at its heart – a 16thC mansion, built of sandy-coloured granite in a privileged position on the main square.

The rather unprepossessing entrance opens into a grand cloistered courtyard, surrounded by granite pillars and arches on two floors. When we visited, dining-tables were laid in the courtyard for a wedding banquet – the effect was spectacular. The usual place to dine is an arched room off the cloisters, divided in two by elaborate wrought iron grilles. There are also two public bars, both underground, one serving tapas.

The hotel does not have all the facilities you expect in a Parador, but it has the character and sense of history that many of them lack. The bedrooms are all irregular shapes but are similarly furnished – embroidered bedspreads, wooden furniture and large bathrooms. Those with little balconies, facing on to the busy square full of outdoor cafés and ice-cream stalls, are rather noisy, at least by day.

~

NEARBY Roman theatre, arena and villa, Alcazaba; Badajoz (60 km), Zafra (65 km), Cáceres (70 km), Trujillo (90 km).
LOCATION on main square (follow signs to town centre); no private car parking
FOOD breakfast, lunch, dinner
PRICES €€
ROOMS 17 double, 24 single, one family room, all with bath; all rooms have central heating, phone
FACILITIES dining room, TV room, 2 bars
CREDIT CARDS V
CHILDREN welcome
DISABLED no special facilities
PETS welcome
CLOSED never
MANAGER Francisco Moro

BADAJOZ

ZAFRA

HOTEL HUERTA HONDA

~ TOWN HOTEL ~

Av López Asme 30, 06300, Zafra, Badajoz
TEL 924 554100 **FAX** 924 552504
E-MAIL reservas@hotelhuertahonda.com **WEBSITE** www.hotelhuertahonda.com

WHEN OUR inspectors first visited Zafra, the castle Parador was surrounded by scaffolding and in the throes of extensive redecoration. So they were delighted to discover, right next door, the Huerta Honda. This white villa, with red-tiled roofs and window-boxes dripping with geraniums, has fine views of the medieval castle. It is not merely a decent substitute for the Parador; in many ways, it is more attractive.

The hotel now has a swimming pool on their third level terrace where you can float admiring the impressive view of the castle next door. Chairs and tables spill out of the bar and sitting room around the pool, and it is a perfect place to enjoy a drink, between potted plants and trailing ivy. If you have had too much sun, you will appreciate the cool sitting room, full of wicker furniture and wonderful ornaments (look out for the wicker pig under the mini grand piano, and the boar's head over the open fire). The dining room is a similar haven, and the *menu del dia* excellent value. The hotel bar is a popular night spot and positively buzzes with activity. In contrast the bedrooms are serene; decorated in pastel shades with every possible comfort. You can be sure of a good night's sleep and of waking to a great view.

~

NEARBY Llerena (40 km), Aracena (90 km).
LOCATION next to castle Parador in heart of town; with car parking
FOOD breakfast, lunch, dinner
PRICES €€€-€€€€
ROOMS 37 double, 29 with bath, 8 with shower; 9 single with shower; one family room with bath; all have central heating, air conditioning, phone, TV, minibar, radio, hairdrier
FACILITIES dining room, 2 sitting rooms, 3 bars, terrace; swimming pool, gourmet product shop
CREDIT CARDS AE, DC, MC, V
CHILDREN accepted
DISABLED access easy; ground floor rooms; lift/elevator **PETS** accepted **CLOSED** never
MANAGER Dario Martinez Doblas

SALAMANCA

LA ALBERCA

LAS BATUECAS

COUNTRY HOTEL

*Carretera Las Batuecas, 37624, La
Alberca, Salamanca*
TEL 923 415188 **FAX** 923 415055
E-MAIL lasbatuecas@teleline.es
WEB www.hotellasbatuecas.com
FOOD breakfast, lunch, dinner
PRICES €€ **CLOSED** Jan to Mar
MANAGER Francisco Hernandez
Hoyos

A POPULAR WEEKEND destination for Madrilueños, Las Batuecas is an
imposing stone building located on the edge of the quaint village of La
Alberca, in the heart of the fascinating Sierra de Francia, with its chest-
nut-woods and picturesque terraces of cherry-trees. The hotel begins on
the first floor with a wide, covered terrace. Behind is a garden with a lawn
and rose-clad trellis, and the rest of the floor is an open-plan lounge-bar-
dining-room. The bedrooms and bathrooms have recently been refurbished and the windows sealed against the cold. A useful base for walking,
cycling or touring.

HOTELS IN CENTRAL SPAIN

AREA INTRODUCTION

The provinces of Segovia, Avila, Madrid, Guadalajara, Toledo, Cuenca and Cjudad Real are covered in this section. Outside Madrid, new recommendations include **Posada de Duraton** (page 124), a great place for outdoor activities, **Hostal de Buen Amor** (page 126), run by the Lopezes with great charm and warmth, and **El Milano Real** (page 128), with its eclectic design and rooms with their own aromatherapy scent.

HOTELS IN MADRID

Although the hotel scene in rural Spain has developed dramatically in the last decade, with many new hotels opening that are perfect for this guide, in Madrid the hotel scene is still depressingly unchanged. The delightful small hotels that are such a feature of Paris, Venice, Florence and even London just aren't there in the Spanish capital, and for this new edition we have struggled to find useful new entries. See however, pages 133, 134 and 135. If you need more addresses in Madrid, you could consider these: **The Arosa** (Tel 91 532 1600) is a stylish building on the Gran Via, close to the Puerta del Sol. The rooms are elaborately decorated and well soundproofed to minimise noise from the busy street below. Also close to the Puerta del Sol is the **Reina Victoria** (Tel 91 531 4500), an old favourite, with 195 reasonably priced rooms. The best of these overlook the pretty little plaza of Santa Ana.

For a once-in-a-blue-moon treat, there is the **Ritz** (Tel 91 521 2857), which has been beautifully restored to reflect its former early-19thC glory. Public rooms are decorated with priceless carpets and tapestries, bedrooms are filled with antiques, service is absolutely immaculate; this is one of Spain's top hotels, a fact reflected in its prices. Nearby is the equally grand but rather less wonderful **Palace** (Tel 91 360 8080), a massive 440-room hotel with an impressive clientele – from matadors to politicians. Service tends to be (not surprisingly) rather impersonal, but like the Ritz it has an excellent location close to the Prado. In contrast, the **Villa Magna** (Tel 91 587 1234) is further from the middle towards the northern district. It is a modern version of the Ritz, and almost as classy. Set in immaculate gardens, it has a glass and steel tower, public rooms decorated in 18thC style, large bedrooms and stylish dining rooms.

Outside the central area, the **Monte Real** (Tel 91 316 2140) is a modern hotel in an exclusive suburb. Ask for one of the rooms that overlooks the pool surrounded by trees in tranquil gardens. The hotel is far more impressive from the inside than from the outside; walls are hung with fabulous works of art and tapestries. **The Barajas** (Tel 91 747 7700) is 14 km from the middle of the city, near the airport. It has excellent facilities.

PARADORS IN CENTRAL SPAIN

The three provinces to the north-west of Madrid have a handful of interesting Paradores. The 71-room one at **Tordesillas** is a low modern building set in a secluded pine-grove, just out of the town; it makes a good base for exploring this very interesting region of castles and medieval towns (Tel 983 770051). Within easy reach of it is the **PT de Segovia** – modern, 106 rooms, on the edge of a lake, views of the town and cathedral (Tel 921 443737). Near Avila is the 15thC **PT Raimundo de Borgoña** (see page 112) and, in the Sierra de Gredos, the **PT de Gredos** near Navarredonda de Gredos, with its beamed ceilings and mounted hunting trophies (Tel 920 348048).

With one exception, the Paradores to the north-east of Madrid (Soria and Sigüenza) and to the south (Chinchon, Toledo, Almagro, Alarcón) are all described in detail in this section. The exception is the unremarkable **PT de Manzanares**, east of Ciudad Real.

Segovia

Pedraza de la Sierra

La Posada de Don Mariano

~ Village hotel ~

Calle Mayor 14, 40172, Pedraza de la Sierra, Segovia
Tel 921 509886 **Fax** 921 509887

IF IT IS A QUIET night, the manager of this archetypal charming small hotel, may offer you a selection of rooms. The trouble is: which one do you choose if all of them are like showpieces from an antiquated Ideal Home Exhibition?

Each is unique, personal, luxuriously carpeted and decorated with English floral wallpaper. Antiques abound. Everything is carefully arranged and prepared so that you could almost forget you are in a hotel. It comes as no surprise to learn that the hotel was designed by the owner of one of Madrid's most famous furnishing shops and was featured in *Elle* magazine. But that does not help you choose your room. Maybe you should just take your chance. How about one of the attic rooms upstairs? Smaller perhaps, but still exquisitely furnished and oozing with character. TVs are only provided on request – otherwise they spoil the decoration.

We had three minor reservations about the hotel: the noise from the bar below seems to travel to the rooms above it; the bathrooms are inadequately lit; and breakfast is disappointing. Otherwise, this is a hotel to remember.

~

Nearby Castle and square (2 mins walk each); scenic road up to Puerto de Navafría in the Sierra de Guadarrama (30 km).
Location near castle in main street; no private car parking
Food breakfast, lunch, dinner
Prices €€-€€€
Rooms 15 double, 3 single, all with bath; all rooms have central heating, phone, TV (on request)
Facilities dining room, sitting room/bar
Credit cards AE, DC, MC, V
Children welcome
Disabled access difficult
Pets not accepted
Closed never
Manager Mariano Pascual

SEGOVIA

SEBULCOR

POSADA DE DURATON

~ VILLAGE HOTEL ~

Calle la Matilla, Sebulcor, 40380 Segovia
Tel 921 521424 Fax 921 521472
E-MAIL info@posadadelduraton.com **WEBSITE** www.posadadelduraton.com

ALMOST TOO CHARMING. Not, in fact, a critical comment, but this is one of many small hotels in this area that have been made over by talented interior designer-architects who might have used the Charming Small Hotel Guides as a textbook. Starting even outside, with the huge flagstones that lead to the front door, not a chance is lost to expose and set off some original feature; everything is a symphony of mellow old stone, gnarled beams, endless lovely country antique furniture, tastefully chosen fabrics and furnishings. The building was in fact once a church - some of the walls are 70 cm thick. Downstairs, public rooms and connecting areas held together with equal care in beautiful mellow brick and honey colours, deep brown and orange brown exposed wood. The dining room is especially charming, with modern chairs and tables offsetting the original irregular wooden pillars supporting the ceiling. Upstairs a passage floor is lined with two vivid lines of blue tiles to offset the usual terracotta. Bedrooms are just as well done, OK for space, and bathrooms are a high standard. We often wonder whether in such places the design might not be covering for a lack of hospitality - but we don't, in fact, believe that's the case here.

The large village of Sepulcor is not especially interesting, but it's a great base for outdoor activities in the Duraton Natural Park. There's a cycle hire depot near the hotel entrance.

~

NEARBY Duraton Natural Park; Sierra de Guaderrama, Segovia, Sepulveda, Pedraza.
LOCATION on street; ample safe car parking on road close to hotel
FOOD breakfast, lunch, dinner
PRICES €€
ROOMS 10; 9 doubles, 1 suite; all rooms have bath, shower, phone, TV, minibar
hairdrier
FACILITIES sitting room, dining room
CREDIT CARDS AE, DC, MC, V **CHILDREN** welcome **DISABLED** one ground floor bedroom
PETS accepted **CLOSED** never **LANGUAGES** Spanish only **PROPRIETOR** Jose Tovar

SEGOVIA

SIGUERUELO

POSADA DE SIGUERELO

~ VILLAGE BED AND BREAKFAST ~

Calle Baden 40, Sigueruelo, Segovia
TEL and **FAX** 921 50 81 35
WEBSITE www.situral.com

WE ARE NOT SURE how long we would want to stop in Siguerelo: there's not much here. But it is a real Spanish village, and probably fine for a stopover. The solidly built *posada* is up a dusty little lane leading away from the main street. By the front door, a hollowed out tree trunk was once a cattle trough. The charm is of the cottagey kind that we like, if not too pretty-pretty, especially when the service is also friendly but unobtrusive. Our inspector was met by the son of the owners, who was manning front of house and the breakfast room: he was in shorts and T-shirt - and why not? The temperature was over 40 degrees C, he was doing three things at once, and he was still friendly and switched on. We describe it as a B & B because of its simplicity, but in fact they do serve dinner in the restaurant.

Everywhere you look is the rich brown colour of exposed beams. Downstairs is a homely breakfast-dining room, and a sitting room where your granny might be entirely at home, triangular wood burning stove tucked neatly into a corner. The first flight of the staircase is almost entirely freestanding, increasing the impression of a forest of timber. Its risers (the verticals between the treads) are faced with charming hand-painted tiles. Bedrooms are similarly charming, continuing the rustic style, with feminine touches such as frilly lampshades offsetting solid free-standing antique wardrobes and delightful pastel patterned bed covers. No televisions, or phones disturb the period feel.

~

NEARBY Duraton Natural Park, Sierra de Guaderrama; Segovia, Sepulveda, Pedraza.
LOCATION easy to find behind main street on gravel track; parking on track by house
FOOD breakfast, dinner
PRICES €€
ROOMS 6, all doubles; all rooms have bath and shower
FACILITIES sitting room, dining room/breakfast room **CREDIT CARDS** MC, V
CHILDREN welcome **DISABLED** no specially adapted rooms or lift/elevator
PETS by arrangement **CLOSED** never **LANGUAGES** Spanish only
PROPRIETOR Concepcion Rodriguez

SEGOVIA

HOSTAL DE BUEN AMOR
~ VILLAGE HOTEL ~

40170 Sotosalbos, Segovia
TEL 921 403 20 **FAX** 921 403022
E-MAIL hosbamor@cempresarial.com **WEBSITE** empresarial.com/hostaldebuenamor

W E HAVE A CLUSTER of four hotels in this area east of Segovia. This is our clear favourite because the couple who run it stand out as natural hosts who have a way with people. They happen to be older than most of the other local owners, but that's not the point. The Lopezes are cultivated and speak several languages - something of a rarity in these parts - and we think that these qualities count if you're running this type of operation. The mellow four-square building stands in the middle of a peaceful village. Most of downstairs is taken up with a long, relaxing sitting room, with reception at the front. The interior is not so heavily designed as many we've seen, but it's furnished very comfortably and with real taste: country furniture, good fabrics, harmonious rustic colour schemes. The bedrooms continue the rustic-but-elegant theme, each individually furnished and decorated. Try No 201, with a view of the Romanesque church; or if you have the cash, No 203, almost a suite, but not allowed to be advertised as such (regulations). The British enjoy number 104 because of its familiar English country house settee. Just across the road is a an award-winning restaurant, El Porche de las Casillas, run by the Lopez's son Alberto, where you can try the local speciality, lamb cooked in the wood burning oven (*horno de asnar*) until so tender it falls from the bone. Buen Amor? The name is from a classic of Spanish literature, the *Libro de Buen Amor*.(The Book of Loving Well) by Hita, who knew the village well.

~

NEARBY Duraton Natural Park, Sierra de Guaderrama; Segovia, Sepulveda, Pedraza.
LOCATION near village entrance with ample car parking on street
FOOD breakfast; affiliated restaurant across road serves lunch and dinner
PRICES €€- €€€€ **ROOMS** 12; 11 doubles, 1 single; all rooms have bath, shower, phone, TV, hairdrier **FACILITIES** living room, conference room, affiliated restaurant; riding arranged **CREDIT CARDS** AE, DC, MC, V **CHILDREN** welcome **DISABLED** 2 rooms on ground floor with wheelchair access **PETS** not accepted **CLOSED** never; restaurant open Fri eve, Sat and Sun lunch, and some special occasions
LANGUAGES English, French, Italian, some German **PROPRIETOR** Dora Lopez

SEGOVIA

TURÉGANO

EL ZAGUAN
~ TOWN HOTEL ~

Plaza de Espana 16, 40370 Turegano, Segovia
TEL 921 501165/56 **FAX** 921 500776
E-MAIL zaguan@el-zaguan.com **WEBSITE** www.el-zaguan.com

THE ROAD THROUGH the little town of Turegano widens dramatically as you reach the centre, forming a roomy plaza, which is pleasantly arcaded and overlooked by an imposing castle, still pretty much intact. Tucked into a corner, with a misleadingly modest facade, is El Zaguan. Inside, with the bar curiously sited right opposite the reception desk, you realize you're in a substantial three-story building. In terms of design, it could hardly be more impressive. As usual, much use is made of exposed timbers as a structural and as a design feature: in a building of these dimensions, there are plenty of them and they have to be supported at intervals by pillars, which usefully define the space. See the dining room, which because of the timber succeeds admirably despite quite simple elements (terracotta floor, exposed stone walls and white paint between the roof beams). The *tour de force* is the second-floor-mezzanine sitting room on three levels. You don't often see hotel architecture as imaginative as this. There's charming country furniture throughout, to be used, not revered. The connecting corridors are nicely decorated, maybe a little dark. Bedrooms, with adequate space, are a nice balance of clean interior design and homely touches, with restful ochres and dull maroon walls, comfortable armchairs, tasteful bed covers; the bathrooms gleam. Prices are fair. However: as in many of the beautiful small hotels we visited in this area, there was slightly static atmosphere and we felt that the owner and reception staff had a rather neutral approach. Reports welcome.

NEARBY Duraton Natural Park, Sierra de Guaderrama; Segovia, Sepulveda, Pedraza.
LOCATION in town centre on main square with ample car parking close to entrance
FOOD breakfast, lunch, dinner
PRICES €€
ROOMS 15; 10 doubles, 2 singles, 3 suites; all rooms have bath, shower, phone, TV, air-conditioning, safe **FACILITIES** sitting room, restaurant **CREDIT CARDS** MC, V
CHILDREN welcome **DISABLED** no specially adapted rooms; lift/elevator
PETS not accepted **CLOSED** never **LANGUAGES** Spanish only **PROPRIETOR** Mario Garcia

AVILA

EL MILANO REAL
~ VILLAGE HOTEL ~

Calle Toledo s/n, 05634, Hoyos del Espino, Avila
TEL 920 349108 **FAX** 920 349156
E-MAIL info@elmilanoreal.com **WEBSITE** elmilanoreal.com

P**URPOSE-BUILT** as a hotel in 1994, up a narrow approach road in a strag-
gling mountain village, this hotel nonetheless has a charm all its own.
The rustic stone exterior, still not particularly mellow, is in deliberate
contrast to the interior, a triumph of eclectic interior design. Downstairs,
the style changes at a brisk pace between the comfortable traditional-rus-
tic galleried sitting room; the two more contemporary dining rooms; and
the central patio. Even the garden offers variety, one section being for
drinks, the other, with a rocky waterfall and pond, for contemplation.
Upstairs, the bedrooms could hardly be more different, and each has its
own aromatherapy scent. In Gredos the air is laden with thyme; in
English, lavender; in Japanese jasmine; in Manhattan, not exhaust fumes,
but apple. All except a couple have the bewitching 180-degree view of the
heights of the Sierra de Gredos. Our inspector stayed in the expansive
Scandinavian suite, with its own sauna. There's a library, an astronomical
observatory, charming corners for slumping with a book in front of windows looking out on to the mountain view, and a cards/chess room. Teresa
Dorn (American) and Francisco Sanchez Rico started in the hotel business from scratch and are wise hosts. The food is well above average and
the cellar has an astonishing 400 wines. Sadly, there's building work going
on outside the hotel which presently somewhat spoils the approach to the
front door, but this was due to finish within a year of this new edition
being published. Anyway you'll forget it once you're inside.

~

NEARBY Sierra de Gredos; wild ibis park; Celtic ruins; Tormes river; Avila 50 mins
by car. **LOCATION** in residential area of village, in own grounds with ample street
parking **FOOD** breakfast, lunch, dinner **PRICES** €€€ **ROOMS** 21; 8 doubles, 5 large
doubles, 8 suites; all rooms have bath, showr, phone, TV, video, fax/modem
connection, minibar, hairdrier **FACILITIES** sitting room, 2 dining rooms, library,
cards/games room, observatory, garden **CREDIT CARDS** AE, DC, MC, V
DISABLED one suite on ground floor; lift/elevator **PETS** not accepted **CLOSED** 24 Dec
LANGUAGES English **PROPRIETORS** Teresa Dorn and Francisco Sanchez Rico

AVILA

NAVARREDONDA DE GREDOS

CASA DE ARRIBA

~ VILLAGE HOTEL ~

Calle de la Cruz, 19, 05635 Navarredonda de Gredos, Avila
TEL 920 348024 **FAX** 920 348386

THIS IS MINUTES away from El Milano Real (page 128), our other recommendation in the Gredos, but offers a very different sort of charm. It's also as different as could be from the forbidding and conventional Parador de Gredos, also close by in the next-door village of Sierra de Gredos. The location is actually a little better than that of the Milano Real, in a quiet lane at the top of the village, and with the same wonderful views. It's a very private, peaceful place, behind metal gates and walls in a slightly overgrown but charming garden, with rustic stone tables and stools. The solid old building has been restored beautifully, even by the high standards we've noted for this new edition. There's a long, cool reception-sitting room; a beamy dining room and on the first floor a memorable landing with gloriously uneven antique floorboards running the width of the house. Bedrooms are better than usual for space, and special care has been taken with various cheerful paint effects for the walls - notice their massive thickness. The atmosphere is almost that of a private house, with low-key but friendly owners who only speak Spanish. There are just eight rooms, so the welcome really can be personal. We believe it's well run, and that a traveller interested in exploring the area and walking the Gredos mountains could be happy here for several days.

~

NEARBY Sierra de Gredos; wild ibis park; Celtic ruins; Tormes river; Avila 50 mins by car.
LOCATION difficult to find, but signposted from main road running through Navarredonda. First sign is legible, but a second, some way on, partially obliterated when we visited; turn left when you get to the top and be prepared to ask your way.
FOOD breakfast, dinner
PRICES ⓔⓔ **ROOMS** 8, all double; all rooms have bath, shower, TV
FACILITIES sitting room, dining room, garden
CREDIT CARDS MC, V **DISABLED** no specially adapted rooms **PETS** not accepted
CLOSED Jan **LANGUAGES** Spanish only **PROPRIETOR** Teresa Pazos

AVILA

SAN ESTEBAN delVALLE

POSADA DE ESQUILADORES
~ TOWN HOTEL ~

Esquiladores, 1-05412 San Esteban delValle, Avila
TEL 920 383498 **FAX** 920 383456

S AN ESTEBAN is an off-the-beaten-track mountain town with a slightly lost feel, and this small hotel is quite hard to find, down an alley near the centre. We think it may suit travellers who like to explore, and who appreciate a genuine 'local' experience. You step through the front door into a large (darkish), reception room, once a shop. It's homely, full of the well-chosen, charming country furniture that is now the making of so many small hotels in Spain; the restoration has been achieved with great skill. We especially liked the dining room, in what was the central patio, covered in by a transparent roof, with an unusual grey-blue floor to emphasize the restful, diffuse lighting. Food - the owner is the chef - is imaginative - concentrating on regional specialities with fresh vegetables from the hotel's garden. Below, a cellar with massive dividing walls has an eating area; and you can breakfast in a sunny outdoor area at the back. Bedrooms are pleasantly low key, with much use of whites, greys and muted colour; hand-painted tiles add character to gleaming bathrooms. The cheapest room is just about OK for space, bearing in mind that this is a town house. When we visited, the place had a slightly curious, subdued atmosphere, maybe something to do with a not-exactly outgoing manager. Historians may like to know that the owner, Almudena Garcia Drake, is indeed descended from Francis Drake, the great 16thC English admiral, and scourge of the Spanish Armada.

~

NEARBY Sierra de Gredos, Cinco villas gully, Roman baths in Pico, castle of Mombeltran, caves of Aguila.
LOCATION in town centre, limited car parking in square immediately adjacent. Difficult to find: where main road through town meets plaza (with bars and statue) take Calle de San Petro Bautista. At next plaza, the posada is a few paces down to right
FOOD breakfast, lunch, dinner **PRICES** ©© **ROOMS** 12; 10 doubles and 2 'special' doubles; all rooms have bath, shower, TV, air conditioning, hairdrier, safe
FACILITIES sitting room, cellar, conference/meeting room; terrace
CREDIT CARDS AE, DC, MC, V **DISABLED** one specially adapted room on ground floor; lift/elevator **PETS** not accepted **CLOSED** Christmas **PROPRIETOR** Almudena Garcia Drake

MADRID

CHINCHON

PT DE CHINCHON
~ CONVERTED MONASTERY ~

Avenida Generalisimo 1, 28370, Chinchón, Madrid
TEL 91 8940836 **FAX** 91 8940908
E-MAIL chinchon@parador.es **WEBSITE** www.parador.es

GATHERED AROUND a light, green, airy courtyard – with tall cypress trees in its corners and pigeons flitting around a fountain and climbing roses – the ground floor of this 17thC monastery is a wealth of colour and detail. The peaceful, glazed-in cloisters form wide passages which are decorated with murals and antiques: clocks, chests, cabinets, even a large old brass still (the town is renowned for its *anis*).

The stately dining room and cool blue bar are both brightly tiled and lit by small windows piercing massively thick walls. Climb the staircase, which has original but fading frescoes on the ceiling above it, and you find landings furnished with comfortable sofas.

The bedrooms are different in style from everything else. They have the austere but romantic atmosphere of a decaying medieval palace; but very clean, light, airy and comfortable. Our most recent reporter noticed the thoughtful and friendly service and thought the food good, even though the menu was somewhat unenterprising. Fair prices, too.

~

NEARBY Plaza Mayor; Royal Palace, Aranjuez (26 km).
LOCATION opposite main square in heart of village; private garage
FOOD breakfast, lunch, dinner
PRICES €€€€
ROOMS 36 double, 2 suite all with bath; all rooms have central heating, air conditioning, phone, TV, minibar, hairdrier
FACILITIES 2 dining rooms, sitting room, bar, terrace
CREDIT CARDS AE ,DC ,MC, V
CHILDREN welcome
DISABLED access not easy; some ground floor rooms
PETS not accepted
CLOSED never
MANAGER Daniel de Lamo

MADRID

MADRID

HOTEL CARLOS V
City hotel

Maestro Vitoria 5, 28013, Madrid
Tel 91 5314100 **Fax** 91 5313761
E-mail recepcion@hotel.carlosv.com. **Website** www.hotelcarlosv.com.

A T FIRST SIGHT this looks like a run-of-the-mill city-centre hotel and indeed the bedrooms, though renovated and spotless, and well-equipped with bright modern bathrooms, are impersonal. Scratch the surface, however, and you will find a family-run hotel that cares for its individual guests. The original owner's grandson, now in charge, eschews organised tour groups.

The hotel has a great variety of bedrooms and family rooms. Some rooms on the first and second floors have small balconies and five rooms at the top of the building have fair-sized, sun-catching terraces for no extra charge. The Carlos V is also one of the few hotels in its class in Madrid to have plenty of double beds. The hotel's greatest asset is its stylish sitting room with its crystal chandeliers, large mirrors and moulded ceiling.

In a pedestrianized street next to the Puerta del Sol ('the centre of Spain'), the Carlos V can be a maddening place to find in a car. The convenient location has its disadvantages. A good night's sleep in summer depends on getting the right balance between ventilation, street noise and the din of the air-conditioning.

Nearby Metro (Callao or Sol, 2 mins walk), Plaza Mayor.
Location on a pedestrianized street near Puerta del Sol; public car parking nearby
Food breakfast
Prices €€€€
Rooms 61 double, 6 single, all with bath; all rooms have central heating, air conditioning, phone, satellite TV, minibar, hairdrier, safe
Facilities sitting room, bar/breakfast room
Credit cards AE, DC, MC, V
Children welcome
Disabled access easy; lift/elevator
Pets not accepted
Closed never
Proprietor Jose Gutierrez

MADRID

ORFILA
~ CITY HOTEL ~

Orfila 6, 28010 Madrid
Tel 91 7027770 **Fax** 91 7027772
E-mail inforeservas@hotelorfila.com **Website** www.hotelorfila.com

If only it wasn't a Relais & Chateau; if only the reception staff weren't in tails; if only the so-called welcome was something like spontaneous, rather than studedly polite; if only the bedrooms (impeccable as they are) were less predictable - then this could be a real charming small hotel city hotel. But Madrid has always been one of the worst European capitals for relaxed, individual, places to stay. Still, the Orfila is housed in a beautiful little mansion parallel to Paseo de la Castellana, the city's smart central north-south axis, and with 32 bedrooms it's quite small for a city hotel. Stepping in from the quiet street you find yourself in a striking entrance chamber, and then comes the handsome reception hall. You could talk yourself into thinking that this has an intimate feel, grand though it is. Off it is a charming tea room and an elegant small dining room. So, on balance, we welcome this hotel to the guide and hope readers have pleasant experiences here.

A safe choice for the middle-aged or elderly, not on a budget. If you're a young, and want something trendier, the Santo Mauro (page 135), a few minutes walk to the north, is a better choice.

~

Nearby Prado, old centre sights.
Location west side of Paseo de la Castellana in quiet semi-residential street; street car parking or hotel garage
Food breakfast, lunch, dinner
Prices €€€€
Rooms 32; 20 doubles, 12 suites; all rooms have bath, shower, phone, TV, video, CD player on request, air conditioning, mini bar, safe
Facilities lobby, sitting room, bar, tea room, dining room, tea room, terrace
Credit cards AE, DC, MC, V
Children accepted
Disabled no specially adapted rooms; lift/elevator **Pets** not accepted
Closed never **Languages** English, French
Manager Elena Bravo

MADRID

MADRID

LA RESIDENCIA DE EL VISO

~ CITY HOTEL ~

Calle Norvión 8, 28002 Madrid
TEL 91 5646370 **FAX** 91 5641963
E-MAIL reserva@residenciadelviso.com **WEBSITE** www.residenciadelviso.com

THE BROCHURE describes this place as an oasis of peace and pleasure in central Madrid. In truth, it is quite peaceful, since it's in a relatively subdued residential street. 'Central' is more fanciful: it's at least 15 minutes in a cab north-east from the old city centre, and our inspector's driver had to ask the way twice. As for pleasure, you may find your mood altered here, but not we hope, by the bland and irritating piped music in the reception area. We include this newish hotel mainly because of the pleasant way the reception/sitting room/bar and the restaurant open via big glass doors on to a flowery internal courtyard. It's light, friendly, and quite informal, much less chic than our other Madrid hotels, but care has been taken to create a sympathetic atmosphere, with a few antiques (and repro pieces) here and there, old prints and oriental rugs on marble floors. Bedrooms, levered into three floors, are smallish, some cramped, but they are decorated individually with bright but anodyne fabrics. Though in joint ownership, it has some of the feel of a family-run enterprise. When we inspected, a double room was 127 euros. Outside the capital you can stay, of course, in twice as good a place for half the money. But compared with the Orfila (page 133, 348 euros for a double) and the Santo Mauro (page 135, 404 euros for a standard double) this is a useful 'budget' address in the capital.

~

NEARBY Museo de Ciencias Naturales, República de Argentina train station.
LOCATION off north end of Paseo de la Castellana
FOOD breakfast, lunch, dinner
PRICES €€€
ROOMS 12, 3 singles, 9 doubles; all rooms have bath, shower, TV, air conditioning, safe
FACILITIES lobby, sitting room, bar, restaurant
CREDIT CARDS AE, DC, MC, V **CHILDREN** accepted
DISABLED no specially adapted rooms; lift/elevator **PETS** not accepted
CLOSED never
MANAGER Myriam Escudero

MADRID

SANTO MAURO
~ CITY HOTEL ~

Zurbano 36, 28010 Madrid
TEL 91 3196900
E-MAIL santo-mauro@ac-hoteles.com

WE CONTINUE moaning about the Madrid hotel scene with this relative newcomer close to the Orfila (page 133) and the Paseo de la Castellana in a smart residential area favoured by the Spanish nobility in the early 1900s. No mistake, it's a lovely hotel, but it could be so much more interesting. You'll find some of what we favour: stylish, distinctive interior decoration; and an enviable situation - the entrance is deeply classy, in an off-street court revealing a clean 18thC style exterior (clearly French-influenced) artfully set off by a splendid green metal and glass porch. Service and welcome are OK, nothing special, in fact we suspect the staff may often be hard pressed. The main frustration, from our perspective, is that this is essentially a hotel, part of a chain, a very public place. Under a private owner-manager, it would have a very different atmosphere. The reception rooms have superb style - modern urban chic skilfully blended with this old building's grand proportions - but are essentially impersonal. Note the magnificent dining room, in what was once the library. Bedrooms are of course stylish, with gleaming bathrooms.

~

NEARBY Pardo, old centre sights.
LOCATION west of Paseo de la Castellana, off semi-residential street
FOOD breakfast, lunch, dinner
PRICES €€€€
ROOMS 51; 5 singles, 14 doubles, 32 suites; all rooms have bath, shower, phone, TV, CD player, modem connection, air conditioning, mini bat
FACILITIES 3 sitting rooms, indoor swimming pool, sauna, terrace, garden
CREDIT CARDS AE, DC, MC, V
CHILDREN accepted
DISABLED some specially adapted rooms; lift/elevator
PETS small ones accepted
CLOSED never
MANAGER Luisa Rodriguez

GUADALAJARA

ALBALATE DE ZORITA

LAS NUBES
~ COUNTRY HOTEL ~

Ctra, de Cabanillas – 19117 Albalate de Zorita, Guadalajara
TEL 949 826897 **FAX** 949 826897
E-MAIL lasnubes@csh.e.telefonica.net

IF IT WERE anywhere else, this place would not be in the guide. It's a some-what harsh modern building; furnishings and fittings, though inoffensive, are modern and lack character, in fact some may come from a hotel chain suppliers. A TV screen dominates part of the living area. Music is piped. The bedrooms, ranged down a corridor, are boxy and not very spacious.

But: Las Nubes (meaning The Clouds) is sited like a peregrine's nest as high as it can be on the crest of a hill rising abruptly from the plain below. The resulting 180-degree views of the Castillian plain, stretching away to the horizon, could keep you gawping for 48 hours. Moreover, it's the most isolat-ed place we've seen in 20 years of hotel inspecting, down a deserted track 9 km from the nearest town, 2 km of which is gravel: its own little world, bespoke tailored for mellowing out. Bikini'd women wander in and out of the living-dining area from the pool. The family atmosphere (young children also drift about) is informal and friendly, and the Sanchez family seem to be nat-ural hosts, running it as a cross-over between private house and hotel. Food (all Spanish dishes) is rather good, with plenty of choice; they keep their own chickens. When we visited there was a polyglot collection of British, German and Spanish visitors, wanting (and getting) food at odd times. The main indoor living space is open plan, split into several levels, well designed for this style of operation, There are plenty of corners for escape, such as the upstairs gallery with chess table.

~

NEARBY Castle and ruins of Recopolis (7 km), Pastrana monastery, Arabigo castle.
LOCATION 9 km along narrow road from Albalate. On main road in Albalate, look for sign for Ctra. Cubilla and at first follow these signs. Signs for Las Nubes start some way on. Towards end, 2 km of road is gravel
FOOD breakfast, lunch, dinner **PRICES** €€€-€€€€ **ROOMS** 6; 5 doubles, 1 suite (with Jacuzzi); all rooms have bath, shower, hairdrier **FACILITIES** living room, dining area, games room, swimming pool, sauna **CREDIT CARDS** AE, DC, MC, V
CHILDREN welcome **DISABLED** no specially adapted rooms; no lift/elevator
PETS accepted **CLOSED** 1 week in Jan **LANGUAGES** English **PROPRIETOR** Sanchez family

TOLEDO

TOLEDO

LA ALMAZARA
~ COUNTRY HOUSE HOTEL ~

Ctra Toledo-Arges km 3.4, 45080, Toledo
TEL 925 223866 **FAX** 925 250562
E-MAIL reservas@hotelalmazara.com **WEBSITE** www.hotelalmazara.com

JUST A FEW kilometres out of Toledo is this hotel on a wooded hilltop over-looking the city. The views are magnificent –and cost half the price of the Parador further around the hill. It is a simple, rustic place, built as a country residence in the 16thC. A gravel courtyard is surrounded on three sides by a solid ivy-clad building.

This is not the sort of place you would want to lounge around in all day, and it does not have a restaurant, but it is the perfect haven after a hot day's sightseeing in much-visited Toledo. 'Absolute peace' writes a contented American visitor. 'The place is charming, the staff are charming, even the cats are charming.' The atmosphere is very laid back.

The huge sitting room looks lived in – comfy sofas around a log fire, piles of magazines and books scattered on tables, and a TV in one corner. Breakfast is served in a delightful arched room that leads on to a small (and rather overgrown) terrace. All the bedrooms are simple, cool and spacious (extra beds can be installed), and are brightened up by locally-made curtains and bedspreads. Bedrooms 1 to 9 all have balconies overlooking Toledo.

NEARBY Toledo – Alcázar, cathedral, El Greco museum, synagogue and Jewish quarter; Madrid (70 km).
LOCATION on hill overlooking Toledo; 3 km from Carretera Circunvalación, on Cuerva road; with car parking in courtyard. Well signposted
FOOD breakfast
PRICES €€€-€€€€
ROOMS 26 double, 2 single, 1 family room, all with bath; all rooms have central heating, phone
FACILITIES sitting room, breakfast room
CREDIT CARDS AE, DC, MC, V
CHILDREN welcome
DISABLED 6 ground floor rooms **PETS** not accepted
CLOSED 10 Dec to 1 Mar
MANAGER Paulino Villamor

TOLEDO

HOSTAL DEL CARDENAL
~ COUNTRY HOTEL ~

Paseo de Recaredo 24, 45004, Toledo
TEL 925 224900 **FAX** 925 222991
E-MAIL cardenal@hostaldelcardenal.com **WEBSITE** www.hostaldelcardenal.com

THIS CLASSY LITTLE hotel was one of the highlights of our latest inspection tour. It occupies a long, pale-brick mansion, built in the 18thC as the summer residence of the archbishop of Toledo, Cardinal Lorenzana. It is set in beautiful shaded gardens, virtually enclosed by the old city walls, rising in three tiers to an impressive, crested doorway. The lowest tier of the garden incorporates an excellent restaurant, now run independently but used by all the guests.

Every room oozes style and character; the sitting rooms contain well-chosen antiques, the stairway has a beautiful sculpted ceiling, bedrooms have old painted-wood bedheads, and bathrooms have hand-painted tiles and old mirrors. There is a clever mixture of old and new throughout; original Moorish corbels support beams in the upstairs corridor, while modern Moorish sculpture surrounds bedroom doors downstairs. There are two brick courtyards, decorated with ferns, terracotta pots and lilies.

This is a magical place to enjoy a warm summer's evening. You need to book well in advance as it is extremely popular, especially with British and American tourists.

~

NEARBY Alcázar, cathedral, El Greco Museum, synagogue and Jewish quarter; Madrid (70 km).
LOCATION within city walls near main gate (Puerta de Bisagra); with garden but no private car parking
FOOD breakfast; lunch and dinner in adjacent restaurant of same name
PRICES €€€-€€€€
ROOMS 22 double, 3 single, 2 suites, all with bath; all rooms have central heating, phone; most have air conditioning, hairdrier, TV
FACILITIES breakfast room, 2 sitting rooms
CREDIT CARDS AE, DC, MC, V
CHILDREN welcome **DISABLED** no special facilities
PETS accepted **CLOSED** never
PROPRIETOR Luis González

TOLEDO

TOLEDO

PINTOR EL GRECO

~ TOWN HOTEL ~

Alamillos del Tránsito, 13, 45002 Toledo
TEL 925 285191 **FAX** 925 215819
E-MAIL elgreco@estancias.es **WEBSITE** www.pintorelgreco.com

YOU COULD HARDLY be closer to the sights of Toledo than in this converted and extended 17th century house in the former Jewish quarter of the city.

Behind the original façade, most of the building is modern but the widespread use of sand-blasted pine, wrought iron and Spanish ceramics preserves the historical feel while allowing light, space and all modern comforts.

You can get a feel of the original building by taking the short flight of steps beside Room 3 (which has a brick arch in its bathroom) down to the entrance of a blocked tunnel which once linked the house to the palace behind, and indeed to the city at large.

Some of the bedrooms overlook the square and gardens in front of the hotel and two of the rooms have views of the hillside across the river. There are six secluded rooms in the attic, two of them large family rooms.

If all the hotel lacks is a dining room, there are plenty of restaurants close by and the owners have their own beyond the city walls.

Prices increase for Toledo's Holy Week celebrations.

~

NEARBY El Greco museum, El Tránsito synagogue, cathedral.
LOCATION next to El Greco museum; no car parking
FOOD breakfast
PRICES €€€€
ROOMS 33 double, one single, all with bath; all rooms have central heating, air conditioning, TV, minibar, telephone, safe, hairdrier
FACILITIES sitting room, breakfast room
CREDIT CARDS AE, DC, MC, V
CHILDREN accepted
DISABLED access difficult
PETS accepted
CLOSED never
MANAGER Mariano Sánchez

CUENCA

PT MARQUÉS DE VILLENA
~ CASTLE PARADOR ~

Avenida Amigos del Castillo, 16213, Alarcón, Cuenca
TEL 969 330315 **FAX** 969 330303
E-MAIL alarcon@parador.es **WEBSITE** www.parador.es

YOU MAY NOT believe your eyes as you approach Alarcón, so improbable is the position of the castle which has guarded the village since Moorish times – overlooking the valley of the deep-green Río Júcar, on the edge of Don Quixote's La Mancha.

You may feel like a wandering knight returning from the Crusades as you step into the quaint little courtyard with its well in the middle. Within the thick castle walls you should sleep well and live in typical Parador style, with your minibar discreetly hidden in a reproduction antique cabinet; the pick of the bedrooms is number 103, with a canopied bed and steps up to a high window where distressed damsels might sit and dream of rescue. The sitting room-cum-cafeteria has everything you could want of a great hall: a circular iron chandelier, an enormous tapestry depicting a coat of arms, a suit of armour and three wooden thrones. The dining room is also a vaulted chamber, with a long slit window.

A lift will whisk you up to the battlements for a view worthy of a feudal baron. The village has several other historical buildings and there are some good walks.

~

NEARBY Castle of Belmonte (70 km), Mota del Cuervo (85 km) and Cuenca (85 km).
LOCATION on huge rock encircled by river, at end of village; car parking outside castle
FOOD breakfast, lunch, dinner
PRICES €€€€
ROOMS 14 double, all with bath; all rooms have central heating, phone, TV, minibar
FACILITIES dining room, bar
CREDIT CARDS AE, DC, MC, V
CHILDREN welcome; special play area
DISABLED access easy; lift/elevator
PETS not accepted
CLOSED never
MANAGER Juan Antonio Choza

CUENCA

CUENCA

POSADA DE SAN JOSÉ
~ TOWN HOUSE HOTEL ~

Calle Julian Romero 4, 16001, Cuenca
TEL 969 211300 **FAX** 969 230365
E-MAIL info@posadasanjose.com **WEBSITE** www.posadasanjose.com

ONCE THE HOME of the in-laws of Velazquez's daughter and later a cathedral choir school, this Posada could hardly offer better credentials. Today – with a 1961 addition – it is a six-tier labyrinth replete with curios, antique furniture and even frescoes. If you like stairs, antiques, history and exploring, this is the hotel for you.

Jennifer Morter, an expatriate Canadian, and her Spanish husband Antonio have lovingly decorated every room with great attention to detail and cleanliness ('you could sit on the floor', Jennifer likes to say). The sheets are pressed and turned back in the old-fashioned way. The 30 rooms are all different and each has been given individual character – you may get a four-poster bed, a Latin inscription on the wall or a dreamy balcony with a magnificent view across the valley. Room 33 is the most popular, with its sloping floor and two balconies.

The rooms themselves are cosy enough to sit in but there is also a rambling breakfast room and bar where tapas is served, with intimate nooks and a sunny terrace, a TV room stranded on its own peculiar floor and a hall with a few antiques and a sofa.

~

NEARBY Cathedral and Casas Colgadas (both within a short walk); Ventano del Diablo (25 km), Ciudad Encantada (35 km).
LOCATION off Plaza Mayor in old part of town, down narrow road past cathedral; no private car parking
FOOD breakfast, light snack suppers
PRICES €€
ROOMS 18 double, 2 single, 2 suite with bath (not all rooms have own bathrooms); all rooms have central heating
FACILITIES breakfast room, TV room, bar
CREDIT CARDS AE, DC, V
CHILDREN welcome **DISABLED** access difficult
PETS accepted in bedrooms **CLOSED** never; bar only, Mon
PROPRIETORS Jennifer Morter and Antonio Cortinas

CUENCA

CASA PALACIO
~ TOWN HOTEL ~

Angustias, 2 - 16450 Uclés, Cuenca
TEL 969 135065 **FAX** 969 135011

IF YOU'RE ON the N111/E901 Madrid-Valencia motorway, south of Madrid, you might ask why you should detour to Uclés, apparently in the middle of nowhere. And when you arrive (in fact quite quickly: it's a fast minor road) at the sleepy small hill town with a vast, eerily deserted monastery-church perched at the top, you may ask again what a decent hotel could be doing here. Which makes Casa Palacio all the more charming when you find it just off a corner of the main plaza. The solid stone town house, several hundred years old, has been beautifully converted into a hushed small hotel. Down one side of the central courtyard is the restaurant, with modern tables and chairs. A wooden gallery at first floor level (supported on antique stone columns at each corner), works the usual charm. A delightful little sitting room on the ground floor has pinkish walls and an elegant, but simple fireplace with logs piled each side, perhaps as you would have them at home. Genuine, unpretentious country antiques and artefacts - here a weighing scales, there a chest - rub shoulders happily with the occasional modern piece - perhaps a steel uplighter or simple bedside lamps. Bedrooms are just about OK for space, done out individually in simple rural style; bathrooms are also smart-rural, with many a hand-painted tile. At the back is a sheltered swimming pool area around which the grass is kept green, even in the furnace of the Castillian summer. Drawbacks: service may not be instant, and (for foreign guests) little or no foreign languages are spoken. But it's a real CSH.

~

NEARBY Carrascosa del Campo, Tarancón, Cuenca (70 km).
LOCATION in centre of town - drive to main square, ample car parking, and ask for directions - it's just off the square, a few paces away
FOOD breakfast, lunch, dinner
PRICES €€-€€€ **ROOMS** 4 double, 3 suite **FACILITIES** sitting room, bar, garden, swimming pool **CREDIT CARDS** AE, DC, MC, V **CHILDREN** accepted
DISABLED no specially adapted rooms; lift/elevator **PETS** accepted **CLOSED** restaurant only Mon-Tue **LANGUAGES** Spanish only **MANAGER** Marie Carmen Guijarro Jimenez

CIUDAD REAL

ALMAGRO

PT DE ALMAGRO

~ CONVERTED CONVENT PARADOR ~

Ronda de San Francisco, 13270, Almagro, Ciudad Real
TEL 926 860100 **FAX** 926 860150
E-MAIL almagro@parador.es **WEBSITE** www.parador.es

ALMAGRO'S PARADOR has ancient origins (it is on the site of a 16thC Franciscan convent) but is almost entirely modern, built just a decade ago. The layout of the building is highly unusual – the rooms are set around fourteen little quads, all different from each other. The first one you come to has ivy-clad walls and fig trees shading a small fountain, the second bamboo trees around a pond, the third rose-bushes, and so on.

It would be easy to get lost inside – every corridor looks the same – if it were not for the lovely hand-painted signs and room numbers on every corner. Such attention to detail runs throughout – there are painted ceilings and bright tapestries in the public rooms, tiled bed-heads and locally made lace covers in the bedrooms, and fresh flowers throughout. The *bodega* is built on two floors in the old cellars of the convent; massive storage jars go up through the floor and are used as table tops on the upper level. Other cosy sitting rooms are dotted about.

Despite its size, this is one of the friendliest Paradors – an interesting place in a picturesque town on the plains of Don Quixote's La Mancha.

~

NEARBY Plaza Mayor, old town, lace-making; Ciudad Real (25 km); Valdepeñas (35 km).
LOCATION in quiet street, near centre of town, signed from main road; with garden and car parking
FOOD breakfast, lunch, dinner
PRICES €€€€
ROOMS 48 double, 2 single, 3 suite; all with bath; all rooms have central heating, air conditioning, phone, TV, minibar
FACILITIES 2 dining rooms, 2 sitting rooms, bar, terrace; swimming pool
CREDIT CARDS AE, DC, MC, V
CHILDREN welcome
DISABLED access easy **PETS** not accepted
CLOSED never
MANAGER José Munoz Romera

TOLEDO/SEGOVIA

TOLEDO

HOTEL ABAD DE TOLEDO

TOWN HOTEL

Real del Arrabal, 1 - 45003 Toledo, TOLEDO
TEL 925 283500 **FAX** 925 283501
FOOD breakfast
PRICES €€€
CLOSED never
PROPRIETORS Vicente Bargueño

A USEFUL, BUT relatively expensive address to consider if our main selections in Toledo are full. A recently and much restored town house on a thoroughfare in the lower art of the city, the downstairs reception area/sitting room is pleasantly informal but nothing special. Bedrooms are a fair size for this type of operation, carved out of eccentric spaces with some ingenuity and character. There are different decorative schemes in each room, and much use of timber and exposed walls.

COLLADO HERMOSO

EL MOLINO DE RIO VIEJO

CONVERTED MILL

Carretera N110, km 172, 40170, Collado Hermoso, Segovia
TEL 921 403063 **FAX** 921 403051
FOOD breakfast, dinner
PRICE €€€
CLOSED 24,25,31Dec and 1 Jan
PROPRIETOR Teresa Primo

T HIS OLD MILL set amongst poplars by the River Viejo makes a perfect base from which to explore the leafy countryside of Segovia. Horses are available to riding enthusiasts. The bedrooms, some with beamed attic ceilings, are all the more cosy for the absence of mini-bar and TV. The dining room is in the old mill room. From Monday to Thursday only pre-requested cold meals are served, but at the weekends you can try the chef's roast lamb and home-made strawberry tart.

Booking is essential. At weekends the hotel is very popular. At other times it may be closed if there are no reservations.

HOTELS IN EASTERN SPAIN

AREA INTRODUCTION

This section covers the provinces of Teruel, Castellon, Valencia and Alicante, with interesting newcomers for this edition on pages 149, 150, and 151.

HOTELS IN VALENCIA

Valencia, Spain's third largest city, is relatively little-visited by tourists. Its international fame rests mainly on paella. In Spain it is also known for its nightlife (facilitated by year-round balmy temperatures), its prolific production of oranges and the spectacular Fallas fiesta in March during which huge papier mâché monuments are burnt in the streets. It is the capital of a large region on the eastern seaboard, including numerous cultural tourist attractions still undiscovered by the hordes.

Most of the city's hotels cater predominantly for trade fair and business visitors. The best are a long way out of town. The purpose-built seaside Parador, **Luis Vives** (Tel 96 161 1186), is on the edge of a nature reserve and surrounded by a golf course. Nearby is another modern hotel, the **Sidi Saler Palace** (Tel 96 161 0411). The luxurious 82-room **Monte Picayo** (Tel 96 142 0100), the choice of VIPs, is a short way inland, (conveniently close to the A7 motorway) and has its own casino and adjacent bullring.

In the city centre, apart from the **Excelsior**, the best of the smaller hotels is probably **Hotel Inglés** (Tel 96 351 6426), housed in an old palace. The art nouveau-style **Reina Victoria** (Tel 96 352 0487), with 94 rooms, retains an air of the *belle époque* in which it was built. A much larger central hotel is the modern **Astoria Palace** (Tel 96 352 6737).

PARADORS IN EASTERN SPAIN

These tend to be modern and functional, with little charm. The **PT Costa del Azahar** at Benicarlo is a box-like building (108 rooms) set in beautiful gardens facing 6 km of gently curving beach (Tel 964 470100). Just south of Valencia, on the narrow sandy peninsula of El Saler is the **PT Luis Vives**, a golf hotel with its own 18-hole course (Tel 96 161 1186). Further down the coast on the Javea peninsula is another unremarkable 1960s creation, the 65-room **PT Costa Blanca** (Tel 96 5790200). The **PT de Puerto Lumbreras**, 80 km SW of Murcia, is not on the coast, despite its maritime-sounding name. It is a plain but smart white hotel (60 rooms) on the main road through the town. Its floors are chequered marble, and the walls are brightened up by local ceramics (Tel 96 8402025).

Of the places further inland, only the **PT La Concordia at Alcañiz** (a hilltop castle with just 12 rooms) gets a full entry here (see page 146). The **PT de Teruel** is a modern hotel overlooking the city which is famous for its integration of Christian, Jewish and Muslim styles of architecture (Tel 978 601800). The **PT de la Mancha**, south of Albacete, is a low, white building on the sprawling plains of La Mancha. It is decorated in rustic style with beamed ceilings and primitive wooden farm tools hanging from the walls – donkey baskets, oxen yokes, ploughshares (Tel 967 229450).

TERUEL

ALCAÑIZ

PT LA CONCORDIA

~ CASTLE PARADOR ~

Castillo de los Calatravos, 44600, Alcañiz, Teruel
TEL 978 830400 FAX 978 830366
E-MAIL alcaniz@parador.es WEBSITE www.parador.es

STILL DOMINATING the town and its green river from the summit of a hill, as it has done since the 12th century, this castle-monastery is the first thing that you see as you approach Alcañiz; it certainly looks too big to have only 12 rooms.

Although monumental in scale, the former home of the Order of the Knights of Calatrava has been converted into an intimate hotel full of historical character. It is furnished in a modern imitation of castle-style, with wrought iron chandeliers everywhere and gold knobs topping the chairs in a dining room fit for medieval banquets. In the bedrooms, however, you can forget that you are in a castle, as evidence of the past has been largely crowded out by new furnishings. There are magnificent views from most of the rooms and the rest look on to the peaceful cloister-garden behind.

The castle is also a tourist attraction and its grounds are open to the public – so it is not a place in which to seek seclusion. The TV in the cafeteria at the entrance, in an elegant vaulted chamber, sometimes intrudes too, but at night the castle returns more or less to its ancestral peace. La Concordia underwent a refurbishment in 2002, so reports would be welcome.

NEARBY Caspe (30 km) – Roman temple, caves of Molinos (40 km), El Parrisal near Beceite (50 km) – wildlife.
LOCATION on hill dominating town (follow Parador signs); with garden and car parking
FOOD breakfast, lunch, dinner
PRICES €€€€
ROOMS 37 double, all with bath; all rooms have central heating, air conditioning, phone, TV, minibar
FACILITIES 1 dining room, 2 sitting rooms, cafeteria
CREDIT CARDS AE, DC, MC, V
CHILDREN welcome
DISABLED access easy; lift/ elevator PETS not accepted
CLOSED never
MANAGER Carmelo Martinez Grande

TERUEL

VALDEROBBRES

TORRE DEL VISCO
~ CONVERTED TOWER HOUSE ~

Apartado 15, 44580 Valderrobres, Teruel
TEL 978 769015 **FAX** 978 769016
E-MAIL torredelvisco@torredelvisco.com **WEBSITE** www.torredelvisco.com

THIS IS A REMOTE 15thC semi-fortified estate house which has been carefully restored by its English owners, Piers Dutton and Jemma Markham, who have lived in Spain for many years. It's a real hideaway: the nearest villages are 7½ miles (12 km) away, and the hotel is reached by gravelled forest tracks. Arriving at the final turn in the track, you see at last the outline of the house, surrounded by 200 acres of farmland. Standing on a steep hillside overlooking the beautiful valley of the river Tastavins, it is a haven of peace, with a warm welcome from the owners. You can walk, ride or mountain bike along the valley or up into the mountains, followed by rest and relaxation on the terrace, in the sitting room with its grand piano and open fire, or in the library. Breakfast is taken in the farmhouse kitchen, while dinner features Mediterranean cuisine using produce from the farm as well as fish bought directly from the quayside and a well stocked wine cellar. The bedrooms are fresh, with modern paintings on the walls and tiled floors, and the whole place feels like a home, not a hotel. A reader writes in exceptionally fulsome terms about the place, emphasizing the value for money. Evening meal is obligatory and included in the price of the room.

~

NEARBY Valderrobres, 7.5 miles (12 km); Morella, 33 miles (53 km), Alcaniz (44km).
LOCATION 7.5 miles (12 km) S of Valderrobres; hotel signposted after 3.5 miles (6 km); in own farmland with ample parking
FOOD breakfast, lunch, dinner
PRICES €€€€
ROOMS 11 double, 3 suites, all with bath; all rooms have central heating, hairdrier
FACILITIES 4 sitting rooms, dining room, library, bodega, terrace, gardens
CREDIT CARDS MC, V
CHILDREN accepted
DISABLED access difficult **PETS** not accepted
CLOSED mid-Jan
PROPRIETORS Piers Dutton and Jemma Markham

CASTELLON

MORELLA

HOTEL CARDENAL RAM
～ CONVERTED PALACE ～

Cuesta Suñer 1, 12300, Morella, Castellón
TEL 964 173085 **FAX** 964 173218
E-MAIL hotelcardenalram@cts.es

CARDINAL RAM's 16thC Gothic palace, set in a commanding position on Morella's medieval porticoed main street, is a local landmark. Its thick walls enclose a variety of spacious rooms. The furnishings have been improved since we last visited. Bathrooms are modern and well-equipped, and the rooms on the second and third floors have magnificent views.

The excellent restaurant is well known for its local delicacies including the succulent *cordero trufado* – lamb stuffed with truffles – the hearty Morella soup, and typical desserts made of sheep milk, *cuajada* and *requesón*. We are glad to report that breakfast is much improved.

The hotel lacks seating and recreational space, but it makes up for this with its age and character. It is arguably overpriced for the level of comfort offered, but you can eat well here and it is as close to the authentic history of Morella as you will get. The management told us that major improvements were being undertaken in 2004 - reports welcome.

～

NEARBY Castle and church; La Balma (25 km), Montalvana – cave paintings (25 km), Mirambel (30 km) – walled village.
LOCATION in heart of Morella, on main street; private car parking
FOOD breakfast, lunch, dinner
PRICES €€€
ROOMS 16 double, 1 single, 2 suites, all with bath; all rooms have central heating, phone, TV, minibar
FACILITIES dining room, hall/sitting room
CREDIT CARDS MC, V
CHILDREN accepted
DISABLED access difficult
PETS not accepted
CLOSED never
PROPRIETOR Jaime Penarroya

VALENCIA

CAMPELLANIA

ENTREVINAS

~ COUNTRY HOTEL ~

Finca El Renegado, Caudete de las Fuentes 46315
TEL 0962 1740 29 **FAX** 0962 1714 32
E-MAIL entrevinas@ainia.es **WEBSITE** www.entrevinas.incitur.com

THE YELLOW-PAINTED building can seem a little austere at first – it is fairly large, all angular lines and wrought-iron railings. Once inside, however, you will find beautiful tiled floors, and pleasing touches such as writing desks in the rooms, and antique farm instruments that reflect the nature of the land that surrounds it. As the name suggests, the hotel is surrounded by 200 hectares of vines (the hotel building happily finds itself right next to the *bodegas*, so you won't have far to go for tastings and wine tours). This is a working estate with plenty of history: if you get the chance, do go on a walk around the farm and woods. Each of the bedrooms is named after a plot of the vineyard, and there are plenty of peaceful spots for reading up on the history. Local specialities are served at dinner, such as stuffed peppers, *ajoarriero* (a spicy poached fish dish) or *morteruelo* (a deliciously heavy meat casserole). Just one warning: they can cater for large groups at times, so be careful to check when booking.

~

NEARBY Valencia.
LOCATION close to town of Campellania, in large vineyard, with ample private car parking
ROOMS 14; 12 double, 2 apartments; all rooms have bath, phone, TV, hairdrier
PRICES €-€€€
FOOD breakfast, lunch, dinner
FACILITIES dining room, swimming pool, garden
CREDIT CARDS DC, MC, V
CHILDREN weolcome
DISABLED some specially adapted rooms
PETS accepted
CLOSED never
PROPRIETOR M. Héras

VALENCIA

LA CASA VEJA
∾ COUNTRY GUESTHOUSE ∾

Horno 4, Rugat, Valencia 26842, Spain
TEL and **FAX** 962 814013
E-MAIL mail@lacasaveja.com **WEBSITE** www.lacasavieja.com

A BRITISH WOMAN HAS owned this hotel for the past seven years, and can lay claim to many loyal visitors (us too now – a chance encounter while in this beautiful, often forgotten, inland region). The 460-year-old building has been fully restored, creating six bedrooms for guests. The largest, at the top of the house, has spectacular views and a private terrace, but our favourite is the smallest, Collado, with its rich blues and airy feel. The bed faces the window, which you will want to keep open in summer to allow the fresh breeze to blow over you. Maris knows the area intimately and can point you in the direction of many walks and drives. The kitchen produces typical Spanish cuisine, using fresh local produce, and has a surprisingly wide wine list for such a small hotel, with good choices from around the country. Sit outside with a tray of local almonds and honey, and you will be charmed – as we were.

∾

NEARBY Gandia, Valencia, Alicante.
LOCATION exit 61 on A7 motorway, behind the church in village of Rugat; street parking outside guesthouse
FOOD breakfast, dinner
PRICES €€€-€€€€
ROOMS 6 doubles; all rooms have bath, hairdrier
FACILITIES swimming pool
CREDIT CARDS DC, MC, V
CHILDREN welcome
DISABLED no specially adapted rooms
PETS accepetd
CLOSED mid Dec to mid Jan
PROPRIETOR Maris Watson

VALENCIA

VALENCIA

ADHOC HOTEL

~ CITY HOTEL ~

C/Boix, 4 Valencia 46003 (Valencia)
TEL 963 919140 **FAX** 963 913667
E-MAIL adhoc@adhochoteles.com **WEBSITE** www.adhochoteles.com

THE LEGENDS OF VALENCIA are well known – the Holy Grail, Hannibal, El Cid. But despite its history, and despite being Spain's third largest city, it's as bad as Madrid and Barcelona in terms of interesting places to stay. To be honest, we wondered whether this hotel should make the grade. It has an excellent location, right next to the cathedral and the Turia Gardens, and it is close to Valencia's traditional fruit and vegetable market (one of the few in Spain of this size and quality). We weren't, however, particularly convinced by the communal areas – the atmosphere is definitely 'hotel' rather than 'home'. On the other hand, the bedrooms are good. Exposed brick walls, well-chosen antiques, each slightly different in shape and use of space. The feeling here is small but chic, and you begin to get the impression of how it must have felt as a well-staffed 19thC town house. The restaurant is fairly small, with an intimate feel, so you need to book ahead.

~

NEARBY Cathedral, Palacio del Temple.
LOCATION city centre, historical Xerea quarter; some private car parking, phone ahead to ensure a space
FOOD breakfast, lunch, dinner
PRICES €€-€€€
ROOMS 28; 23 doubles, 5 singles; all rooms have bath, phone, TV, internet connection, air conditioning
FACILITIES parking, restaurant, bar
CREDIT CARDS DC, MC, V
CHILDREN accepted
DISABLED access in all common areas; lifts/elevators to all floors
PETS accepted
CLOSED never
PROPRIETOR Louise Garcia Alarcon

VALENCIA

XATIVA

HOSTERIA DE MONT SANT
～ COUNTRY HOTEL ～

Subida al Castillo, s/n, Xativa, Valencia
TEL 96 2275081 **FAX** 96 2281905
E-MAIL montsant@servidex.com **WEBSITE** www.servidex.com/montsant

A DELIGHTFUL LITTLE ochre-red country house, well restored, set in love-ly grounds, with great views down on to Xativa and above to the Moorish castle: with just six bedrooms, this is essentially a charming restaurant with rooms. The welcome is warm, the atmosphere relaxed; the service is faultless and every detail has been thought out - all in a way that a larger place could not imitate. It is recommended by two widely-travelled readers, who were impressed by the friendly atmos-phere, spotless maintenance, efficient organization, large beds and all-round comfort.

There's a spacious sitting room with French windows making the most of the views; an intimate dining room with doors to a terrace for eating outside. The menu is 'excellent' and reasonably priced. Bedrooms, all decorated indivually, are simply furnished in Spanish period style. The Castle Room has particularly good views. It would be worth pausing here for more than just one night in order to explore his-toric Xativa, and to mellow out beside the secluded swimming pool.

～

NEARBY Xativa, Valencia, Alicante.
LOCATION near the castle; in own large gardens, with car parking, signposted
FOOD breakfast, lunch, dinner
PRICES ©©©©
ROOMS 16, four double, two suites in the main building,10 in newly constructed wooden cabins inn the garden all with air conditioning, central heating
FACILITIES sitting room, dining room, terrace, swimming pool.
CREDIT CARDS AE, MC, V
CHILDREN welcome
DISABLED one room suitable
PETS accepted
CLOSED never
PROPRIETOR Javier Andreas Cifre

ALICANTE

CASTELL DE CASTELLS

PENSION CASTELLS

~ VILLAGE GUEST HOUSE ~

Calle San Vicente 18, 03793, Castell de Castells, Alicante
TEL AND FAX 96 5518254
E-MAIL pensioncastell@terra.es **WEBSITE** www.mountainholidays/spain.com

HAVING CONVERTED an old village house and found themselves with a surplus of rooms, previous owners Jan and Eric Wright decided to put them to profitable use. New owners Sarah and Gary Neal, also English, are continuing to run things along the same lines.

From the street you step directly into the sitting-cum-dining room with its wood-burning stove creating a cosy atmosphere during the winter months. At the window end, by the street door, is the table around which everyone eats together. At the other end comfy armchairs are arranged by the hearth. Upstairs are four simple but cosy rooms, each a different shape; all of them furnished with a loving touch. Two of them have sloping beamed roofs. The top one, dubbed 'the Casita', is the favourite: by the bed are a shelf of books and a tea-maker. The staircase ends in a sunny terrace at rooftop level.

Although Castell de Castells is not far from the Costa Blanca it gets few tourists and the principal attraction is rural peace. Many of their guests come to walk in the surrounding mountains, although potential visitors are warned that there is little for children to do in the area. If you don't mind sharing your table with whoever else happens to be staying, this is one definition of the charming small hotel.

~

NEARBY natural rock arches (5km); Jalon valley vineyards (20km); Castell de Guadalest (33km); Costa Blanca (35km).
LOCATION in a narrow street in the centre of the village: park near the church and ask for directions
FOOD breakfast, lunch, dinner
PRICES €€
ROOMS 3 twin, one double, all with shower and toilet; all rooms have central heating
FACILITIES sitting/dining room; guided walks, mountain bikes available for hire and guided mountain bike rides, 9 seater mini-bus for collection to and from airport
CREDIT CARDS none **CHILDREN** accepted
DISABLED access difficult **PETS** not accepted **CLOSED** Jul and Aug
PROPRIETORS Sarah and Gary Neal

ALICANTE

MORAIRA

SWISS HOTEL MORAIRA

SEASIDE RESORT HOTEL

Urbanización Club Moraira,
03724, Moraira, Alicante
TEL 96 5747104 **FAX** 96 5747074
E-MAIL brapahotel@telefonica.net
FOOD breakfast
PRICES €€€€
CLOSED mid Dec-mid Jan
MANAGER Santiago Bravo

THE SWISS WATCHES on sale in the lobby and the private hair salon set the tone for this hotel which goes for luxury at the expense of personality.

Set in an estate of holiday villas a short way back from the coast, its central feature is the large swimming pool surrounded by a sun-trapping terrace onto which all rooms have views and more or less direct access. The bedrooms are spacious, especially the 'semi-suites' and suites, and lavishly equipped – all newly furnished, although in predictable grand hotel style. The staff are discreet and faultlessly formal. Only breakfast is served.

HOTELS IN ANDALUCIA

AREA INTRODUCTIONS

Andalucia is well known to most travellers as the broad swathe of Mediterranean Spain that includes the provinces of Huelva, Seville, Cordoba, Jaen, Granada, Almeria, Cadiz and Malaga. In this new edition we have too many new entries in Andalucia to do justice to in a brief list, but among the many highlights are **Hotel Cortijo Aguila Real** on page 171, **Hotel Carmen de Santa Ines** on page 191, **Hotel Marquez de Torresoto** on page 210 and **Hotel la Fuente de la Higuera** on page 231.

HOTELS ON THE COSTA DEL SOL

'Charming' and 'small' are not the first adjectives that spring to mind when considering hotels along the Costa del Sol. It has taken some searching to find such places along this 200 km holiday playground, and many of the hotels we describe in detail are not actually on the coast but behind it, hidden away in the mountains. Anyone who wants to be on the coast itself might consider the **Hurricane** on page 215 and those listed below.

The pick of Gibraltar's hotels is the **Rock** (Tel 350 73000), a large, rather old-fashioned establishment serving traditional British food.

Just outside San Pedro de Alcántara is the **Cortijo de los Caballos** (Tel 952 886767), a complex of 9 bungalow apartments around a swimming-pool and one of the few places in Spain not to accept children.

The true heart of the Costa del Sol is Marbella, the most up-market of the resorts. One of the more stylish places to stay here is the **Marbella Club** (Tel 952 822211) which is set in luxuriant gardens.

Further round the coast, after the package holiday resorts of Fuengirola and Torremolinos, comes Málaga. More than an airport it is a sprawling city which is best avoided in high season. If you have to stay here, the **Palacio** – luxurious, with a roof-top pool (Tel 952 215185) – and **Casa Curro** (Tel 952 227200) – central, comfortable – are good alternatives to the Parador. Most hotels run a bus service to the airport.

East of Málaga the coast is less built up. The famous view from the **Balcón de Europa**, in Nerja, is definitely worth stopping for.

The 47-room **Los Fenicios** (Tel 958 827900), in the small resort of La Herradura stands out from the blocks around it because of its original architecture and its unusual brass and glass lift.

The holiday strip ends in the dry province of Almeria. In the city of Almeria, the **Torreluz IV** (Tel 950 234999) is brashly modern with white leather sofas, a spiral staircase and a roof-top swimming pool.

PARADORS IN ANDALUCIA

The two Paradores in Huelva are both modern. The 35-room **PT Costa de la Luz at Ayamonte**, on the Portuguese border, is a sprawling white building high above the city, with magnificent views (Tel 959 256422). Cádiz's Parador is a six-storey white complex called the **Atlántico**, on the south side of the isthmus. Ask for a room with a sea view (Tel 956 226905).

The Costa del Sol has three Paradores. Two are close to Málaga – as well as the **PT de Malaga-Gibralfaro** (see page 226) there is the self-explanatory **Golf**, a little way west of the town (Tel 952 381255). The third is at Nerja: large and modern but attractive, with well-furnished rooms and an elevator down to the beach (Tel 95 2520050). North-east of Almería is **PT Reyes Católicos** at Mojácar (Tel 950 478250), more intimate than its 98 rooms would suggest.

Inland, the Paradores at Antequera, Arcos de la Frontera, Carmona, Granada, Jaén and Úbeda have detailed entries. The modern 83-room **PT de la Arruzafa at Córdoba** is 3 km from the city (Tel 957 275900). The dismal **PT de Bailén** has little to recommend it apart from its pool (Tel 953 670100).

HUELVA

HOTEL TORUÑO
~ VILLAGE HOTEL ~

Plaza de Acebuchal 22, 21750 El Rocio, Huelva
TEL 959 222323/442626 **FAX** 959 442338
E-MAIL hoteltoruno@eresmas.com

A MADE-IN-HEAVEN hotel for nature lovers, but especially for bird watch-ers. Not only is it in Rocio, the best of the centres for visiting the famous Coto Doñana nature reserve, but it stands just 15m from the famous Rocio marshes, with (for twitchers, at least) life-enhancing views from the public area and many of the bedrooms of flamingos. little and cattle egrets, Eurasian spoonbills, white storks and whiskered terns, to mention only the highlights. The building is pleasingly white and four-square, with pretty iron balcony railings. Some reliable reporters describe the ambience as friendly and relaxed; bedrooms unexceptional but simple and tasteful. Public areas are much as you would expect, comfortable and unpretentiously traditional. It's more hotel-like than home-like, and a large function room can hold up to 200 people for celebrations, but it's still the best place to stay in Rocio. With 30 bedrooms, it is not especially small, but the overall experience should more than compensate. Rocio has a frontier-village feel, with wide sandy-dusty streets (no tarmac or pave-ments) and the hussle and bustle of 'real Spain'. It's also a pilgrimage cen-tre (booked solid in late May/early June) to which surrounding communi-ties bring their *virgens* on ox-drawn carts.

~

NEARBY Ermita del Rocío, Matalascañas beach, Almonte y el Contado.
LOCATION in village
FOOD breakfast, lunch, dinner
PRICES €€
ROOMS 30, 28 double, 2 single; all rooms have bath, phone, TV, air conditioning
FACILITIES sitting room, restaurant, conference room, guided visits to the Doñana reserve and riding arranged
CREDIT CARDS AE, DC, MC, V
CHILDREN welcome
DISABLED no special facilities **PETS** by arrangement
CLOSED never
PROPRIETORS Cooperative Marismas del Rocío

HUELVA

LOS MARINES

FINCA BUENVINO

~ COUNTRY HOTEL ~

21293, Los Marines, Huelva
TEL 959 124034 **FAX** 959 501029
E-MAIL buenvino@facilnet.es **WEBSITE** www.buenvino.com

A S OUR INSPECTORS discovered, this is not an easy place to find; the lovely modern villa, built in 18thC style on the top of a hill, is hidden away in the heart of a National Park, amid chestnut forests, fruit trees and bubbling springs.

Sam and Jeannie Chesterton, an English couple, stress that this is their home and that you are expected to join in with the family (who are very easy-going). They keep Iberian pigs, sheep, goats and chickens, and have three dogs. Everyone eats together – on the terrace in summer or in the panelled dining room. Jeannie is a trained cordon bleu cook, and produces mouth-watering dinners and salad lunches, accompanied by liberal amounts of wine. Drinks taken at other times – and perhaps consumed before the huge fireplace of the sitting room or in the airy conservatory – are recorded in an 'honesty book'.

The bedrooms are all bright and comfortable. The two attic rooms have hand-stencilled walls and wonderful views over the woods. The other two rooms are smaller; one has its own bathroom and dressing room, the other requires a trip across the landing. There is also a self-catering cottage with its own small plunge pool, for those seeking greater seclusion.

~

NEARBY Aracena (caves and castle); Zafra (85 km).
LOCATION in heart of woodland, km 95 of N433 Seville-Lisbon road, W of Los Marines, itself W of Aracena; with garden and shaded car parking
FOOD breakfast, dinner
PRICES €€€€
ROOMS 4 double, two with bath; all rooms have central heating, hairdrier, kettle
FACILITIES dining room, sitting room, conservatory; swimming pool
CREDIT CARDS MC, V
CHILDREN welcome
DISABLED access difficult **PETS** not accepted
CLOSED Christmas and New Year (check by phone before visiting)
PROPRIETORS Sam and Jeannie Chesterton

SEVILLE

ALCALA DE GUADAIRA

HOTEL OROMANA

∼ ANDALUCIAN VILLA ∼

Avenida de Portugal, 41500, Alcalá de Guadaira, Seville
TEL AND FAX 95 5686400
E-MAIL reservas@hotelormana.com **WEBSITE** www.hoteloromana.com

OUR INSPECTOR had trouble finding the Oromana; it is on a hill opposite the town, in an area (of the same name) which is rapidly being developed for residential purposes, eating into the pine woods that surround the hotel. The tranquillity is not yet lost; a long winding drive takes you away from the building sites to the rounded knoll where this impressive white hotel, complete with bell-tower, overlooks the meandering Guadaira river.

There is a particularly Spanish feel to the lofty public rooms; reception leads into a vaulted sitting room of marble columns and ornamental Spanish vases. Its large French windows open on to a bougainvillaea-clad terrace where guests can sit and enjoy the view. Next door is a small cosy bar, serving *tapas* at red-and- white checked tables. The more formal dark green dining room has sombre pictures of matadors on the walls. All service comes with a smile.

The bedrooms are in the main building and in a new extension which overlooks the swimming pool. The rooms, decorated in light tones, vary in size but not quality. Some have balconies – a welcome extra in the heat of the Andalucian summer. A recent visitor was unenthusiastic about the food, and thought a worn stair carpet might be dangerous. Reports welcome.

∼

NEARBY Seville (15 km) – cathedral and palaces.
LOCATION amid pine trees, on hill overlooking town and river; with gardens and ample car parking
FOOD breakfast, lunch, dinner
PRICES €€€€
ROOMS 31 doubles, all with bath; all rooms have central heating, air conditioning, phone, TV
FACILITIES dining room, 2 sitting rooms, bar/cafeteria, terrace; swimming pool
CREDIT CARDS MC, V **CHILDREN** welcome
DISABLED access difficult **PETS** not accepted **CLOSED** never
MANAGER Antonio Contreras

SEVILLE

ALMUDENA

LA CASA DEL MAESTRO
∼ TOWN HOUSE HOTEL ∼

Almudena 5,.41003 Seville
TEL 954 500007 **FAX** 954 500006
E-MAIL patriciaz@lacasadelmaestro.com **WEBSITE** www.lacasadelmaestro.com

IN THE WARREN of narrow streets of Seville's 'Old Town' stands the unassuming Casa del Maestro. You could be forgiven for walking straight past the front door: there are few outward signs that this is a hotel. Once inside, you'll be glad you didn't.

As with many of Seville's old houses, the building goes up, not out, to accommodate the rooms. This gives a feeling of space and airiness, important in the searing heat of summer. You breakfast in the cool hall and relax in a cosy little sitting room where you can listen to CDs and help yourself to the honesty bar.

Beautiful antique matador outfits adorn each floor and there are dozens of prints illustrating Andalusia's bull fighting heritage. The bedrooms are small but immaculate, with gleaming bathrooms. Some have small balconies offering views of the lively back streets.

A roof terrace can also be used for breakfast, actually far preferable to the hall because of its magnificent views over Seville and its cathedral. Next door to the hotel is Santa Catalina, a beautiful old church, and nearby a choice of small restaurants serving *tapas* and drinks.

∼

NEARBY Santa Catalina, Cathedral, La Giralda, Jewish quarter.
LOCATION just off Avenido Mendez Pelayo, opposite Santa Catalina; parking in square. Hotel 2 minute walk from square
FOOD breakfast
PRICES €€€€-€€€€€
ROOMS 11 doubles all with shower; all rooms have central heating, air conditioning, phone, TV.
FACILITIES sitting room, bar, roof terrace
CREDIT CARDS AE, DC, MC, V
CHILDREN welcome
DISABLED not suitable **PETS** no
CLOSED Aug
DIRECTOR Patricia Zapardiel Arteaga

SEVILLE

HACIENDA DOS OLIVOS
~ COUNTRY GUEST HOTEL ~

Aznalcazar, Seville
TEL AND FAX 95 575 05 62
E-MAIL j.beattie@teleline.es

THE NAME REFERS to the only two olive trees which had to be cut down to build this typical estate house a decade or so ago. A mixture of Andalucían, Moorish and modern, it is surrounded by a sea of olive groves which are farmed by the owners. Within easy reach of Seville, the property borders the vast Doñana National Park, and in the evening you can see eagles circling above.

Hacienda Dos Olivos is run very much as a private home. Meals are taken communaly, either in the candle-lit dining room, or, on fine evenings, beneath an olive tree in the gardens. The two guest bedrooms, grouped around an inner patio, are simply furnished, with tiled floors and high sloping beamed ceilings. It is possible to take the whole property for a single party, including La Casita, a little self-catering house within the courtyard which sleeps four (two supplementary beds can also be added).

The *raison d'être* of the Hacienda is its magnificent horses. Johanna Beattie-Batista is a renowned Classical dressage rider, and while staying here you can, if you wish, take lessons. Two discordant notes from a British reader: First, despite a deposit paid and reservation confirmed, the Hacienda was full; alternative rooms in La Casita did not please. Second, the drive is apparently somewhat rough. ~

NEARBY Seville, 22 miles (35 km); Doñana National Park; Christopher Columbus sights on the Costa de la Luz.
LOCATION outside Aznalcazar, 22 miles (35 km) SW of Seville; in own grounds with ample parking. Difficult to find. Get directions from reception
FOOD breakfast, lunch, dinner
PRICES €€-€€€
ROOMS 5 double and twin, one with bath, 4 sharing 2 bathrooms; all rooms have heating
FACILITIES sitting room, dining room, courtyard, terraces, gardens, swimming pool
CREDIT CARDS not accepted **CHILDREN** welcome **DISABLED** rooms on ground floor
PETS not accepted **CLOSED** never **PROPRIETOR** Johanna Beattie-Batista

SEVILLE

CALLE REAL

HOTEL HACIENDA SAN YGNACIO

~ TOWN HOTEL ~

Calle Real 190, Castilleja de la Cuesta, 41950 Seville
TEL 954 169290 **FAX** 954 161437
E-MAIL reservas@haciendasanygnacio.com **WEBSITE** www.haciendasanygnacio.com

THIS OLD JESUIT monastery, converted in the 19th century, is just 15 minutes outside Seville, and so offers the comfort and space of a *hacienda* while being really close to the action.

The courtyard is surrounded by mature palm trees so tall that they almost dwarf the building. You can sit in their shade and enjoy drinks or *tapas* in the evening. There are numerous places to dine within the hotel, depending on how many people you are with. The Almazara restaurant (Andalusian, Basque or International dishes) has been renovated from an old olive mill and still has its original vaulted ceiling.

Bedrooms are small, but pleasantly cool in hot weather; some have views over the courtyard. The hotel is close to the road and we were worried about traffic noise, but the owners have put a great deal of time into double glazing the windows, so expect a peaceful night's sleep. Our only real problem with the rooms was the piped music – but you can ask for it to be switched off.

The grounds aren't especially large, but there is a decent-sized pool complete with sun loungers. When we visited the place was being re-decorated, so reports will be especially welcome.

~

NEARBY Seville, Huelva.
LOCATION head to Huelva on A49 come off on exit 3, hotel is at bottom of Calle Real with very limited car parking in own grounds
FOOD breakfast, lunch, dinner
PRICES ©©©©
ROOMS 18; 17 doubles, 1 for 4 people all with bath and shower; all rooms have central heating, air conditioning, phone, TV, minibar, safe
FACILITIES dining room, sitting room, bar, garden, swimming pool, patio
CREDIT CARDS AE, DC, MC, V
DISABLED access difficult **CHILDREN** welcome **PETS** one room available
CLOSED never
PROPRIETOR Ramon Gutierrez

SEVILLE

CAZALLA DE LA SIERRA

LA CARTUJA DE CAZALLA

~ CONVERTED MONASTERY ~

41370 Cazalla de la Sierra, Seville
TEL 954 884516 **FAX** 954 884707
E-MAIL cartujsv@teleline.es **WEBSITE** www.skill.es/cartuja

A FORMER CARTHUSIAN monastery nestled deep in the Sierra Norte north of Seville, La Cartuja is guaranteed to surprise, an amusing mish-mash of styles and tastes, eccentric but delightful. The main part of the property is the monastery itself, which houses paintings and sculptures and is also used regularly for concerts and recitals as the acoustics are excellent. One wing of the building is dedicated to the paintings of Espinoza and his daughter; if you want to learn about them, just ask the formidable Senora Guevara.

Adjacent to this wing are some of the bedrooms and the suites. We can't say that huge amounts of effort have been put into their decoration and furnishing, but they are a fair size, with comfy beds and quite roomy showers. Another wing, has much smaller rooms, in fact you could call them cramped.

The main body of the house accommodates the small restaurant and the dining room, whose menus are mainly organized around chicken, lamb, eggs and vegetables from the monastery garden - wholesome but not ambitious. Close by is a charming courtyard, with strutting peacocks, and a bubbling spring that never dries up. There are two beautiful swimming pools with spectacular views. Senorä Guevara can organize riding, or you can join one of the art classes she runs – often taught by her resident artist.

~

NEARBY Cazalla de la Sierra, Seville, Cordoba.
LOCATION go through Cazalla de la Sierra heading for Constantina on the A455. The hotel is on the left sign posted for 'Villa Turistica' on the 2.5 km mark with ample car parking in own grounds
FOOD breakfast, lunch, dinner
PRICES €€€€€
ROOMS 15; 4 doubles with sitting room, 6 doubles, 2 singles, 1 small cottage with 3 bedrooms, with bath; all rooms have TV, mini bar, air conditioning, heating
FACILITIES restaurant, dining room, bar, sitting room, garden, 2 swimming pools
CREDIT CARDS AE, DC, MC, V
Children by arrangement **DISABLED** unsuitable **PETS** by arrangement
CLOSED Christmas day for 4 days **PROPRIETOR** Carmen L. De Guevara

SEVILLE

CAZALLA DE LA SIERRA

LAS NAVEZUELAS

~ COUNTRY HOTEL ~

A.P.Correo no 14, 41370 Cazalla de la Sierra, Seville
TEL 954 884764 **FAX** 954 884594
E-MAIL navezuela@arrakis.es **WEBSITE** www.arrakis.es/~navezuela

THIS ANCIENT MILL dating from the 16th C has bundles of original charm: rooms, a reception area and a swimming pool have been added with skill and good taste. It's located in the Sierra Natural Park and you get sweeping views of olive and cork tree groves. Wild pigs and goats roam nearby, and the place has a natural, earthy atmosphere. The owner, Luca, can arrange for you to explore this beautiful countryside on horse back, on foot or by car.

It's a shame that the restaurant is soulless and uninspiring (under redecoration as we go to print). Although the food is OK – simple and hearty – you'd do better to eat in the nearby town of Cazalla de la Sierra, which has some lovely little restaurants that serve *tapas*, and you might even stumble across some live music if you're lucky.

The bedrooms are unremarkable, but cheery enough and perfectly comfortable, with good sized bathrooms. All of the rooms have little kitchen areas; some of the studios and suites have balconies where you can enjoy breakfast, lunch or dinner whilst drinking in the view.

~

NEARBY Cazalla de la Sierra, Seville, Cordoba,
LOCATION leaving Seville on the A432, take the turning just before reaching Cazalla de la Sierra on the km 43 mark, ample car parking in own grounds
FOOD breakfast, lunch, dinner (seasonal)
PRICES €€€
ROOMS 11; 2 suites, 4 doubles, 4 studios, 1 appartment (can sleep 4/6 people), with shower; all rooms have TV, phone, air conditioning, heating
FACILITIES dining room, sitting room, reading room, garden, swimming pool
CREDIT CARDS DC, MC, V
CHILDREN welcome
DISABLED access difficult but possible to some suite/studio rooms
PETS by arrangement
CLOSED 3rd Jan – 25th Feb
PROPRIETOR Luca Cicorella

SEVILLE

CRUCE DE LAS CABEZAS

HACIENDA DE SAN RAFAEL
~ COUNTRY HOTEL ~

Apartado 28, Carretera Nacional IV (Km 594)
TEL 955 872193 **FAX** 955 872201
Bookings only through TRI Hotel Marketing, London, Tel 020 8563 2100 Fax 020 8563 2300

A DISCRIMATING London couple, not to mention one of our regular reporters, recommend this stunning place less than an hour south of Seville. One small negative is the inauspicious approach from the main-road, the NIV, and the setting in flat farmland. But once down the drive, the charm takes over: the two-storey building, formerly an olive farm and press, has impeccably white outside walls contrasting with windows and cornices picked out in tasteful cream-ochre: come the golden light of a fine evening, the whole place glows. A young Sloany girl may greet you on arrival; most of the guests are British.

Most of the rooms are set around the large, oblong, pleasingly paved interior courtyard, with the old well neatly restored at its centre. Public rooms offer exemplary Hispanic rustic chic. There's a pleasant atmosphere in the grand drawing room, where you help yourself to drinks. Dinner is a pricey set menu, but the French chef ensures that it's all delicious. The split-level bedrooms have simply-patterned rugs on tiled floors, and home-ly-but-smart patchwork quilts in artfully muted colours; 'galleries' give sitting areas under exposed beams. Breakfast is brought to one's private terrace. A recent visit reconfirmed that this is an exclusive experience.

It's a major outing to get anywhere – but you can always just relax by one of the two pristine pools or browse for leather goods in the little shop.

~

NEARBY Seville, Jerez, Arcos, Ronda.
LOCATION just off the NIV south of Seville, signposted; in own grounds with car parking. Directions given on booking.
FOOD breakfast, lunch, dinner
PRICES €€€€-€€€€€
ROOMS 11; 9 double, 2 twin; all with bathrooms
FACILITIES drawing room, dining room, garden, 2 swimming pools, paddle tennis, library, TV room
CREDIT CARDS none. **CHILDREN** discouraged. **DISABLED** one specially adapted room
PETS not accepted **CLOSED** end Oct - 1st Feb **PROPRIETORS** Tim and Kuky Reid

SEVILLE

GERENA

CORTIJO EL ESPARRAGAL
~ COUNTRY HOTEL ~

Carretera de Merida km 795, 41860 Gerena, Seville
TEL 955 782702 **FAX** 955 782783
E-MAIL cortijoelesparragal@elesparragal.com **WEBSITE** www.elesparragal.com

IF YOU LIKE SEVILLE, but don't like the bustle of the city, here is a great alternative. It's a grand old Cortijo just 20 minutes from town, but in pleasant rolling countryside, with lush gardens and its own private bull ring.

We think that it has adapted beautifully to its reincarnation as a hotel. Mares and foals graze placidly in the fields either side of the drive – the place is in fact very much a working farm. The reception area leads to a magnificent courtyard (covered in bad weather) decorated with buffalo heads and other hunting paraphernalia. A small fountain trickles peacefully and birds dart from the lush flowers cascading from the walls.

As in many Spanish hotels, the bedrooms are quite sparse, with dark, heavy furniture, however they are roomy with spacious bathrooms; some have balconies that look down into a small (but also enchanting) courtyard that leads to a stunning private chapel. The food is a mixture of Spanish and European dishes served in a cool, light dining room. After dinner you can retire to the impressive drawing room for a drink served by the friendly staff.

~

NEARBY Seville, Gerena.
LOCATION on the N630 to Merida/Santaponce, take the Gerena exit and turn right at first roundabout. Hotel is 1.5km on right with ample car parking in own grounds
FOOD breakfast, lunch, dinner
PRICES ⓔⓔⓔⓔ
ROOMS 18; 5 junior suites, 13 doubles; all have en-suite bath and shower; all rooms have central heating, air conditioning, TV, phone
FACILITIES dining room, 2 sitting rooms, bar, reading room, garden, heated swimming pool, tennis court, chapel, bull ring
CREDIT CARDS AE, DC, MC, V
DISABLED not suitable
PETS welcome by arrangement
CLOSED never
PROPRIETOR Familia Oriol e Ybarra

SEVILLE

GUILLENA

CORTIJO TORRE DE LA REINA
~ COUNTRY HOTEL ~

Paseo de la Alameda, s/n Torre de la Reina, Guillena, Seville
TEL 955 780136 **FAX** 955 780122
E-MAIL info@torredelareina.com **WEBSITE** www.torredelareina.com

YOU COULD EASILY miss this Cortijo as you drive through Torre de la Reina: it's guarded by large green gates and solid walls. Once through you find the building crammed close to the gate, which belies the spaciousness of the interior and the spreading gardens behind.

A stunning floral lined internal courtyard leading through to the gardens makes the place feel like a tropical paradise. Beautiful sculpted water ways and box hedges divide the immaculate gardens into elegant spaces. Not surprisingly, it's very popular for weddings. The public rooms are grandly decorated with sumptuous furnishings, fabrics and the walls are adorned with historical paintings and an impressive collection of books.

Each bedroom is decorated individually with taste and style. There's every modern comfort, yet all is in keeping with the history of the building and most have the bonus of exquisite views of Seville.

This old fortress has interesting royal connections: it was the rearguard settlement for King Ferdinand III's camp during the conquest of Seville and towards the end of the 13th century the home of Queen Maria of Molina. Parts of the original building (dating back to the 12th century) have been preserved and it is the only rural building of that period in the Seville region.

~

NEARBY Seville, La Algaba, Merida.
LOCATION on the SE188 from Seville heading north, go past La Algaba on A431 turn left for Torre de la Reina, hotel is before the village on the left with limited car parking in own grounds
FOOD breakfast, lunch, dinner
PRICES €€€€
ROOMS 6 double and twin, 6 suites all with bath and shower; all rooms have central heating, air conditioning, mini bar, fax service, phone, satellite TV
FACILITIES dining room, sitting room, bar, reading room, garden, swimming pool, tennis court **CREDIT CARDS** AE, DC, MC, V
CHILDREN welcome **PETS** No **CLOSED** never **PROPRIETOR** Jose Maria Medina

SEVILLE

SEVILLE

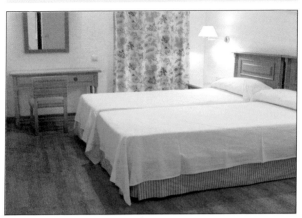

HOTEL ALCANTARA
~ CITY HOTEL ~

Calle Ximenez de Enciso 28, 40114 Sevilla
TEL 954 500595 **FAX** 954 500604
E-MAIL info@hotelalcantara.net **WEBSITE** www.hotelalcantara.net

IN SEVILLE'S OLD CENTRE, in the former Jewish quarter called the Barrio de Santa Cruz, the Hotel Alcántara occupies a distinguished 18th-century Moorish mansion, its windows veiled in traditional metal grilles and narrow wrought-iron balconies. The old house, accessed through its former coach entrance, overlooks narrow, paved alleys overhung with bright flowers; and it encloses, Moorish style, a large central patio surrounded by palms and potted shrubs, and furnished with tables and chairs. On hot Andalusian days it is delightful to breakfast here and to while away a sultry evening hour or two. Adjoining the patio is a modern extension with a big, glass-walled breakfast room/lounge.

The Alcántara is a bed-and-breakfast hotel. The rooms are cool (airconditioned), crisply decorated in shades of white, with unfussy wooden furniture. There are a few singles and some generous-sized rooms for families and groups of three or four friends. Finding somewhere for lunch and dinner in Seville is never a problem – there are bars and restaurants aplenty in nearby streets and a shopping centre just opposite.

With the Cathedral and its Giralda, the Alcázar and other famous sights of this exhilarating city just a stroll away, the Alcántara is a magnet for foreign visitors. Yet the hotel is quiet: no traffic can pass along its flanking alleys. From another perspective, that can be a problem – guests have to pay to use the public car park, a short walk away.

~

NEARBY Ruins of Itálica Roman town, with amphitheatre, bath house, theatre (8 km).
LOCATION in the Santa Cruz district in Seville's old centre, next to Murillo Gardens
PRICE €€-€€€
ROOMS 4 single, 11 double, 3 triple, 3 family rooms (with double beds and room for 2 extra beds); all with bath, shower, TV, clock/radio, phone, PC jack, air conditioning
FACILITIES reception, breakfast room, lift, patio
CREDIT CARDS AE, DC, MC, V **CHILDREN** welcome **DISABLED** one room with disabled access and shower **PETS** not accepted **CLOSED** never
PROPRIETOR Paloma Calvo

SEVILLE

CASA IMPERIAL
~ TOWN HOTEL ~

Imperial 29,.41003 Seville
TEL 954 500300 **FAX** 954 500300
E-MAIL info@casaimperial.com **WEBSITE** www.casaimperial.com

THIS GEM, a beautifully converted 16th century palace, is right in the heart of Seville. Formerly the home of the Villafranca family, (their coat of arms is still above the main entrance) the place blends history, good taste and modern comforts.

You enter by a typical Andalusian courtyard, where you can have breakfast if you don't want it in your bedroom, or on your own private balcony/patio. An exquisitely Sevillan style Pisan staircase leads up to the bedrooms, which are all decorated individually, and reflect the different cultures of Seville. Of special note are the bathrooms, which have fantastically decorated baths: some are deep blue, contrasting with cranberry-coloured walls; others are vibrating deep greens and purples. Made in a typical Andalusian way, they need regular upkeep, but are luxuriously roomy and deep.

There's something to look at, and a charming corner for everyone here, from the interesting little patios dotted around, to the beautiful Hispano-Moslem pond on the second floor. Plans for a pool on the terrace will make it all the more popular, providing a wonderful city-centre respite for hot and bothered travellers.

~

NEARBY Santa Catalina, Cathedral, Jewish quarter.
LOCATION just off Plaza Pilatos on Imperial. Hotel is on right hand side of the church down a narrow alley; very limited parking by hotel, bigger car park in Plaza Ponce de Leon
FOOD breakfast, lunch, dinner
PRICES €€€€€
ROOMS 26; 16 suites, 10 junior suites all with bath and shower; all rooms have hairdriers, TV, phone, safe, modem points on request, air conditioning
FACILITIES dining room, bar, terrace, open courtyard
CREDIT CARDS AE, DC, MC, V
CHILDREN welcome **DISABLED** not suitable **PETS** No **CLOSED** never
MANAGER Leticia Cienfuegos

SEVILLE

SEVILLE

LAS CASAS DE LA JUDERIA

~ TOWN HOUSE HOTEL ~

Callejún de Dos Hermanas, 7, 41004, Seville
TEL 95 4415150 **FAX** 95 4422170
E-MAIL juderia@casasypalacios.com **WEBSITE** www.casasypalacios.com

THIS IS THE LARGEST and best known of the several Sevillan mansions to have been converted into stunning but affordable hotels during the 1990s. Book well in advance. The interconnected houses, dating from the 17thC, are most memorable for their beautiful mustard-and-green courtyards, awash with pot plants, urns and statuary. The cool main patio, where wicker chairs are set around a tiled fountain under marble pillared arcades, is a strong contender for the prettiest spot in the city.

Bedrooms, with parquet floors and prints of old Seville, are exceedingly tasteful. Many have sitting areas, and much more besides – a pillar here, old tilework there, maybe a mini, private patio (such as number 29). Generally, first floor rooms are preferable, since they have french windows opening on to small balconies overlooking the courtyards.

The hotel's location – down a cul-de-sac alley in the Santa Cruz or Jewish quarter – is hard to beat: very quiet yet as central as can be. Though only breakfast (good buffets) is on offer, endless tapas bars lie a short walk away. The place is professionally run: for example, if you're having trouble finding the hotel by car (which is more than likely), you can call a porter to pick up your vehicle and park it for you.

NEARBY Cathedral, La Giralda, the Alcázar, Jewish quarter.
LOCATION In the heart of the Santa Cruz district on Avenida de Mendez Pelayo; underground car park for small cars, public car park off Pelayo (2 min walk)
FOOD breakfast, dinner
PRICES €€-€€€€€
ROOMS 97; 57 double, 13 single, 3 suites, 24 junior suites all with bath; all rooms have central heating, TV (satellite), phone, air conditioning, minibar
FACILITIES breakfast room, piano bar
CREDIT CARDS AE, DC, M, V
CHILDREN welcome
DISABLED lift/elevator, but limited access **PETS** no **CLOSED** never
MANAGER Maria Luisa Tortolero

SEVILLE

SEVILLE

LAS CASAS DEL REY DE BAEZA

∽ TOWN HOUSE HOTEL ∽

Calle Santiago, Plaza Jesus de la Redenciùn, 2, 41003, Seville
TEL 95 4561496 **FAX** 95 4561441
E-MAIL lacasasdelreydebaeza@hospes.es **WEBSITE** www.hospes.es

THIS NEW HOTEL, which opened in 1998 under the same dynamic owner-ship as the Casas de la Juderìa (see page 169), is a slick conversion of an 18thC apartment block. Depending on your taste, you'll either find it a stylish fusion of old architecture and modern design, or a mite contrived. It focuses around three whitewashed, cobbled patios. They are decorated with baskets of oranges and stone flour grinders, are candlelit at night, and surrounded by wooden galleries painted a washed blue. Bedrooms, most of which overlook the patios, are equally eye-catching. Colourful rugs cover black granite floors, armchairs come in plush leather, and bath-rooms in orange and grey marble. Lighter rooms have french windows and small balconies looking across the little square in front of the hotel to a former convent.

The hotel has limited facilities – beyond the bedrooms, there is just a small rooftop swimming pool and a breakfast room/bar. However, you can expect good buffet breakfasts with freshly-squeezed orange juice. The location, in a little-visited part of the Barrio Santa Cruz, has a lot going for it. The big sights are just a ten-minute walk away, while the nearby tapas bars are full of locals rather than tourists.

∽

NEARBY Casa de Pilatos, Jewish quarter, shopping district.
LOCATION overlooking small square off narrow street called Santiago; with limited car parking
FOOD breakfast, lunch, dinner
PRICES €€€-€€€€
ROOMS 37 doubles, 5 suites, all with bath; all rooms have central heating, air conditioning, TV (satellite), phone, minibar, CD, DVD (some rooms)
FACILITIES breakfast room, bar, swimming pool
CREDIT CARDS AE, DC, M, V
CHILDREN accepted **DISABLED** lift/elevator, but access difficult **PETS** No
CLOSED never
MANAGER Marta Perez Asiain

SEVILLE

HOTEL CORTIJO AGUILA REAL

~ COUNTRY HOTEL ~

41210 Guillena, Seville
TEL 955 785006 **FAX** 955 684330
E-MAIL hotel@aguilareal.com **WEBSITE** www.aguilareal.com

MANY OF THE HOTELS we've selected in this part of Spain have breathtaking views, but this one is exceptional. On a clear day, the Cortijo, and its surroundings (which you can explore on horseback) offers amazing views of the country around Seville, and of the city itself.

On arrival, you may well be greeted by the charming manager, David Venegas, in the large, whitewashed courtyard where blazing-hot-pink flowers are festooned from the walls. Just off the courtyard is the sitting room, which may strike you as a little drab after the brilliant scene outside, but actually it's comfortable and cosy, especially in winter. In summer, guests prefer to sit and read or drink on the terrace, with its fabulous views and spectacular sunsets – heliophiles please note.

When we visited, a new restaurant/dining room was under construction, which also promised great views of the plains and gardens – we'd be interested in reports on how this turns out.

The bedrooms are round the side of the Cortijo, overlooking the garden in a charming, small courtyard, quite close together, useful for families or groups of friends. Down a few steps from here is the substantial pool, complete with honesty bar and changing rooms.

~

NEARBY Guillena, Seville, Jabugo, Aracena.
LOCATION on the SE30 out of Seville, take Guillena exit. The hotel is the second turning on the right with ample car parking in own grounds
FOOD breakfast, lunch, dinner
PRICES €€€€
ROOMS 13; 8 doubles, 4 junior suites, 1 superior suite, all with bath and shower; all rooms have central heating, air conditioning, TV, phone, modem points
FACILITIES dining room, sitting room, bar, reading room, swimming pool, bull ring, riding
CREDIT CARDS AE, DC, MC, V **CHILDREN** welcome
DISABLED 2 rooms possible **PETS** No **CLOSED** never
MANAGER David Venegas

SEVILLE

SEVILLE

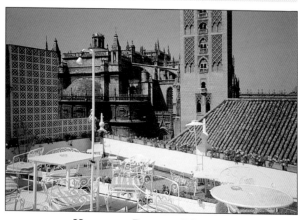

HOTEL DONA MARIA
~ TOWN HOUSE HOTEL ~

Don Remondo 19, 41004, Seville
TEL 95 4224990 **FAX** 95 4219546
E-MAIL reservas@hdmaria.com **WEBSITE** www.hdmaria.com

IMAGINE LYING by a swimming pool which overlooks one of the biggest cathedrals in the world – just one of the perks of staying at the Doña María in the heart of Seville. The hotel is built in an old town house, in a cobbled alley-way off the cathedral square – very convenient for sightseeing, not so convenient for parking, unless you get a space in the underground car park.

The hotel has no dining room, but serves large buffet breakfasts downstairs, and has two bars – one wood-panelled, adjoining the sitting room, the other on the roof-terrace (in summer only). The other public rooms are elegant and comfortable – the sitting room has dark red sofas between brick pillars, the landings are crammed with antiques and portraits, the corridors are lit with blue and white glass lamps; and there is a tiny tropical garden in the middle of the building.

Each bedroom is different, apparently decorated by the Marchioness de San Joaquin herself and named after eminent Sevillian ladies. If possible, ask to see several rooms and choose carefully, as some are disappointing and not cheap. The roof-terrace certainly makes up for it – there are not many places where you get a view of Gothic spires as you swim.

~

NEARBY Cathedral, La Giralda, the Alcázar, Jewish quarter.
LOCATION in narrow alley-way, leading from square in front of cathedral; underground parking for 9 cars
FOOD breakfast
PRICES €€€-€€€€€
ROOMS 35 double, all with bath; 14 single, 12 with bath, 3 with shower; all rooms have central heating, phone, TV, radio; swimming pool on roof
FACILITIES 2 sitting rooms, bar, breakfast room
CREDIT CARDS AE, DC, MC, V
CHILDREN welcome
DISABLED lift/elevator **PETS** accepted in 2 bedrooms
CLOSED never **MANAGER** Isabel Moreno

SEVILLE

SEVILLE

HOTEL MURILLO
~ TOWN HOUSE HOTEL ~

Calle Lope de Rueda 7 & 9, 41004, Seville
TEL 95 4216095 **FAX** 95 4219616
E-MAIL reservas@hotelmurillo.com **WEBSITE** www.hotelmurillo.com

To FIND THE Hotel Murillo you need a good sense of direction and a detailed map; it is lost in the historic Barrio de Santa Cruz, a maze of tiny pedestrian passages behind the Alcázar. From the outside, it is a typical Sevillian town house, painted mustard-yellow and white, with wrought-iron grilles and balconies.

From the inside, it is an extraordinary place, a treasure trove of peculiar objects and antiques. Suits of armour guard the entrance to a long, dim room crammed with furniture –leather sling chairs around carved tables, elaborate screens and glass cabinets along the walls, a sedan chair in front of the bar. The panelled ceiling gives you the feeling that you are in the cabin of a medieval ship. This room serves as a sitting, eating and reception area, and there is another small sitting room for families or groups.

In contrast, the bedrooms upstairs are rather plain. Second floor rooms have small balconies looking on to the street, third floor rooms have arched windows. Furniture is functional and bathrooms small. The room keys are attached to miniature paint pallets, emphasizing the connection with the Sevillian artist Murillo, after whom the hotel is named.

~

NEARBY Cathedral, La Giralda, the Alcázar, Jewish quarter.
LOCATION in a maze of tiny streets, north of cathedral, approachable only by foot; garages nearby
FOOD breakfast
PRICES €€-€€€
ROOMS 47 double, all with bath; 10 single, with bath; all rooms have central heating, air conditioning, phone
FACILITIES sitting room
CREDIT CARDS AE, DC, MC, V
CHILDREN accepted
DISABLED no special facilities **PETS** not accepted
CLOSED never
MANAGER Enrique Ysasi

SEVILLE

PALACIO DE SAN BENITO

～ TOWN HOUSE HOTEL ～

Cazalla de la Sierra, 41370 Seville
TEL 954 883336 **FAX** 954 883162
WEBSITE www.palaciodesanbenito.com

A RIOT: RICH FABRICS, pulsating colour schemes; eccentric combinations of style - but pleasing all the same. Everything in this hotel screams flamboyance, reflecting the character of the owners, who can be seen in photographs meeting celebrities, but who remain very much in the background. We particularly enjoyed the riotous pink and red Chinese sitting room, with its Oriental/French decorative scheme and profusion of prints; and the luscious blue velvet four-poster bed in one of the bedrooms. You get the feeling that you are going to be truly spoilt – and you are. From the spoiling surroundings, to the service from the staff, we were not disappointed.

You can get away with an over-the-top collection of colour, fabrics and decorative artefacts if they are contrasted with a plain backdrop – and that is just what the owners have done here: there are plain, stylish flagging on the floors and lovely cream shades for the walls. An unusual welcoming touch is washbags in all the bathrooms.

The hotel is in the heart of Cazalla de la Sierra, and some of the rooms have views over the picturesque town; others look down on to the pool, fountain and terrace area. This would be the perfect place for a party: there are three dining rooms, all splendid in their own way, whilst the food is a mixture of Mediterranean and traditional Andalusian, cooked to a high standard.

～

NEARBY Cazalla de la Sierra, Seville, Cordoba.
LOCATION in the centre of Cazalla de la Sierra, on the main street, with limited street car parking
FOOD breakfast, lunch, dinner **PRICES** €€€€
ROOMS 9; 7 doubles, 2 suites, all with bath and shower; all rooms have air conditioning, heating, TV, phone, modem points, (4 rooms have patios)
FACILITIES 3 dining rooms, sitting room, bar, reading room, patio garden, swimming pool, gym, sauna
CREDIT CARDS AE, DC, MC, V **CHILDREN** welcome **DISABLED** one room suitable **PETS** no
CLOSED never **PROPRIETOR** Manuel Sanchez de la Madrid and Manuel de Matta

SEVILLE

SEVILLE

TRASIERRA
~ COUNTRY HOTEL ~

Cazalla de la Sierra, 41370 Seville
Tel 954 884324 **Mobile** (UK) 07887 646336 / (Spain) 609 550600
Fax 954 883305

'VERY MUCH THE family-run hotel: friendly relaxing and spoiling' says a recent reporter. Charlotte Scott brought up her five children at the Trasierra, teaching them the business and it feels as much like a home as a hotel. All 11 rooms are individually decorated, with taste and style: the blue and white *toille de jouie* room was our favourite. Not all the rooms are particularly large, but clever decoration and lighting has made each exceptionally charming and comfortable in its own way.

The breakfast room is lavishly stocked with delicious fruits, cereals and juices. If you want a fried breakfast, just walk in to the kitchen and ask – but it will have to be in Spanish. For lunch or dinner you can sit on your own private terrace or by the pool, or for larger parties, under the fragrant verandah by the main door. The ingredients come from the hotel's own organic garden and there's an interesting wine list. Swimming, tennis and ping pong is on hand, and Charlotte can organize painting courses, wine cellar tours, wildflower walks and biking if you book in advance. Likewise massage, yoga or flamenco dancing. On the other hand, doing nothing in a place such as this is also very attractive.

~

Nearby Cazalla de la Sierra, Seville, Cordoba.
Location through centre of Cazalla de la Sierra from the north, turn right at the roundabout and head over the hill. Look out on the right for a large upturned amphora; take the dirt track here to the hotel which has ample car parking in its own grounds
Food breakfast, lunch, dinner
Prices €€€€
Rooms 11; all doubles with bath and shower
Facilities dining room, sitting room, bar, garden, swimming pool, tennis court
Credit cards DC, MC, V
Children welcome
Disabled access difficult **Pets** no **Closed** Jan – Easter (still do B + B so give a ring on the off chance) **Proprietor** Charlotte Scott

SEVILLE

SEVILLE

PATIO DE LA CARTUJA/PATIO DE LA ALAMEDA

~ TOWN HOUSE APARTMENTS ~

CARTUJA: Lumbreras, 8-10, 41002, Seville. **TEL** 95 4900200 **FAX** 95 4902056.
ALAMEDA: Alameda de Hèrcules, 56, 41002, Seville. **TEL** 95 4904999 **FAX** 95 4900226
E-MAIL informacionalcliente@patiosdesevilla.com **WEBSITE** 4www.patiosdesevilla.com

WE'VE LUMPED these two apartment hotels together because they are under the same management, are just 150 yards apart, and offer virtually identical accommodation at the same (bargain) prices. The Cartuja is a rebuilt 19thC apartment block around a wedge-shaped courtyard (or patio), while the Alameda, set around three cool, ochre-coloured patios, was formerly a mansion, then a hospital. At both, almost all the apartments overlook the patios so are peaceful (avoid the few facing the busy roads). All are furnished in a cheerful modern style, and have a large sitting room with a sofabed, plus kitchenette and compact bedroom. The area, albeit on the up, is slightly seedy: hence the low rates.

~

NEARBY Macarena, Isla Magica, city centre 20-minute walk away.
LOCATION on busy streets in the Alameda de Hercules; underground garages
FOOD breakfast
PRICES €€€-€€€€
ROOMS 34 apartments at Cartuja, 22 at Alameda, all with bath; all have central heating, TV, phone, air conditioning
FACILITIES breakfast room at Cartuja
CREDIT CARDS AE, DC, M, V
CHILDREN welcome
DISABLED some ground floor rooms
PETS not accepted
CLOSED never
MANAGER Jose Luis Garcia Baquero

SEVILLE

SEVILLE

SAN GIL

~ TOWN HOUSE HOTEL ~

Calle Parras, 29, 41002, Seville
TEL 95 4906811 **FAX** 95 4906939
E-MAIL sangil.reservas@fp-hoteles.com **WEBSITE** www.fp-hoteles.com

ANOTHER SEVILLAN mansion turned hotel – this time dating from the early 20thC and located in the earthy Macarena district (take a taxi rather than walk around here late at night). Memorable features include the riot of colourful tiles covering the walls in the public areas, and large, tranquil courtyard garden, with olive trees, palms and an old cypress. You can also chill out by the small rooftop swimming pool.

Bedrooms are spread through the mansion, an old converted factory and new block, all of which surround the courtyard. They are simply decorated but notably light and spacious, with a sofabed and kitchenette, and some are split over two floors.

~

NEARBY Macarena sights, Andalusian Parliament; city centre 20-minute walk away.
LOCATION on Macarena backstreet; garage nearby
FOOD breakfast
PRICES €€€€-€€€€€
ROOMS 48 double, 12 junior suites, 1 suite all with bath; all rooms have central heating, TV (satellite), phone, air conditioning, minibar, safe, hairdrier
FACILITIES bar, breakfast room, swimming pool, solarium, cafe
CREDIT CARDS AE, DC, M, V
CHILDREN welcome
DISABLED no special facilities
PETS no
CLOSED never
MANAGER Aquilino Fraile

SEVILLE

HOTEL SIMON
~ TOWN HOUSE HOTEL ~

García de Vinuesa 19, 41001, Seville
TEL 95 4226660
E-MAIL info@hotelsimon.com **WEBSITE** www.hotelsimon.com

Don't be put off by the neon sign outside; once inside the white wrought iron gates, you find yourself transported back in time. Behind them is the typical Andalucian courtyard of a beautiful Moorish town house – a perfect place to cool down among the ferns and marble busts after a busy morning's sightseeing in this spectacular city.

Decoration in the hotel is reminiscent of a mosque; the walls are covered in pretty Moorish tiles and gilded mirrors. Glass chandeliers hang down between the slender marble pillars. The stairway and corridors have tiled walls and floors, period furniture and cabinets full of silver. Bedrooms tend to vary in size and quality and are the original rooms of this lovely 18thC house. Some have small balconies looking on to the street, while others are rather small and airless. Bathrooms also vary, but all are spotlessly clean.

The staff are friendly and helpful, and obviously take great pride in this unusual hotel. The Simon has only two disadvantages – it can be noisy inside and there's no car parking immediately outside. But it is possible to park nearby and the hotel could not be more central.

~

NEARBY Cathedral, La Giralda, the Alcázar, Jewish quarter.
LOCATION on small street, just west of cathedral; no private car parking
FOOD breakfast
PRICES €€€
ROOMS 19 double, with bath, 5 single with shower; 5 suites with bath; all rooms have central heating, phone, air conditioning
FACILITIES dining room, sitting room, patio
CREDIT CARDS DC, MC, V
CHILDREN accepted
DISABLED some ground floor rooms
PETS accepted in bedrooms
CLOSED never
MANAGER Francisco Aguayo

SEVILLE

UTRERA

HACIENDA DE ORAN

~ COUNTRY HOTEL ~

Don Rodrigo KM4, Utrera, Seville
TEL AND FAX 955 815994 **MOBILE** 696 930204
E-MAIL haciendadeoran@hotmail.com **WEBSITE** www.haciendadeoran.com

THIS IS SET IN a rather arid and non-descript plot of land just outside Utrera and you may think at first that you've taken a wrong turn. However, doubts will soon melt away.

The interior is full of charm and cosiness with tasteful, cheerful furnishings and fabrics. Bedrooms are a successful 'rustic chic', with wall hangings from India and bathrooms with beautiful Moorish tiles and basins. It all hangs together very successfully to create an 'International eclectic' feel.

Going out to the extensive gardens you pass through a delightful little patio with plump, soft cushions where you can be served *tapas* or cocktails. Surrounding the inviting pool are (almost too immaculate) gardens, alive with colour and scent. The substantial internal courtyard is lined with stables whose beautiful grey horses can be ridden by guests and which may also take you for a carriage ride and picnic in the surrounding countryside. Next to the stables is a carriage museum, worth a visit if you want to learn about Andalusian history. The staff speak mainly Spanish only, so bring a phrase book. In the top price bracket, but you get what you pay for here.

~

NEARBY Seville, Utrera.
LOCATION 10 km N of Utrera on A473, take Don Rodrigo exit. Hotel is 9km on left, ample car parking in own grounds
FOOD breakfast, lunch, dinner (on request)
PRICES €€€€
ROOMS 13; 7 doubles, 2 mini suites, 2 junior suites, 2 suites all with shower; all rooms have phone, TV, air conditioning, central heating
FACILITIES dining room, sitting room, garden, swimming pool
CREDIT CARDS AE, DC, MC, V
CHILDREN welcome
DISABLED not suitable
PETS no
CLOSED never
MANAGER Rafael Vazquez Jimenaz

CORDOBA

CORDOBA

HOTEL GONZALEZ

~ TOWN HOUSE HOTEL ~

Manriquez 3, 14003 Cordoba
TEL 957 479819 **FAX** 957 486187

HIDDEN AWAY in one of the narrow, white-washed streets in Córdoba's old Jewish quarter, just a stone's throw from the beautiful Mezquita, is this unusual little hotel, built in the remains of a 16thC Moorish palace. The only 'remains' we could see were a rectangular stone doorway and one stone capital, but Joaquín and Manuel González have added plenty of Moorish touches, such as arabesque arches on the patio. They also run a souvenir shop adjoining the hotel, full of gaudy Moorish vases, but this does not affect (or reflect) the character of the hotel, which is run with a happy blend of informality and efficiency.

Our first impression was of a cool marble interior and a charming receptionist. The hall leads through the arches to a lovely patio, packed with pretty red and white dining-tables and copious flowers and greenery. Geraniums hang down from every possible ledge and balcony. There is also a modern bar where breakfast is served. Upstairs, the bedrooms are simple and comfortable; most have small balconies looking over the patio. An (otherwise impressed) reader thought the food uninteresting and recommends El Churrasco, five minutes' walk away. Another (likewise impressed) reports night-time noise, possibly from a compressor. Another complained of heat in his bedroom, thin mattresses and uninterested reception staff.

~

NEARBY Mezquita, Alcázar, old Jewish quarter.
LOCATION in quiet street behind Mezquita (best found on foot); no private car parking – public car park
FOOD breakfast, lunch, dinner
PRICES €€
ROOMS 15 double, 2 single, 3 family rooms, all with bath; all rooms have central heating, air conditioning, phone, satellite TV, radio
FACILITIES dining room/patio, sitting room, cafeteria/bar, souvenir shop
CREDIT CARDS AE, MC, V, DC
CHILDREN welcome **DISABLED** no special facilities **PETS** not accepted **CLOSED** never
PROPRIETOR Joaquín and Manuel González

CORDOBA

PALMA DEL RIO

HOSPEDERIA DE SAN FRANCISCO

~ CONVERTED MONASTERY ~

Avenida Pio XII, 14700, Palma del Rio, Córdoba
TEL 957 710183 **FAX** 957 710236
WEBSITE www.intergrouphoteles.com **E-MAIL** hospederia@casasypalacios.com

THIS 15THC Franciscan monastery stands on a small square at the centre of a confusing one-way system. If you get lost, don't hesitate to ask for directions; everyone knows where the Hospedería is, as it becomes a focus of attention at fiesta time (the staff dress up as monks and run a bar behind the church).

The Moreno family converted the monastery into a hotel five years ago. The care they took is immediately obvious as you enter the main court-yard; tables are set up in the cloisters, where you can watch pigeons nesting in the bell-tower as you eat. The main dining room is a high-ceilinged hall, dominated by a huge fireplace. All the sitting areas are comfortable, especially the tiled bar, with its beamed ceiling and old paintings. Some of the bedrooms were once monks' cells and are fairly small and basic, but what they lack in luxuries they make up for in character, with beautifully hand-painted basins and bed-covers woven by local nuns.

Chef Iñaki has an excellent reputation, and his caricature (round, moustached and wagging a long finger) adorns the constantly changing menu, which reflects his Basque origins.

~

NEARBY Córdoba (55 km); Seville (90 km); churches and palaces in Écija and Carmona.
LOCATION on quiet square in heart of town; car parking
FOOD breakfast, lunch, dinner
PRICES €€€€€
ROOMS 35 double, all with bath; all rooms have central heating, air conditioning, phone, TV, safe
FACILITIES dining room, sitting room, bar, 3 patios, cloisters, swimming pool, garden
CREDIT CARDS AE, MC, V
CHILDREN welcome
DISABLED no special facilities **PETS** not accepted
CLOSED never
MANAGER Jesus Rojas

JAEN

MOLINO DE LA FARRAGA
~ CONVERTED MILL BED AND BREAKFAST ~

C/ Camino de la Hoz Apdo. De Correos no 1, 23470 Cazorla, Jaen
TEL and FAX 953 721249
E-MAIL: farraga@teleline.es **WEBSITE:** www.molinolafarraga.com

PERCHED ON the mountainside above the narrow, winding streets of the Arabic/Andalusian town of Cazorla, this mill is hard to reach but worth the effort. About 200 years old, it was a working grain mill until 30 years ago. Parts of the mechanism have been preserved and make an interesting feature when lit up at night.

The breakfast rooms are somewhat dark and old fashioned, as are the bedrooms, but they are cool and spacious, and some have conservatories with an almost 360 degree view of the surrounding nature reserve where you can see wild boar and goat, golden eagles and Egyptian vultures. The mill's best feature is in fact the gardens, with their rich selection of plants, mainly unique to the area. You'll find plenty of secluded corners where you can relax completely hidden by walls of vegetation. Various paths lead to the pool, which has spectacular views of the countryside and back on to the Molino itself.

Reaching the mill you have to park your car about 100 metres below, and the climb with your bags could be a strain in hot weather. If you walk up to reception (without your bags) and announce yourself, someone will probably be happy to help.

~

NEARBY Jaen, Cazorla town centre, natural reserves, Castillo de Yedra.
LOCATION take the A319 into Cazorla, follow the street Hilario Marco, turn right on to Dr Munoz and follow this to Plaza de Santa Maria. Then follow the signs for the Molino, park below in public car park, and walk up
FOOD breakfast
PRICES €€€
ROOMS 9; 7 double, 2 suites, all with bath and shower; suites have TV, phone
FACILITIES dining room, sitting room, garden, swimming pool
CREDIT CARDS AE, DC, MC, V
CHILDREN welcome
DISABLED access difficult **PETS** by arrangement
CLOSED 10th Dec – 1st Mar **PROPRIETOR** Teresa Fernandez

JAEN

ÚBEDA

PT CONDESTABLE DAVALOS

~ TOWN MANSION ~

Plaza de Vázquez de Molina 1, 23400, Úbeda, Jaén
TEL 953 750345 **FAX** 953 751259
E-MAIL ubeda@parador.es **WEBSITE** www.parador.es

SOMEWHAT OVERSHADOWED by the lovely façade of the 16thC chapel next door to it, Úbeda's stately Parador stands on the Renaissance square of Vázquez de Molina. Its internal courtyard is delightful; sixteen slender pillars (on both floors) enclose a stone-flagged patio set with tables and chairs. Striking blue-and-white patterned tiles half cover the walls around the outside. A sweeping staircase leads to the glass-enclosed gallery, past suits of armour and a spectacular light inside a double-headed glass eagle. Some bedrooms are around the gallery, others look on to smaller leafy quads or the ornamental garden. There is more attention to detail here than in the average Parador – carved bed-heads, hand-painted mirrors and wooden writing desks.

Guests have the choice of two bars, the underground taberna or a bar-cum-sitting room on the way to the gardens. Red-tiled floors with little picture inlays are found in all public rooms, including the attractive dining room. It is a friendly and animated place, in which it is easy to relax – perhaps in the shade of giant ferns in the courtyard, or under pine trees in the garden. It seemed half the size of its 31 rooms, without being cramped – a great base for exploring this historic town. 'Just sitting in the patio is worth the price – which is saying something,' writes a much-impressed U.S. reader.

~

NEARBY Plaza, palaces, churches; Baeza (10 km); Jaén (55 km).
LOCATION on square in historic part of town; follow signs; with car parking
FOOD breakfast, lunch, dinner
PRICES €€€€
ROOMS 34 double, 2 suites, all with bath; all rooms have central heating, air conditioning, phone, TV, minibar, hairdrier
FACILITIES 1 dining room, TV room, bar, cafeteria
CREDIT CARDS AE, DC, MC, V
CHILDREN welcome
DISABLED access difficult **PETS** not accepted, except guide dogs
CLOSED never **MANAGER** Juan de la Torre Alcala

JAEN

UBEDA

PALACIO DE LA RAMBLA
∽ ARISTOCRATIC MANSION ∽

Plaza del Marqués 1, 23400, Úbeda, Jaén
TEL 953 750196 **FAX** 953 750267
E-MAIL palaciorambla@terra.es **WEBSITE** www.rusticae.es

THERE COULD be no more appropriate place to stay in the historic city of Úbeda than in this 16th century urban stately home, part of which has been opened to guests by the present Marquesa de la Rambla in order to help with the upkeep. More a seignorial guest house than a hotel, the door of the Palacio de la Rambla is kept locked and you have to summon the caretaker via an intercom.

The central feature is the patio, dripping with ivy, which is one of Úbeda's Renaissance treasures. Around it are the four original rooms which are decorated with old engravings and family antiques. One has an old-fashioned blue bath on legs; the other has its own fireplace. The two other rooms on the ground floor have less character. Another four rooms have been added upstairs at the front of the house.

Breakfast – 'whatever you want'– is brought to your room or served at one end of the salon. The grand piano at the other end holds the family photograph collection. 'Delightful'; 'warm and welcoming atmosphere' writes a recent visitor.

∽

NEARBY monuments of Úbeda; Baeza (11km); Cazorla Nature Reserve (55km).
LOCATION in the town centre; 4 garage places available
FOOD breakfast (other meals for groups only by prior arrangement)
PRICES €€€€
ROOMS 7 double, 1 suite, all with bath; all rooms have central heating, TV, minibar, telephone, hairdrier
FACILITIES sitting room
CREDIT CARDS AE, V
CHILDREN accepted
DISABLED access difficult
PETS not accepted
CLOSED 15 Jul to 15 Aug
PROPRIETOR Elena Meneses de Orozco

GRANADA

ALPUJARRA

ALQUERIA DE MORAYMA
~ COUNTRY HOTEL ~

18440 Cadiar Alpujarra, Granada
TEL 958 343221 / 958 343303 **FAX** 958 343221
WEBSITE www.alqueriamorayma.com

A PLACE WITH A WARM heart, run by charming people. Arriving after a long day on the road, our inspectors were met by concerned, generous and gregarious staff, quick to offer free bottles of wine made in the small *bodega* next to the hotel.

The hotel's layout is quite spread out and disjointed, but every area is charming in its way. One of the rooms has been converted from an exquisite little church, without losing its character, or indeed most of its decorations and relics. The other 18 rooms are not quite as unusual, but delightfully rustic, with stunning views: the hotel is on the side of a mountain overlooking the dramatic countryside.

A beautiful cobbled walkway separates the main part of the hotel from the *bodega* which is stuffed with vats of red and white wine and air-cured legs of ham, which you have of course to try. The restaurant is not especially cosy, but you can eat outside on the lawn, where you can sit and gaze out at Cadiar and the nearby Sierra Nevada mountains.

~

NEARBY Granada, Las Alpujarras, Cadiar.
LOCATION just off the A348 on the km 52 mark between Cadiar and Torviscon, in own grounds with ample car parking
FOOD breakfast, lunch, dinner
PRICES €€
ROOMS 19; 14 doubles, 2 triples, 2 quadruples, 1 single, 2 appartments for 4, 5 with bath rest with shower; all rooms have TV, phone, some with terrace 2 with kitchen
FACILITIES dining room, sitting room, bar, garden, swimming pool, library, working room, carpentry
CREDIT CARDS AE. DC. MC, V
CHILDREN welcome
DISABLED one room
PETS by arrangement
CLOSED never
DIRECTOR Mariano Cruz Farjardo

GRANADA

BAZA

CUEVAS AL JATIB
~ CAVE HOTEL ~

Arroyo Curcal, s/n 18 800 Baza, Granada
TEL 958 342248 **MOBILE** 667 524219
E-MAIL info@aljatib.com **WEBSITE** www.aljatib.com

YOU COULD HARDLY find a more historic – or unique a place to stay. It's a 'Troglodyte' or cave dwelling – one of several in this area. Luc Compoint and his wife Isabel opened the Cuevas in 2001 after seven years of hard graft. The result is a fabulous Arabesque place of relaxation. Every corner turned brings a fresh surprise. On the right of reception is the cosy little cave restaurant that serves delicious Arab/Andalusian and French dishes. On the left behind reception is the Moroccan tea room, complete with low cushions, tables and wonderful aromatic smells. The Arab baths and massage rooms are deeper still into the rock: don't miss out on these.

The bedrooms are next to the main cave in exquisitely beautiful mini caves: these can (variously) sleep between two and 11 people. All are stylishly decorated, with their own bathrooms. For the children, the Compoints have built a magical subterranean playground and maze of tunnels that all end on squashy mattresses. The nearby town of Baza is well worth a visit: it has a famous 4th century AD statue (The Lady of Baza) and the oldest Arab baths in Europe, dating from the 10th century.

~

NEARBY Baza, Arab baths, Guadix.
LOCATION leave the A92 at the Baza Este exit. The road doubles back on itself: follow the sign for Camino de Oria – a dirt track. Soon pick up signs for the caves, which have ample off-road car parking
FOOD breakfast, lunch, dinner
PRICE €€€€-€€€€€
ROOMS 5 caves; 2 caves sleeping 2, 1 sleeping 4, 1 sleeping 6, 1 sleeping 11, all with bath; all rooms have TV, phone, kitchen, washing machine, private terrace
FACILITIES dining room, sitting room, bar, garden, Arab baths, chill out room, massage room, play caves for children
CREDIT CARDS MC, V
CHILDREN welcome
DISABLED one cave suitable **PETS** no **CLOSED** never
PROPRIETORS Luc and Isabel Compoint

GRANADA

BENALUA

CUEVAS LA GRANJA
~ CAVE HOTEL ~

Camino de la Granja S/N 18.510 Benalua, Granada
TEL 958 676000 **FAX** 958 684433
E-MAIL cuevas@granada.net **WEBSITE** www.cuevas.org

THIS IS YET ANOTHER of Southern Spain's cave hotels (see also page 186 and 189). It's much the smartest of the caves we've seen, with very modern interior furnishings and much of the walls plastered to a smooth finish – unlike some cave hotels, which make a point of letting bits of rock face show through. However the effect is intimate and cosy and has a certain charm. All of the 11 caves have a sitting room, kitchen, TV and phone; the bedrooms themselves are comfy enough, but lack the kind of individuality we favour – a shame considering the uniqueness of their situation.

This is essentially a self-catering operation, but there's a restaurant next to the caves. It's not especially charming or full of character, but the food is acceptable. Like other cave hotels, La Granja doesn't need air conditioning – it's naturally cool in the summer and in winter it's deceptively warm with open fires and animal skin/fabric wraps to make you feel even cosier.

Gaudix, with its historical monuments is worth a visit; so is the Sierra Nevada National Park, and, of course, Granada, which is 45 minutes by car.

~

NEARBY Guadix, Granada, Almeria, Sierra Nevada.
LOCATION just off the A92 between Granada and Guadix. Go into Guadix and follow the signs. The caves have ample private car parking
FOOD breakfast, lunch, dinner
PRICE €€€-€€€€
ROOMS 11 caves, 4 single bedrooms, 5 caves sleeping 2, 1 cave sleeping 3, 1 suite, all with bath and shower; all caves have TV, phone, kitchens
FACILITIES restaurant, sitting rooms, garden, kitchens, swimming pool
CREDIT CARDS AE, DC, MC, V
CHILDREN welcome
DISABLED one cave
PETS no
CLOSED never
PROPRIETOR Francisco Riveria

GRANADA

VILLA TURISTICA DE BUBION
~ TOURIST VILLAGE ~

Barrio Alto s/n, Bubión, Granada
TEL 958 763111 FAX 958 763136
E-MAIL albujarr@ctb.es WEBSITE www.ctb.es.albujarr

THIS IS THE FIRST in a new concept of accommodation in Andalucia: a cluster of self-contained apartments built in the local style. The Villa Turística, run by a co-operative, recreates the architectural atmosphere of an Alpujarran village with its low-rise, flat topped houses, singular chimneys and shady alleyways. Compare it to the real thing in Bubión only a stone's throw down the hill.

There are three models of apartment, the largest having two bedrooms, two bathrooms and a sitting/dining room. All are decorated similarly, using local textiles and ceramics. Each has a fireplace – vital in the Alpujarras in winter – which room service will attend to. When we inspected, the authenticity of the rooms was only let down by the veneered kitchen cabinets, which we understand are being replaced.

The central block near the car-park houses reception, the dining-room/bar and a rather impersonal sitting room upstairs – the sofas in front of reception are more inviting.

On weekdays the manager offers a reduced price to readers who present a copy of this guide.

~

NEARBY walks in the Alpujarras; Bubión; Capileira (2km); the Veleta, by unsurfaced road to over 3,000 metres (25km).
LOCATION above the village; car parking and garden
FOOD breakfast, lunch, dinner
PRICES €€€
ROOMS 43 apartments, all with bath; all rooms have fireplace, TV, fridge, telephone
FACILITIES sitting room, dining room, bar; mountain bikes
CREDIT CARDS AE, DC, MC, V
CHILDREN accepted
DISABLED easy access
PETS accepted at extra charge
CLOSED never
MANAGER Victor Fernandez

GRANADA

GAUDIX

CUEVAS PEDRO ANTONIO DE ALARCON
~ CAVE HOTEL ~

Bda. San Torcuato S/N, Gaudix, Granada
TEL 958 664986 **FAX** 958 661721
E-MAIL cavehotel@infonegocio.com **WEBSITE** www.andalucia.com/cavehotel

FROM OUTSIDE, the whitewashed fronts of these little cave rooms sparkle dazzling white in the sun, in beautiful contrast to the duller colours of the Tufa hillside in which they are set. The interiors are an eclectic mix of simple Mexican and Spanish decoration making the place feel homely and cheerful. Some of the caves have two or more bedrooms created by hanging up vibrant Mexican drapes, not great for privacy but a fun alternative to a conventional partition. Each cave has a working fire, kitchen and a bathroom – it's mainly a self-catering operation, but there is a rather soulless little restaurant down by the pool serving traditional Spanish dishes, wine and cold beer. One downside: there's a noisy motorway within earshot of the swimming pool. Still, once inside your cave, you're completely insulated from road noise.

One reason for staying in a cave hotel is, of course, to sample an experience which is completely unique to this part of Spain. Another would be that the area is full of interesting things to do and see. Guadix boasts an awesome Moorish castle and a 16th–18th C cathedral. It also claims to be the most important centre for cave dwellings in Europe and a short drive through town will bring you to a community of private cave dwellings and a cave museum. We feature two other cave hotels in the area on pages 186 and 187.

~

NEARBY Guadix, Granada, Almeria, Sierra Nevada.
LOCATION from Almeria head towards Granada on the A92. Leave at the Guadix – Benalua exit and go left towards Murcia. The caves are on your left with ample car parking in own grounds
FOOD breakfast, lunch, dinner
PRICES €€
ROOMS 23; some with 1 bedroom others with 2 or 3 with a 6 person maximum per cave, all with bath; all rooms have kitchen, TV, phone
FACILITIES restaurant, sitting room, garden, swimming pool, working fireplaces
CREDIT CARDS MC, V **CHILDREN** welcome **DISABLED** one cave suitable
PETS by arrangement **CLOSED** never **PROPRIETORS** Cuevas Pedro Antonio de Alarcon

GRANADA

GRANADA

HOTEL AMÉRICA
～ TOWN HOUSE HOTEL ～

Real de la Alhambra 53, 18009, Granada
TEL 958 227471 **FAX** 958 227470
E-MAIL reservas@hotelamericagranada.com **WEBSITE** www.hotelamericagranada.com

TUCKED AWAY between the Alhambra and Granada's Parador, this delightful family-run hotel offers a perfect location at an affordable price. It is a small, friendly place, built around a vine-covered patio. In the summer months, the patio doubles as a dining room – pretty tiled tables are set out, and you dine by the light of hanging lanterns to the sound of running water. The choice of dishes is limited, but everything is home-cooked, and if the smells coming from the kitchen when we visited are anything to go by, the food is delicious; it is also reasonably priced.

The bedrooms are small but comfortable and clean, and overlook either the patio or the gardens of the Alhambra. They are brightened up by colourful woven bedspreads and curtains. The sitting area next to the reception is crammed with pottery, ornaments, screens, sofas and rocking chairs – leaving hardly enough room to sit down. It is a small, busy hotel, and not the kind of place you would want to linger in all day. But with the Alhambra on your doorstep, there is more than enough to keep you busy. 'A friendly, but casual welcome,' says a recent reporter. Popular with our German readers.

～

NEARBY Alhambra, Generalife and gardens, cathedral; Sierra Nevada (35 km), Costa del Sol (65 km).
LOCATION inside walls of Alhambra (follow road past entrance); car parking not allowed in square. Use Alhambra car park (15 mins walk) – reduced fee.
FOOD breakfast, lunch
PRICES €€€€
ROOMS 10 double, 6 single, 1 suite, all with bath; 4 single, 2 with bath, 2 with shower; all rooms have central heating, air conditioning, phone
FACILITIES dining room, sitting room
CREDIT CARDS MC, V
CHILDREN accepted
DISABLED 2 ground floor rooms **PETS** not accepted
CLOSED 1 Dec to 28 Feb
PROPRIETOR Rafael Garzón

GRANADA

GRANADA

HOTEL CARMEN DE SANTA INES
~ TOWN HOTEL ~

Placeta de Porras 7/San Juan de los Reyes, 15 18018 Granada
TEL 958 226380 **FAX** 958 224404
E-MAIL sinescar@teleline.com **WEBSITE** www.palaciosantaines.com

'WONDERFULLY DECADENT; oozes shabby chic' writes a recent reporter. In fact, the Carmen de Santa Ines is so romantic that you're tempted not to leave the premises at all. The garden, reached via the main entrance courtyard, bursts with lush vegetation and beautifully tended plants and trees. Fountains trickle peacefully in the background. You can have breakfast underneath a pergola with an awesome view to the Alhambra.

Most of the bedrooms share the spectacular views over the Alhambra and are beautifully decorated with minimum of fuss: expect fresh flowers and charming antique furniture. The bathrooms, although clean and functional, are on the small size. Our favourite, the Oratory Room, has wonderful old, incredibly comfortable, wooden sleigh bed. The hotel is in Granada's Arab quarter, the Albayzin, and the Islamic influence on the architecture is obvious and pleasing to the eye. The Albayzin's shops and stalls are just a few hundred yards' walk – worth a visit if you enjoy bargain hunting. Do not miss the Cathedral, one of Granada's most famous sights, although a little further away.

~

NEARBY Alhambra, Cathedral, Albayzin, Plaza Nueva.
LOCATION from Granada's Plaza Nueva, take the Carrera del Darro, and turn left on San Juan de Los Reyes; the hotel is well signposted; no car parking so use the public car parks on the Gran Via
FOOD breakfast
PRICES €€€€
ROOMS 9; 8 double (3 with small salon), 1 suite, all with bath; all rooms have air conditioning, mini bar, phone
FACILITIES dining room, sitting room, garden
CREDIT CARDS AE, DC, MC, V
CHILDREN welcome
DISABLED not suitable **PETS** small dogs by arrangement
CLOSED never
PROPRIETOR Nicolas Garrido

GRANADA

GRANADA

CASA MORISCA
TOWN HOTEL

Cuesta de la Victoria 9 18010, Granada
TEL 958 221100 **FAX** 958 215796
E-MAIL info@hotelcasamorisca.com **WEBSITE** www.hotelcasamorisca.com

JUST OFF THE Plaza Nueva in the heart of Granada, overlooked by the Alhambra: you could not ask for a better location. All around are the narrow, exotically fragrant streets of the Albayzin (Arab Quarter), where vendors sell, haggle and smoke their *shishas*.

The building dates back to the 15th century: the name Morisca alludes to its Moslem inhabitants, who stayed in Granada after the Arab conquest of Spain. The decoration of Morisco houses is unique, vibrant and incredibly stylish, and this is no exception. The inner courtyard has its original Morisco pool, and is lined in authentic Moorish style with columns supporting the upper floor. All are individually decorated, with Moorish beamed ceilings and deliciously comfortable beds. Some of them have views of spectacular scenery, and some of the bathrooms are decorated in wonderful Moorish tiles.

Off the courtyard is the beautiful vaulted breakfast room that leads on to the patio and garden where you get a spectacular view of the great Comares Tower of the Alhambra. There is no shortage of places to eat and visit in the neighbourhood and the friendly reception staff are happy to point you in the right direction.

NEARBY Alhambra, Albayzin, cathedral.
LOCATION in the heart of Granada just off the Plaza Nueva on the left of the Carrera del Darro with very limited street car parking
FOOD breakfast
PRICES €€€€
ROOMS 14; 11 doubles, 2 suites, 1 semi-suite, all with bath and shower; all rooms have phone TV, air conditioning, heating, safe
FACILITIES dining room, sitting room, bar, garden
CREDIT CARDS AE, DC, MC, V
CHILDREN welcome
DISABLED one room suitable **PETS** no **CLOSED** never
MANAGER Maria Jesus Candenas

GRANADA

GRANADA

PT SAN FRANCISCO
~ CONVERTED CONVENT PARADOR ~

Real de la Alhambra, 18009, Granada
TEL 958 221440 **FAX** 958 222264
E-MAIL granada@parador.es **WEBSITE** www.parador.es

'BOOK AT LEAST three months in advance' was the advice that the management of this extremely popular Parador asked us to pass on; 'and more in high season', we would add. The attraction of this converted 14thC convent, set in the gardens of the famous Alhambra, is easy to see – especially when the day-trippers have disappeared – and the results are predictable.

Although the hotel is rather big and impersonal, it has some lovely touches – the chapel where Isabella of Spain was originally buried, now open to the sky, is used as a patio, and the adjoining courtyard full of plants and flowers is a place to sit and relax in lovely old rocking-chairs. Alcoves in the corridors and stairways are decorated with carved wooden figures of saints, and the stone-flagged floors are covered in bright Granadan rugs. The bedrooms are fairly standard, with large, tiled bathrooms; 32 of them have superb views over the Alhambra and the Generalife. Public rooms are comfortable, and there are seating areas on the terraces. The dining room gets very busy – but any hotel near the Alhambra attracts crowds, and at least here you can sit and wait in glorious surroundings.

~

NEARBY Alhambra, Generalife and gardens, cathedral; Sierra Nevada (35 km), Costa del Sol (65 km).
LOCATION in Alhambra gardens (follow road past entrance); with garden and garage for 17 cars
FOOD breakfast, lunch, dinner
PRICES €€€€
ROOMS 36 double, all with bath; all rooms have central heating, air conditioning, phone, TV, minibar, hairdrier
FACILITIES dining room, sitting room, bar, garden, terrace
CREDIT CARDS AE, DC, MC, V
CHILDREN welcome
DISABLED some ground floor rooms **PETS** not accepted
CLOSED never **MANAGER** Juan Antonio Gianello

GRANADA

GRANADA

PALACIO DE SANTA INÉS
~ TOWN HOUSE HOTEL ~

Cuesta de Santa Inés, 9, 18010, Granada
TEL 958 222362 **FAX** 958 222465
E-MAIL sinespal@teleline.es **WEBSITE** www.palaciosantaines.com

THE PROBLEM with staying on the Alhambra hill is that it's hard to escape from the thousands of fellow tourists. Consider instead basing yourself in the Albaicìn, the mysterious, white washed Moorish quarter that tumbles down the hillside opposite.

Here you'll find the Palacio de Santa Inès, a 16thC mansion that manages to be both grand yet intimate, and combines the old and the new to great effect. Its centrepiece is its enclosed patio, where half-revealed frescoes – said to be by a student of Raphael – and marble pillars are offset by chic soft furnishings. Upstairs, wooden galleries decorated with modern art lead to striking, beamed bedrooms, furnished with wrought-iron beds and more art. Standard double rooms are generally small, however, so it might be worth splashing out on a suite. The grandest (the Alhambra) has a fabulous mudèjar ceiling, while others have roof terraces with sensational views of the Alhambra over the Albaicìnis jumble of terracotta roofs.

The owners have recently opened a second hotel in the Albaicìn, the Carmen de Santa Inès (tel 958 226380), a 16th century Arab house converted in similar style, with a lovely garden to boot. Unfortunately there are still problems here with 'missing' reservations, reconfirm before arriving.

~

NEARBY Albaicìn; Alhambra a 10-minute walk away.
LOCATION up a quiet back alley 200 yards from the main Plaza Nueva; parking 5-minute walk away in public car park
FOOD breakfast
PRICES €€€€-€€€€€
ROOMS 35 double, 4 suites, all with bath; all rooms have central heating, TV (satellite), phone, air conditioning, minibar
FACILITIES breakfast room, sitting room
CREDIT CARDS AE, DC, M, V
CHILDREN welcome **DISABLED** access difficult, one special room **PETS** small dogs
CLOSED never **PROPRIETOR** Nicolas Garrido Berastegui

GRANADA

LA ALPUJARRA

HOTEL AUBERGUE DE MECINA
⌁ VILLAGE HOTEL ⌁

Calle La Fuente 18416, Mecina Fondales La Alpujarra, Granada
TEL 958 766254/958 766241 **FAX** 958 766255
E-MAIL victor@hoteldemecina.com **WEBSITE** www.ocioteca.com/hoteldemecina

WE HAVE MIXED feelings about this place. The building is unexciting, and so is the interior. But there's a wonderfully relaxed and friendly atmosphere and the food is traditional, honestly priced and good. The staff could not be more helpful and friendly, and will fix you up with riding, help you with walking routes, mountain biking, or trout fishing on the nearby Trevelez river.

Locals are encouraged to use the bar and restaurant, which gives the place a pleasant extra buzz, instead of having to venture out to get a taste of the local atmosphere, it comes to you. Adjacent to the restaurant is the swimming pool: it's a good size, but rather close to the road. The bedrooms and well equipped bathrooms have adequate space, large, comfortable beds and are decorated in cheerful colours, equipped with fridges and sinks. Some have lovely views over the small town of Mecina Fondales and others look out on to the peaceful rolling hillsides of the Alpujarra. On balance, we're glad to welcome Aubergue de Mecina to the guides, especially as prices are fair – but would welcome readers' reports.

⌁

NEARBY Granada, Motril, Almeria, Costa del Sol.
LOCATION just off the GR 421 follow signs to Mecina Fondales down the hill and hotel is on the left just before the centre of town, with ample car parking in own grounds
FOOD breakfast, lunch, dinner
PRICES €€
ROOMS 21; 12 quadruples, 5 triples, 4 doubles, all with bath and shower; all rooms have TV, phone, kitchenette
FACILITIES dining room, sitting room, bar, garden, swimming pool
CREDIT CARDS AE, DC, MC, V
CHILDREN welcome
DISABLED all public rooms and some bedrooms accessible
PETS by arrangement
PROPRIETOR Victor Fernandez Garces

GRANADA

LOJA

LA BOBADILLA
~ ANDALUCIAN VILLA ~

Finca La Bobadilla, 18300, Loja, Granada
TEL 958 321861 FAX 958 321810
E-MAIL labobadilla.comercial2@barcelo.com WEBSITE www.la-bobadilla.com

ARCHES, TILES, WHITE walls, iron grilles, fountains, plants, patios and balconies: La Bobadilla resembles a labyrinthine Andalucian village, set in its own 350-hectare grove of olives and evergreen oaks. More than one visitor has described it as the best hotel in Spain, indeed as one of the best in Europe and an inspection visit before this edition went to press confirmed that standards remain as high as ever.

There are 60 rooms: but what rooms. Most of them are enormous, with private garden or terrace. Every room is decorated with an abundance of marbles, silks and woodwork. The columns of the main hall are reminiscent of the mosque at Cordoba. There are concerts in the hotel chapel.

For outdoor entertainment, there is archery and clay-pigeon shooting; or you can ride, or drive a 4x4, through the olive groves. If you are still in need of variety, you can relax in the Turkish baths. There is not a corner, patio or corridor which does not boast some atmospheric detail: splashes of greenery, the gurgles of water seem to greet you at every turn. 'An incredible hotel' writes a well-travelled visitor, 'but we thought, given the sky-high prices, the food at both restaurants was disappointing.' Recently prices have come down and the food has been winning awards.

~

NEARBY Archidona (18km); Antequera (35 km); Granada (70 km).
LOCATION 3 km on the C334 from Salinas to Iznajar; car parking
FOOD breakfast, lunch, dinner
PRICES €€€€
ROOMS 42 casitas, all with bath; all rooms have air conditioning, phone, minibar, TV (satellite), CD
FACILITIES 2 restaurants, bar, meeting room; 2 swimming pools, terrace, sauna, Turkish baths, massage; tennis court, mountain bikes; shops, chapel, beauty salon, hairdressers
CREDIT CARDS AE, DC, MC, V
CHILDREN accepted **DISABLED** 2 rooms with special facilities **PETS** only in rooms
CLOSED never **MANAGER** Miguel del Valle

GRANADA

MONACHIL

LA ALMUNIA DEL VALLE

~ COUNTRY HOTEL ~

Pago de la Umbria, 1 E-18193 Monachil, Granada
TEL 958 308010 **FAX** 958 308010
E-MAIL laalmunia@infonegocio.com **WEBSITE** www.laalmuniadelvalle.com

T HIS IS AN adorable little hotel in a great location, just outside the
sprawling metropolis of Granada in tranquil countryside. The owner,
Patricia Merino, is charming but doesn't speak much English. She has
decorated the place with style, flair and very good taste. Both dining room
and sitting room are done out in a rich red, with beautiful pictures and
objets d'art on the tables and mantlepieces. The bedrooms all have generously sized double beds that take up most of the somewhat limited space.
To compensate, Patricia has created a feeling of space with warm, light
colours and carefully placed hangings and pictures.

The bathrooms are immaculate, with large, well-lit mirrors, and in
many, original stone walls. Outside on the terrace you have fabulous views
of the Natural Park. The food is traditional, prepared with fresh ingredients. You can eat in the dining room or outside on the terrace and hope
for a magnificent sunset.

~

NEARBY Granada, Motril, the Alhambra, Sierra Nevada.
LOCATION leaving Granada on the N323, take exit 2 to Monachil, bypass Monachil
and follow signs to Camino de la Umbria up a dirt track. The hotel is on the left,
with ample car parking in own grounds
FOOD breakfast, dinner
PRICES €€€€
ROOMS 9; all doubles, with bath; all rooms have TV, phone, mini bar
FACILITIES dining room, sitting room, bar, reading room, garden, swimming pool
CREDIT CARDS MC, V
CHILDREN no
DISABLED access difficult
PETS by arrangement
CLOSED Christmas
PROPRIETORS Jose Manuel Plana and Patricia Merino

G R A N A D A

MOTRIL

C A S A D E L O S B A T E S
~ COUNTRY HOTEL ~

18600 Motril, Granada
TEL 958 349495 **FAX** 958 349122
E-MAIL rusticae@rusticae.es **WEBSITE** www.casadelosbates.com

THIS PLACE has a bizarre mixture of good, and indifferent qualities: over-the-top grandeur; somewhat surly staff; and a stunning out look to the sea and of the impressive outline of Salobrena Castle. The stately 19th century house is set right in the heart of Granada's 'tropical coast', and it is refreshing to escape the barrenness of the Costa del Sol for this oasis of lush greenery whose micro climate allows the cultivation of plants and fruits you would not expect to find. The gardens are a haven of palms, tropical flowers, and peaceful fountains and waterfalls.

You can eat breakfast or dinner on the stylish covered terrace. Fresh tropical fruit juices are the speciality, the fruit picked from the garden and squeezed straight into your glass. For the colder days, or to escape the sun, there is a rather grand, yet comfortable sitting room crammed with antiques and opulent fabrics.

The bedrooms are large, if a little soulless, but fresh flowers picked from the garden help them along. Two suites, on the top floor, have marble floors (perhaps again a little too grand) and large terraces with heart-stopping views of the surrounding countryside. As you're so close to Granada, and to the sea, there's plenty to keep you busy.

~

NEARBY Granada, Motril, Almeria.
LOCATION off the N340 between Salobrena and Motril, once on that road keep sharp look out for km 329.5 and a small signpost directing you down a very well hidden drive to the hotel on your left, with ample car parking in own grounds
FOOD breakfast, dinner
PRICES €€€€€
ROOMS 5; 2 suites, 3 doubles, all with bath and shower; all rooms have TV, phone, air conditioning, heating
FACILITIES dining room, sitting room, bar, reading room, garden, swimming pool, golf nearby **CREDIT CARDS** AE, DC, MC,V
CHILDREN welcome **DISABLED** suitable access to public rooms and some bedrooms
PETS by arrangement **CLOSED** never **PROPRIETOR** Inaqui Rodriguez Marlin-Feriche

GRANADA

ORGIVA

HOTEL TARAY
～ COUNTRY HOTEL ～

Ctra. Tablate-Albunol, Km 18, 18400 Orgiva (Granada)
TEL 958 784525 **FAX** 958 784531
E-MAIL tarayalp@teleline.es

EVEN BY LOCAL standards, the Taray has a great location. The single-storey building is on a shelf high in a steep valley of the Alpujarra mountains, with a terrific outlook over the fertile river plain below and beautiful, barren sierras beyond. It's on the edge of the market town of Orgiva, in well-planted gardens, with a river nearby. A London reader noted the friendly reception and 'pleasant service', spacious public rooms and adequate bedrooms. Whitewashed walls and terracotta floors dominate the interior, predictably, but happily. Food, from the hotel's own farm, is 'good but not exceptional'. The bedrooms, some with their own sitting rooms and private terraces, are spread along a common terrace which in turn gives on to the lawns. Walk through the gardens to a pond with turtles and ducks to find the large swimming pool with a generous shallow area for children. A reliable, reasonably-priced base for exploring the Alpujarra and its villages.

～

NEARBY Cave country, Granada.
LOCATION on southern outskirts of Orgiva, own grounds and car parking
FOOD breakfast, lunch, dinner
PRICES €€
ROOMS 27; 12 double, 15 in cottages in grounds, all with air conditioning, TV, heating, minibar
FACILITIES TV/music room, cafe-bar, two dining rooms, garden, swimming pool
CREDIT CARDS AC, DC, MC, V
CHILDREN welcome
DISABLED some rooms suitable
PETS not accepted
CLOSED never
PROPRIETOR Eladio Cuadros

ALMERIA

AGUA MARGA

HOTEL EL TIO KIKO

∾ BEACH HOTEL ∾

C/Embarque s/n, 04149 Agua Marga, Almeria
TEL 950 138080 **FAX** 950 138067
WEBSITE www.eltiokiko.com

'SEASIDE CHIC' is what this place is about. From the outside, it looks like a rather non-descript bungalow whose lazy gardener couldn't be bothered to plant much in the flower beds, apart from cacti. But once inside, you will be pleasantly surprised.

Most of the rooms, public and private, overlook the nearby Almerian coastline, and some have a view of the pool and the coast beyond that. The bedrooms are generally cool and airy, with private terraces. Terracotta flag stones underfoot, whitewashed walls and a tasteful use of wood soothes the eyes and other senses. The bathrooms are also very stylishly done out, with clever use of stone, and personal touches such as fresh flowers, beautifully folded towels and sometimes bowls of fruit.

Breakfast and dinner are to a high standard and the view from the dining room is gobsmacking. If you have the energy to get out and about, you won't be disappointed. The Almerian coast line is stunning and relatively unspoilt by tourism, and if you look hard enough, you'll find enchanting and (almost) deserted little beaches.

∾

NEARBY Almeria, Nijar.
LOCATION on the N344 between Almeria, and Huercal-Overa take the N341 in the direction of Carboneras. Take the turning to Agua Amarga. The hotel is in the town on the right with ample parking in own grounds
FOOD breakfast, dinner
PRICES €€€€
ROOMS 27 doubles, all with bath; all rooms have phone, satellite TV, air conditioning, heating
FACILITIES restaurant, sitting room, garden, swimming pool, tennis court, gym, massage
CREDIT CARDS AE, MC, V
CHILDREN no
DISABLED not suitable **PETS** not accepted **CLOSED** Nov-Mar
PROPRIETOR Jose

ALMERIA

PECHINA

BALNEARIO DE SIERRA ALHAMILLA

~ SPA HOTEL ~

04259, Pechina, Almeria
TEL 950 317413 **FAX** 950 160257
WEBSITE www.gratisweb.com/sierra-alhamilla

Nothing could be more relaxing after a day in the car than to slip into this spa hotel's heated swimming pool with its underwater massage jets.

Inside the hotel you can shut yourself away from the bleak surroundings of arid mountains and relax in modest comfort. Peace reigns day and night: the only sound in the patio is the trickle of a fountain.

The original building was raised in 1777 by the Bishop of Almeria on the site of Roman baths. A few years ago the ruins were faithfully reconstructed by the present owner, the polite and quietly-spoken Isidro Pérez.

The dining room is in a barrel-vaulted chamber decorated with patterned tiles and Mudejar plasterwork. The food is well-intentioned and daintily presented on octagonal plates but not of outstanding quality. Breakfast is served under the brick dome of the Bishop's former chapel, looked down upon by an altarpiece.

The bedrooms are old-fashioned with double doors and arched ceilings. Some of the bathrooms suffer from a few niggling, though unimportant, defects.

~

NEARBY Las Millares neolithic necropolis (20km); Mini-Hollywood film sets (22km); solar power station (35km).
LOCATION turn off N 340 for Chuche; hotel is signposted from Pechina; car parking
FOOD breakfast, lunch, dinner
PRICES €€€-€€€€
ROOMS 12 double, 4 suites, 1 special suite, all with bath; all rooms have central heating, TV, telephone
FACILITIES sitting room, dining room, breakfast room, spa facilities
CREDIT CARDS MC, V
CHILDREN accepted
DISABLED easy access
PETS not accepted
CLOSED never
PROPRIETOR Isidro Pérez

ALMERIA

SAN JOSÉ
~ BEACH HOTEL ~

Correo s/n, 04118, San José Almería
TEL 950 380116

SPAIN'S EXTREME south-east corner has escaped the excesses of package holiday tourism and this hotel is ideally located to enjoy some of the last unspoilt beaches on the Mediterranean coast.

The house, reminiscent of a Swiss chalet, was formerly a warehouse for *esparto* – a grass traditionally used to make shoes and baskets.

Large semi-circular windows illuminate the sitting room and allow you to look down on the beach or gaze out to sea. The whole place is full of entertaining details. A parrot in a large cage on a pedestal is kept covered up to stop it talking. Beyond the dining room an intimate salon has a rustic cot, an old barber's chair and a collection of sea urchins and shells.

The best bedrooms are the two on the second floor facing the sea. All the rooms have character with their antique tiled floors and colonial ceiling fans. But the enormous bathrooms are marred by their antiquated plumbing and fittings – which may convince you that the hotel is overpriced.

Tourists fill San José in the summer months. In the winter the place is dead, or peaceful, as you prefer, but the climate is still warm and sunny.

NEARBY Cabo de Gata nature reserve; Almeria (40km).
LOCATION on the beach in San José; garden and car parking
FOOD breakfast, lunch, dinner
PRICES €€€-€€€€
ROOMS 8 double with bath; all rooms have ceiling fan, safe, TV
FACILITIES dining room, bar, meeting rooms; terrace, private beach, solarium, sitting room
CREDIT CARDS MC, V
CHILDREN accepted
DISABLED access difficult
PETS not accepted
CLOSED Oct to Mar
MANAGER Eduardo G. Zárate

ALMERIA

FINCA LISTONERO
~ COUNTRY HOTEL ~

Cortijo Grande, Turre, Almeria
TEL and FAX 950 479094
E-MAIL listonero@wanadoo.es

RUN BY TWO delightfully eccentric ex-restaurateurs, David and Graham, Finca Listonero is a little haven cluttered with curiosities and trinkets. The building is a converted 300-year-old farmhouse, which adds to the already overwhelming character of the place. The views over the Sierra Cabrera mountains above Mojacar and the natural reserve that surrounds the property are stunning and can be seen from certain rooms in the house and from the pool/garden area. Both the energetic, and the not so, will find plenty to do: with three golf courses in close proximity this is a putter's paradise. However there is also riding, walking, four-wheel drive off-road tours and the beautiful beach at Mojacar is only 20 minutes away. You might not even feel like leaving the Finca, as it really is extremely relaxing. The decoration is riotous and fun, with a stuffed swan in the entrance hall, drapes from the rafters or the naughty prints in the dining room. The public rooms are wonderfully cosy and comfortable - and there's a terrace. The food cooked by David is ambitious, delicious and complemented by an interesting wine list. The bedrooms are all individually decorated and bursting with colour and warmth, as are the bathrooms (don't be surprised to find a hidden shower behind large double mirrors).

~

NEARBY Mojacar, Sierra Cabrera, Nijar.
LOCATION come off the N340 at junction 520 to Mojacar, along that road look out for signs to Cortijo Grande, take that turn and the Finca is along that road on the right with ample car parking
FOOD breakfast, lunch, dinner
PRICES €€€-€€€€
ROOMS 5 doubles, all with bath and shower; all rooms have air conditioning, heating, phone **FACILITIES** dining room, sitting room, bar, reading room, garden, swimming pool **CREDIT CARDS** MC, V **CHILDREN** preferable over 15 years old
DISABLED access difficult **PETS** by arrangement **CLOSED** kitchen on Sundays
PROPRIETORS David Rice and Graeme Gibson

CADIZ

ARCOS DE LA FRONTERA

LA CASA GRANDE

~ TOWN HOTEL ~

Maldonado 10, Arcos de la Frontera, 11630 Cadiz
Tel 956 703930 **Fax** 956 717095
E-mail lacasagrande@lacasagrande.net **Website** www.lacasagrande.net

BUILT IN 1729 by Fransisco Javier Nunez de Prado Lopez Maldonado, the Casa Grande is concealed behind a massive and magnificent metal-studded wooden door. It's a stylish little haven, compared to some of the rather minimalist traditional Spanish interiors we've seen.

Don't be put off by the hotel's very small size, or the way decorative objects seem to be piled at will in corners and crannies, as this is part of the charm. The decoration seems to be Moroccan-influenced, and is remarkably successful. A small sitting room/library is crammed with books and has a quirky working fireplace, little Moroccan lamps create a pleasing glow and the chairs are deliciously comfortable.

You have to climb quite a few stairs to reach the top-floor bedroom – not ideal for those with small children, or for the elderly or disabled. The bedrooms are small, but boldly decorated in vibrant colours; fabrics are fun and stylish. All have mosquito nets hanging over the beds: even if you don't need them, they're an attractive feature. Bathrooms are a better size, and a model of how to combine modern equipment with traditional good taste.

Finally, you get to the roof terrace, which has spectacular views of the vale of the River Guadalete and (close at hand) the sandstone towers of the churches of Santa Maria and San Pedro.

~

NEARBY churches of Santa Maria and San Pedro, Jerez, Seville, views from the 'Pena de Arcos'.
LOCATION set in small street ('Maldonado') beside the churches of Santa Maria and San Pedro; limited car parking in main square, ten minute walk to the hotel
FOOD breakfast
PRICES €€€
ROOMS 5; 3 doubles, 2 suites with bath; all rooms have air conditioning, central heating, phone, mosquito nets, hairdriers (on request), TV, radio
FACILITIES sitting room, reading room, terrace
CREDIT CARDS V **CHILDREN** welcome **DISABLED** not suitable **PETS** No **CLOSED** Jan-Feb
PROPRIETOR Elena Posa

CADIZ

CORTIJO BARRANCO
∼ COUNTRY HOTEL ∼

El Bosque km 5.700, 11630 Arcos de la Frontera
TEL 956 231402 **FAX** 956 231209
E-MAIL reservas@cortijobarranco.com **WEBSITE** www.cortijobarranco.com

JUST A FEW kilometers away from Arcos de la Frontera is Cortijo Barranco, converted from a traditional Andalusian olive mill dating from 1754. The bedrooms and bathrooms are sparsely decorated but comfortable, typical of an Andalusian Cortijo, yet clean and cool. Some have inter-connecting doors, perfect for families. Most of the rooms have exceptional views of the surrounding countryside. All are on the second floor, which looks down into the beautiful lush internal courtyard, where you can eat, drink or just relax in the shade with a book.

A games room on the bedroom floor offers plenty of games and books to entertain all ages on the occasional rainy day. From here you can see down into the well-kept garden with its sizeable pool, which has a convenient soft drinks machine. It is essential to request in advance which meals you wish to eat here as this is a small operation and the staff need time to prepare. To one side of the Cortijo are some cosy self-catering cottage/appartments sharing access to the pool and other facilities. For the energetic, the Cortijo can organize riding, hiking, mountain biking and golf.

∼

NEARBY Arcos de la Frontera, Jerez (35 min), Seville (1 hour).
LOCATION just off the A372 from Arcos de la Frontera on the way to El Bosque, hotel is 5 km on the left with ample car parking in own grounds
FOOD breakfast, lunch, dinner (book in advance)
PRICES €€€
ROOMS 15 doubles (with the option of up to 6 beds in some), 5 apartments all with bath; all rooms have fans
FACILITIES dining room, sitting room, games room, garden, swimming pool, tennis court (planned for next year)
CREDIT CARDS MC, V
CHILDREN welcome
DISABLED not suitable **PETS** welcome by arrangement
CLOSED never
PROPRIETOR Genaro Gil Amian

CADIZ

CORTIJO FAIN

~ ANDALUCIAN VILLA ~

11630, Arcos de la Frontera, Cádiz.
TEL 956 231396 **FAX** 956 231961
E-MAIL cortijofain@eresmas.com **WEBSITE** www.cortijofain.es.eresmas.com

THIS LANDOWNER'S residence, or cortijo, stands in the middle of a vast olive grove not far from one of the most spectacular of the White Towns. The silence is only broken by the odd tractor ploughing between the trees.

The house and outbuildings enclose a pretty courtyard with a well and drinking trough in the middle. Most of the rooms are upstairs in the main house. They are of varying shapes and sizes but all warmly furnished with antiques, iron or brass bedsteads, crocheted bedspreads, books and flowers. On the first floor landing is a small household chapel.

Equally inviting are the rustically decorated public rooms littered with oil paintings and more antiques. The cafeteria is in the old stables. From the sitting room, a door leads into the library: an even more relaxing room lined with 7,000 leather-bound volumes. The dining room has a glass-enclosed porch opening on to the garden.

From the back of the house a path leads across the lawn between the olive trees to a large, curving swimming pool crossed by a hump-backed bridge.

~

NEARBY Arcos de la Frontera (3km); Grazalema (53km). Carretera de Algar, Km 3.
LOCATION from Arcos take the road towards El Algar and turn off left (signposted) after 3 km; garden and car parking
FOOD breakfast, lunch, dinner
PRICES €€€€
ROOMS 3 double, 1 single, 2 suites, 1 apartment, 3 family rooms all with bath; all rooms have air conditioning, radiator
FACILITIES dining room, sitting room, bar, swimming pool
CREDIT CARDS AE, MC, V
CHILDREN welcome
DISABLED 3 ground floor rooms
PETS accepted
CLOSED never
PROPRIETOR Soledad Gil

CADIZ

ARCOS DE LA FRONTERA

EL CONVENTO
~ CONVERTED CONVENT ~

Calle Maldonado 2, 11630, Arcos de la Frontera, Cádiz
TEL 956 702333 **FAX** 956 704128

WE HAVE LONG counted this hotel, in part of a convent in the old town of Arcos, as one of our favourites in Andalucia. Readers have subsequently confirmed this judgement: a recent reporter says it would 'live long in any visitor's memory'; the only carping note is from those who notice its inclination for self-congratulation. Extensive changes have been made to provide more spacious public areas and a café.

Certainly the owners, José Antonio Roldán and his wife María Moreno, could not be more welcoming; but neither does Sr Roldán miss an opportunity to promote his enterprise. The restaurant walls (and others) display numerous press cuttings.

The bedrooms are homely, and sometimes decorated with ingenuous taste. Each year one of them is formally dedicated to a 'famous' son of Arcos. Six of the rooms have terraces and most enjoy panoramic views to rival those of the nearby Parador. Breakfast is served in the convent's former sacristy – a white arched chamber – and there is bar service during the day. For other meals you have to stroll round to the Roldán's garlanded restaurant, one minute's walk away, in the attractive 16th century Valdespino palace. Specialities include asparagus soup, partridge in almond sauce and home-made desserts.

~

NEARBY churches of Santa María and San Pedro; Jerez (30 km).
LOCATION on a tiny back street, past church and Parador; car parking in main square
FOOD breakfast, lunch, dinner
PRICES €€-€€€
ROOMS 10 double, 1 single, all with bath; all rooms have central heating, air conditioning, phone, satellite TV, hairdrier
FACILITIES 2 dining rooms, bar, 2 terraces
CREDIT CARDS AE, DC, MC, V
CHILDREN welcome **DISABLED** access difficult
PETS not accepted **CLOSED** never
PROPRIETOR María Moreno

CADIZ

HACIENDA EL SANTISCAL
~ COUNTRY HOUSE HOTEL ~

Avda. El Santiscal, 129 (Iago de Arcos), 11630 Arcos de la Frontera, Cadiz
TEL 956 708313 **FAX** 956 708268
E-MAIL reservas@santiscal.com **WEBSITE** www.santiscal.com

T HIS HAS BEEN a regrettable ommission from earlier editions of the guide, but we're pleased, on the recommendation of Jenny Rees, author of our *Southern France* and *Ireland* guides, to include it in this new edition. It's a well-restored, dignified, whitewashed 15thC manor house – but that's only the start. Jenny was struck by its lovely position, with views over the nearby lake, and of nearby Arcos; and by the charm of its owners, Hussein, an Egyptian, and his Andalucian wife, Franchesca. They also have a restaurant in Arcos, which, along with the Hacienda, of course, is supplied with fresh vegetables and herbs from the Hacienda's garden. The public spaces are decorated in authentic Hacienda style, offering the understated good taste that we value much more than plush smartness. The conservatory eating area is a particularly charming, somewhat unusual structure. Bedrooms are of a similar standard, all individual, air conditioned, and with views of the lake or hills. For amusement, there's the (circular) swimming pool, riding, biking or walking.

~

NEARBY Arcos; Jerez, Gibraltar, Ronda, Malaga and Seville within driving distance.
LOCATION ten minutes from Arcos, signposted from the the N-342 outside the town; in own grounds with private car parking
FOOD breakfast, lunnch, dinner
PRICE €€€
ROOMS 11 double, 1 suite, all with bath, heating, air conditioning.
FACILITIES sitting room, dining room, bar, gardens, swimming pool.
CREDIT CARDS AE, DC, MC, V
CHILDREN over 12
DISABLED not suitable
PETS only small dogs by agreement in advance
CLOSED never
PROPRIETORS Franchesca Gallardo Carrasco

CADIZ

ARCOS DE LA FRONTERA

HOTEL LOS OLIVOS
∼ TOWN HOTEL ∼

Paseo de Boliches 30, 11630, Arcos de la Frontera, Cádiz
TEL 956 700811 **FAX** 956 702018
E-MAIL losolivosdelc@terra.es **WEBSITE** twww.losolivos.profesionales.org

THE RECEPTIONIST at the Olivos told us (in good English) that the hotel is usually full; it is easy to see why. It is an attractive place, even from the outside – built in typical Arcos style with whitewashed walls, yellow tiled roofs and iron grills over the windows, and equipped with pots of geraniums on arched balconies. But it is the interior that really captivates.

The rooms are built around an internal courtyard; café-style tables and chairs are set out in the middle, under a palm tree. The breakfast room is decorated in the same dark green furniture and doubles up as a bar; it looks on to a tiny patio containing an old stone well. Behind the glass arches surrounding the courtyard is a cosy alcove with wicker sofas and armchairs, and bowls of fresh flowers.

The bedrooms are light and airy – comfortable, but not cluttered with furniture. All have different cane bedsteads, pale covers and curtains, and mats covering stone-tiled floors. The two front bedrooms have balconies with sweeping views over the plains and the nearby olive-groves from which the hotel takes its name.

∼

NEARBY churches of Santa María and San Pedro, castle; Jerez, Cádiz, Ronda within driving distance.
LOCATION on road up to Parador, overlooking Guada-lete plains; car parking in garage (Pts 700 per 24 hours)
FOOD breakfast,buffet
PRICES €€-€€€
ROOMS 17 double, 2 single; all with bath and shower; all rooms have central heating, air conditioning, phone, TV, minibar, radio
FACILITIES sitting rooms, TV room, bar/breakfast room
CREDIT CARDS AE, DC, MC, V
CHILDREN welcome
DISABLED ground floor rooms **PETS** not accepted
CLOSED never
PROPRIETOR Jose A Roloan

CADIZ

HOTEL MARQUES DE TORRESOTO
~ TOWN HOTEL ~

Calle Marques de Torresoto 4 11630 Arcos de la Frontera, Cadiz
TEL 956 700717 **FAX** 956 704205
WEBSITE www.hmdetorresoto.com/www.hmdetorresoto.yahoo.es

ARCOS DE LA FRONTERA is a delightful warren of narrow streets and (confusing) one way systems. Getting around by foot is a joy (although there are some steep places): there are plenty of interesting corners to discover by accident – as indeed we did with the Marques de Torresoto. Its lavishly decorated *capilla* (chapel) caught our eye as we walked past, complete with icons and strewn flowers.

But the main selling point of this hotel is the views from the bedroom windows over the Guadalete plains and beyond. The rooms themselves are nothing special – decorated in the typical, rather sparse Spanish style - but clean, cool and well equipped. Bathrooms are large, and share the spectacular views.

Downstairs, off the courtyard with its fountain, there is a rather charming small bar that can be reached through the hotel or from the street. It's manned by the cheerful manager of the hotel.

Breakfast, lunch and dinner can be eaten in the delightful tiled courtyard or in your bedroom. There are also some great eating places in the neighbouring streets, which we recommend you visit – and don't miss the view from the main square.

~

NEARBY Seville, Jerez, Cadiz.
LOCATION set down a small side street not far from the main square (5 minute walk) where you should park your car
FOOD breakfast, lunch, dinner
PRICES €€
ROOMS 15; with bath; all rooms have TV, phone, air conditioning, hairdrier
FACILITIES dining room, sitting room, bar
CREDIT CARDS DC, MC, V
CHILDREN welcome
DISABLED not suitable **PETS** No
CLOSED never
PROPRIETOR Juan Diaz

CADIZ

EL PUERTO DE SANTA MARIA

HOTEL DUQUES DE MEDINACELI
~ TOWN HOTEL ~

Plaza de los Jazmines No2-11500 El Puerto de Santa Maria, Cadiz
TEL 956 860777 **FAX** 956 542687
EMAIL dmedinaceli@jale.com **WEBSITE** www.jale.com/dmedinaceli

ON THE FACE OF IT, this is a rather grand five-star hotel with a stuffy restaurant and rather bland bedrooms: one we wouldn't normally include. However: it has an atmospheric location, at the entrance to the historic quarter of Puerta Santa Maria, and was once the home of the Dukes of Medinaceli, the family whose history was for some 400 years (until the early 18thC) so closely linked with that of Cadiz. In more recent times, various families have had tenure, the latest being the Irish Terrys, who built up a notable wine collection and constructed a beautiful *bodega* that can be seen from the cosy library. Museum-worthy works of art and historic costumes line the walls. And the hotel has an impressive botanical garden which has just won an award.

The bedrooms are somewhat ordinary, but the bathrooms are glitzy, with showers that massage and enough toiletries to fill a second wash bag.

If you don't want to dine in the restaurant, there are some great seafood restaurants down by the port: you can hand-pick your fish and choose how you want it cooked. Breakfast is unusually generous, with apparently endless choices of pastries, fruit and cooked dishes.

~

NEARBY Arcos de la Frontera, Cadiz, Seville, Jerez.
LOCATION from the NIV from Seville go through Puerta Santa Maria on the main street, bear right at the square and the hotel is on the left before the large roundabout, with ample car parking in own grounds
FOOD breakfast, lunch, dinner
PRICES €€€€€
ROOMS 28; 4 doubles, 5 superior doubles, 18 junior suites, 1 Presidential suite all with bath and shower; all rooms have satellite TV, phone, mini bar, safe, modem points
FACILITIES dining room, sitting room, bar, reading room, terrace, botanical gardens, swimming pool, library, sauna, chapel
CREDIT CARDS AE,DC, MC, V **CHILDREN** welcome
DISABLED facilities available **PETS** no **CLOSED** never
MANAGER Juan Sendra

CADIZ

CASA CONVENTO DE ALMORAIMA
~ COUNTRY HOTEL ~

La Almoraima, 11350, Castellar de la Frontera, Cádiz
TEL 956 693002 **FAX** 956 693214
WEBSITE www.la-almoraima.com

IN THE HEART OF Los Alcornocales Park, this magnificent building has an interesting history dating back to 1603 when the then Countess of Castellar founded the convent for the Order of the Merced. Two and a half centuries later, the Count of Castellar (Duke of Medinaceli) turned the convent into a hunting palace. Relics of both are still prominent, with a rather grand ornate *capilla* (chapel) tucked off the courtyard and numerous hunting spoils proudly adorning the walls. The bedrooms are large and exceedingly spacious, although not decorated in the best of taste, and the same can be said of the bathrooms. However, the rooms have working fire places for the winter and much-needed air conditioning for the summer. You can't get bored. If you like snooker, there are two billiard rooms; there's also golf and plenty of board games plus a pool and a tennis court, and Land Rovers in which to drive around the National Park. The nearest town, Castellar de la Frontera, is 8 km away. The food relies heavily on game, as you would expect, but is well prepared; there's a reasonable wine selection. Settle down afterwards in one of the comfy sitting rooms, which have roaring fires in the winter. There are plans to add extra bedrooms, which will increase the size and perhaps change the atmosphere of the place – reports especially welcome.

~

NEARBY Estepona, Jimena de la Frontera, Rhonda, Algeciras.
LOCATION in Castellar de la Frontera turn left at roundabout with a fountain, cross over bridge and take the first right. The hotel is up that road on the right, in own grounds with ample car parking
FOOD breakfast, lunch, dinner
PRICES €€€€
ROOMS 17; 13 doubles, 4 singles, with bath and shower; all rooms have air conditioning, TV, phone, heating
FACILITIES 2 dining rooms, 2 sitting rooms, bar, garden, swimming pool, tennis court, chapel, 2 billiard rooms, mini golf **CREDIT CARDS** AE, DC, MC, V **CHILDREN** welcome **DISABLED** not suitable **PETS** No **CLOSED** never **PROPRIETOR** Juan Montoya

CADIZ

SANLUCAR DE BARRAMEDA

POSADA DE PALACIO
~ TOWN HOUSE ~

Calle Caballeros 11, 11540, Sanlúcar de Barrameda, Cádiz
TEL 956 365060 FAX 956 365060
E-MAIL posadadepalacio@terra.es WEBSITE www.posadadepalacio.com

ANTONIO AND RENATA Navarrete set up this pension in 1986, when they moved from Switzerland. It is a typical Andalucian town house, near the Bombadilla sherry bodegas in the old part of the town. In fact, one of the *bodegas* has just been turned into a resaturant for the hotel serving traditional Spanish dishes. If you get lost, follow your nose; an overpowering smell of Sanlúcar's famous manzanilla lingers around the warehouses.

The guest-house is built around a courtyard of original stone floor-tiles. Most of the bedrooms are in this part of the building, including two ground floor suites. All the rooms are clean and comfortable – and unconventional, adding to their charm. Those we saw were very spacious – we had a cavernous bathroom, even bigger than our bedroom. We ate a superb home-made breakfast in our room overlooking the tiny garden.

The public rooms are full of interesting objects that the couple have collected over the years; an old grinding wheel hangs next to modern film posters in the bar, miniature pictures decorate the walls, and fresh flowers abound. You are constantly reminded that this is a home as well as a hotel. Tables are set outside under the wistaria, and up ivy-covered steps, four new rooms look on to a large stone sun-terrace. 'Truly enchanting', says a reader.

~

NEARBY Castle, palace, sherry *bodegas*, beach.
LOCATION near castle and palace, in old part of town; car parking on street
FOOD breakfast, dinner
PRICES €€€-€€€€
ROOMS 32 double, all with bath; all rooms have phone
FACILITIES sitting room, TV room, bar/breakfast room, terrace, dining room, swimming pool, restaurant
CREDIT CARDS MC, V
CHILDREN welcome
DISABLED ground floor rooms **PETS** accepted
CLOSED Jan and Feb
PROPRIETOR Carmen Diez Brasero

CADIZ

TARIFA

HOTEL DOS MARES

∼ BEACH HOTEL ∼

11380 Tarifa, Cadiz
TEL 956 684035 **FAX** 956 681078
E-MAIL info@dosmares .com / reservas@dosmares .com

WITH 46 ROOMS this place is well outside our normal size limit, but it's here because of its undoubted charm. Right on the edge of the beach, you can roll out of bed on to the sand for kite surfing and windsurfing (Tarifa is rated Europe's top windsurfing location). The bedrooms (apart from the ones in the hotel building) are in small bungalows with private terraces and their own bathrooms. All are decorated individually in bright, vibrant colours that are not over the top and seem to suit the atmosphere of the place beautifully.

The exterior, like the interior, is bursting with colour and life. The restaurants overlook the beach and are small and intimate, serving delicious variations of Mediterranean food and an impressive array of cocktails. Next to the hotel are the stables: you can gallop the horses up and down the beach in the early morning or evening. After the tennis court, paddle court, beach volley ball or gym, you may need to finish off the day with a relaxing float in the pool, or a massage. If you want to get out and about, Tarifa town is only a ten minute drive away, with lovely little shops and delicious fresh seafood restaurants.

∼

NEARBY Seville, Tarifa, Cadiz, Algeciras, Gibraltar, Morrocco.
LOCATION just off the N340 above Tarifa by Km 79.5, with ample car parking
FOOD breakfast, lunch, dinner
PRICES €€€€
ROOMS 46; all doubles with some rooms having 3/4 beds for families, 4 suites, all with bath and shower; all rooms have TV, phone, air conditioning
FACILITIES sitting room, 2 bars, garden, swimming pool, tennis court, paddle court, volley ball, horse riding, 2 restaurants, watersports
CREDIT CARDS AE, DC, MC, V
CHILDREN welcome
DISABLED access possible to some rooms **PETS** No
Closed never
PROPRIETORS Roberto Van Looy and Eugenia Nunez

CADIZ

TARIFA

HURRICANE
~ BEACH HOTEL ~

Carretera de Málaga a Cádiz, 11380, Tarifa
TEL 956 684919 **FAX** 956 680329

WELL-HEELED thirty-somethings make up the clientele of the hip and casual Hurricane Hotel. Its name more than hints at the prime attraction. Strong winds make the southern end of the Costa de la Luz the best windsurfing spot in mainland Europe, and you can learn to ride or hire a board at the windsurfing school right next to the hotel.

The Hurricane's snazzy gym and riding stables also lure sporty landlubbers, and the hotel offers many enticements for indolent types too. A gorgeous palm, hibiscus and eucalyptus filled garden envellops two swimming pools (one set aside for adults only), and leads to a narrow but pretty and secluded sandy beach. The Spanish/Italian food has a good reputation, especially for its fish dishes. When it's warm, dinners are served under towering Moorish arches on a romantic terrace overlooking the main pool, and the beach café does excellent salads and pastas for lunch.

Standard bedrooms are simple but tasteful; avoid those facing inland as they suffer from their proximity to the busy main road. Suites are worth paying extra for. They either come with private gardens, or are grand and exotic – maybe with keyhole arches over the bath and bold pictures of tigers on the walls.

~

NEARBY Tarifa (7km); Bolonia Roman ruins (16km); Gibraltar (50km).
LOCATION Between N340 coastal road and beach, 7km northwest of Tarifa; ample car parking
FOOD breakfast, lunch, dinner
PRICES €€-€€€€
ROOMS 38; 33 double and single, 3 family suites, 2 luxury suites all with bath and shower; all rooms have phone, air conditioning, minibar; suites have TV
FACILITIES 2 bars, dining room, 2 swimming pools, gym, sauna, windsurfing, horse riding, mountain bikes, massage, yoga
CREDIT CARDS AE, DC, M, V
CHILDREN welcome **DISABLED** limited access **PETS** accepted **Closed** never
PROPRIETOR Michael, Peter and James Whaley

CADIZ

TARIFA

HOTEL PUNTA SUR

∼ BEACH HOTEL ∼

11380 Tarifa, Cadiz
TEL 956 684326 **FAX** 956 680472
E-MAIL puntasur@cherrytel.com

Something of a gamble, this: when we visited, the Punta Sur was undergoing major restoration and redecoration so we could not get a full impression of how it would turn out. It will be the sister hotel to the well-known Hurricane, also at Tarifa, and likewise under the management of the capable Whaley brothers. There's no reason to think that it won't be as good as the Hurricane.

The rooms are a fair size, with ample beds and bathrooms, some with small terraces and views over the beach, which is a five-minute walk away. Breakfast, lunch and dinner will be served in the restaurant – typical Spanish food, plus an eclectic selection of European and Mediterranean dishes. Or you could have a pool-side barbecue. Spreading gardens, an impressive pool and a tennis court dominate the back of the hotel.

Tarifa is a very popular place: on our last visit every hotel in the vicinity was fully booked and even the Punta Sur had reservations for the next season while still under restoration. So please book early to avoid disappointment. We'll be especially interested to hear of readers' experiences here.

∼

NEARBY Tarifa, Algeciras, Gibraltar, Morocco.
LOCATION just off the N340 at Km 76, with ample car parking in own grounds
FOOD breakfast, lunch, dinner
PRICES €€€€-€€€€€
ROOMS 32; 22 double, 10 suites, all with bath
FACILITIES restaurant, bar, garden, swimming pool, tennis court, patio
CREDIT CARDS AE, MC, V
CHILDREN welcome
DISABLED easy access to bedrooms and restaurant
CLOSED never
PROPRIETORS Whaley Brothers

CADIZ

TARIFA

LA SACRISTIA
~ TOWN HOTEL ~

San Donato 8. 11380 Tarifa, Cadiz
TEL 956 685182 **FAX** 956 685182
E-MAIL tarifa@lasacristia.net **WEBSITE** www.lasacristia.net

IN THE HEART of Tarifa's old quarter is this delightfully small but impeccably done out hotel, with a refinement that's rare along this coast. Downstairs by reception you will find tables and chairs crammed together and spilling outside: a charming, informal area for drinks and nibbles. The floor is transparent, with old amphora underneath – you think you're about to step into them.

Moroccan lamps, trinkets, belts and other clothes are sold in a small shop on the ground floor and used for decorations in other parts of the hotel. If something catches your eye, ask if it's for sale – you might be pleasantly surprised. Up a very narrow wooden staircase are the bedrooms. Although some are smallish, a feeling of space is maximized by the clean lines of the furnishings and the simple good taste of the decoration. Wrought-iron or wooden bed frames are swathed with mosquito nets and the bathrooms have mosaic tiles echoing the Moroccan theme downstairs.

Breakfast and dinner can be eaten in the fragrant little courtyard. Or you can explore Tarifa's waterfront with its fresh fish restaurants.

~

NEARBY Morocco, Gibraltar, Algeciras.
LOCATION in Tarifa's old town. Park in the town centre wherever possible as cars cannot get down the narrow streets leading to the hotel. Approx 5 minute walk
FOOD breakfast, dinner
PRICES €€€€
ROOMS 10 doubles, all with bath and shower; all rooms have phone, air conditioning, central heating
FACILITIES dining room, sitting room, bar, terrace
CREDIT CARDS AE, DC, MC, V
CHILDREN welcome
DISABLED not suitable
PETS small dogs by arrangement
CLOSED never
PROPRIETORS Miguel Aguerri and Bosco Herrero

CADIZ

100% FUN

~ BEACH HOTEL ~

11380 Tarifa, Cadiz
TEL 956 680330 **FAX** 956 680013
E-mail 100x100@tnet **WEBSITE** www.tarifanet/100fun

A HOTEL FOR THE young, or the young at heart. If you're looking for culture, repose or exquisite restaurants, don't come here: it's a lively place, a cross between a hostel (because of the informal, youthful atmosphere) and a beach hotel – guests stay in huts spread out across beautiful gardens close to the sea.

Reception is in a surf shop offering a great collection of bikinis, boardies and other surfing paraphernalia, and where you can book windsurfing, kite surfing and many other sea and sand activities. Our only real reservation about 100% Fun is its position right on the Cadiz–Tarifa main road. But just the other side is the great stretch of beach which is the place's *raison d'etre*.

The thatched huts are named after maritime terms such as Wind and Wave, and painted a fun terracotta colour. There are small terraces in front; some have bathrooms, others showers. The restaurant has a Tex Mex feel, and the menu consists mostly of themed food, although there is a choice of more interesting dishes. If you want to head into town for a slightly more sophisticated dinner, Tarifa is about ten minutes away by car.

~

NEARBY Tarifa, Gibraltar, Algeciras.
LOCATION just off the N340 from Cadiz to Tarifa around the 76km mark, in own grounds with ample car parking
FOOD breakfast, lunch, dinner
PRICES €€€€
ROOMS 22; mixture of double, triple, quadruple and superior double rooms, all with bath or shower; all rooms have TV, fan
FACILITIES bar, garden, restaurant, swimming pool
CREDIT CARDS DC, MC, V
CHILDREN welcome
DISABLED suitable **PETS** by arrangement
CLOSED Nov-Mar
PROPRIETOR Barry J. Pussell

CADIZ

VEJER DE LA FRONTERA

CONVENTO DE SAN FRANCISCO

~ CONVERTED CONVENT ~

La Plazuela, 11150, Vejer de la Frontera, Cádiz
TEL 956 451001 **FAX** 956 451004

VEJER IS A DELIGHTFUL medieval town crowning a solitary hill near the coast. In the old part of town, the Felipe brothers have lovingly converted a 17thC convent into an unusual hotel; a set of photographs in the echoing *taberna* tell the story of the renovations. Many of the remains have been preserved – a Roman mosaic in the hall, a cabinet of medieval pottery on the stairs, the old choir stalls and frescos in the sitting room. The bedrooms still have their original stone arches visible in the walls and the furniture has been designed in harmony – arched bed-heads, stripped pine desks, wooden shutters. The result is effective – the simplicity of a nun's cell with the facilities of a modern hotel.

The refectory still serves as a dining room, still with wooden benches and tables lining the walls. Bright modern cushions and abstract modern paintings add a splash of colour. Our inspector's meal, the *menu del dia,* was excellent, piping hot and served by cheerful staff. Outside the dining room is an obscure metal sculpture, two floors high. The centre-piece of the Convento is the 'choir hall' – a great place to sit when the sun filters through the windows in the early morning.

~

NEARBY Castle, churches, Jewish Quarter.
LOCATION on small square in old part of town, round corner from main street on cliff edge; car parking on main street
FOOD breakfast, lunch, dinner
PRICES €€-€€€
ROOMS 18 double, 5 single, one family room; all with bath; all rooms have electric heating, phone, TV
FACILITIES dining room, sitting room, cafeteria, bar
CREDIT CARDS DC, MC, V
CHILDREN welcome
DISABLED lift/elevator **PETS** not accepted
CLOSED never
MANAGER Jesús Felipe Gallego

M A L A G A

BENALMADENA PUEBLO

L A F O N D A D E B E N A L M A D E N A
⮞ BEACH SIDE HOTEL ⮜

Calle Santo Domingo, 7 29639 Benalmadena Pueblo, Malaga
TEL 952 568324 **FAX** 952 568273
E-MAIL lafonda@fondahotel.com **WEBSITE** www.fondahotel.com

Luckily, this hotel is just outside sprawling, smelly Malaga. Hidden away in a corner of Benalmadena Pueblo, a picturesque little town on the outskirts, you may lose heart trying to find it in the maze of little streets: but don't despair - helpful locals will show you the way.

The exterior is nothing special, with a small café and parking in front and underneath. Inside, you will be pleasantly surprised. From all corners of the inner courtyard hang fresh flowers, which soften the otherwise stark entrance hall. The balconies, breakfast room and most of the bedrooms have spectacular panoramic views over the beach and ocean, perfect for catching some rays. If you can't be bothered with the beach, there is a generously sized pool surrounded by the bedrooms on different levels and open to the elements so you can make the most of the sun.

The bedrooms are ordinary - a bit chintzy and stark - but comfortable, light and cool in the heat of summer. Downstairs is the charming little restaurant, serving food prepared by the Benalmadena catering school (typical Andalusian dishes) at lunch time only. Reception will advise on where to go for dinner, and outdoor activities: golf, riding and watersports.

⮝

NEARBY Malaga, Fuengirola, Marbella.
LOCATION leave the N340 at the Benalmadena exit and follow signs for the town. Once in the town, turn on to Calle Santo Domingo and follow the road for approx 600 metres and hotel is on the left with ample car parking in own grounds
FOOD breakfast
PRICES €€€€
ROOMS 26; all doubles with bath; all rooms have phone, air conditioning, heating
FACILITIES dining room, bar, swimming pool
CREDIT CARDS AE, DC, MC, V
CHILDREN welcome
DISABLED not suitable **PETS** No
CLOSED never
PROPRIETOR Jose Antonio Garcia

MALAGA

BENAOJAN

MOLINO DEL SANTO
~ OLD WATER MILL ~

Barriada Estación, 29370, Benaoján, Málaga
TEL 952 167151**FAX** 952 167327
E-MAIL molino@logiccontrol.es **WEBSITE** www.molinodelsanto.com

A SHORT DRIVE (or train-ride) from Ronda is the sleepy village of Benaoján, perched on a herb-scented mountainside, surrounded by olive and almond groves. Its water-mill, beside the bubbling stream below the village, was converted into a hotel in 1987 by a young English couple, Andy Chapell and Pauline Elkin, who fled the rat-race in favour of this idyllic spot. We could see why as soon as we arrived, on a timeless Sunday morning when the guests were eating a leisurely buffet breakfast under the willow trees on the stone terrace. Dinner is also served out here in the summer (a delicious-sounding set menu with plenty of choice and vegetarian options). To the amusement of the locals, guests also get a real English tea with home-made cakes.

Inside, the rooms are comfortable and home-like; the sitting-area still has some of its original trappings – such as the old grinding stones. The bedrooms vary in size (some take extra beds) and are simply furnished, with bright locally made rugs. Fifteen have small terraces overlooking a beautiful swimming pool, shaded by willow, fig and quince trees.

Andy and Pauline provide information for excursions to all the local sights.We've just heard from a couple who visited three times in three years and still 'can't praise it highly enough.'

~

NEARBY cave of La Pileta – paleolithic art; white towns.
LOCATION near railway station; with gardens, car parking
FOOD breakfast, lunch, tea, dinner
PRICES €€€-€€€€€
ROOMS 18 double all with bath, 5 suites/family rooms; all rooms have central heating, air conditioning, tea and coffee facilities
FACILITIES dining room, bar, terrace; solar heated pool
CREDIT CARDS DC, MC, V
CHILDREN welcome
DISABLED access difficult **PETS** not accepted **CLOSED** 19 Nov to 18 Feb
PROPRIETORS Andy Chapell and Pauline Elkin

MALAGA

ESTEPONA

ALBERO LODGE
~ TOWN/BEACH HOTEL ~

Calle Tamesis 16, 29689 Estepona, Malaga
Tel 952 880700 **Fax** 952 885238
E-mail info@alberolodge.com **Website** www.alberolodge.com

DEFINITELY CHARMING and small, except for the location. It's right in the centre of the Costa Del Sol in Estepona, next door to Malaga, the tourist honey pot of southern Spain and therefore highly commercialized.

Fortunately, the hotel itself is in a small, leafy suburb two minutes walk from the beach. The owner, Marian, did all the decoration of the hotel herself over the last ten years and her individual, eccentric taste really brings the place to life. All the bedrooms are a fair size and all decorated in a geographical theme. The Madras room is kitted out with trinkets, *objets d'art* from India and some serene-looking Buddhas. Many of the other rooms are decorated in calming, restful styles, except the New York room. This looks like a typical Yankee batchelor pad, with a zebra skin bedspread, a bath in the bedroom with a fabulous view, a disco ball in the fireplace and even a small chill-out room behind the bed.

The gardens are lush, with a great pool to lounge by, but if you prefer the sea, take a two-minute walk down around supper time and have dinner overlooking the beach. Take Marian's advice on eating places – the Barraka Beach Restaurant is good, but some of the others are dubious.

~

Nearby Malaga, Sotogrande, Marbella.
Location just off the N340, take the exit after the sign for 164.5 km, loop round on yourself and follow the signs, in own grounds with limited car parking
Food breakfast
Price €€€€
Rooms 9 doubles all with bath and shower; all rooms have modem points, satellite TV, air conditioning, central heating, phone, safe, mini bar
Facilities sitting room, garden, swimming pool, private room terraces
Credit cards AE, DC , MC ,V
Children accepted but more suitable for adults
Disabled couple of ground floor rooms but no special facilities **Pets** No
Closed10th Jan-10th Feb
Proprietor Marian

MALAGA

FRIGILIANA

HOTEL RURAL LA POSADA MORISCA

~ COUNTRY HOTEL ~

29788 Frigiliana, Malaga
TEL 952 534151/952 534336 FAX 952 534339
E-MAIL info@laposadamorisca.com WEBSITE www.laposadamorisca.com

'THE ESSENCE OF a charming small hotel' writes a recent reporter. Oozing charm and personality, this place really stands out for its simple, yet, flawless design and understated good taste. The bedrooms are in small, whitewashed cottages named after herbs, each with its own entrance giving a feeling of seclusion. Every room also has a terrace, with great views of the local town, a wood-burning stove and a bathroom. The decoration is very natural and warm: light bed covers, large earthenware slabs on the floor and hand-made tiles in the bathrooms.

The restaurant is small, but breakfast or dinner can also be had on the terrace in good weather under the shade of calico umbrellas. All the dishes have a Mediterranean twist, with the freshest ingredients from the vegetable garden. Leading on from the terrace is a delightful little pool with great views over the local town of Frigiliana, which is worth exploring. The Costa del Sol is also very close beach life should you want, and Malaga and Marbella are less than an hour away. For the golfers (the Costa del Sol is also known as the Costa del Golf) there are many courses in the area: just ask at reception for information.

~

NEARBY Nerja, Granada, Malaga.
LOCATION take exit 292 off the N340 to Frigiliana, by pass Frigiliana and head towards Torrox. The hotel is on that road (MA105) signposted on the right with limited car parking in own grounds
FOOD breakfast, dinner (restaurant closed on Mondays)
PRICE €€€
ROOMS 12; 2 doubles, 10 twin; all with bath; all rooms have TV, fireplace, phone
FACILITIES dining room, garden, swimming pool
CREDIT CARDS AE, DC, MC ,V
CHILDREN welcome
DISABLED unsuitable PETS by arrangement
CLOSED Jan
PROPRIETOR Sarah Navas Sanchez

MALAGA

LA ALMUNA
~ COUNTRY GUEST HOUSE ~

Apt de Correos 2029480 Gaucin, Malaga
TEL 952 151200 **FAX** 952 151343
WEBSITE www.andalucia.com/gaucin/almuna

'HIGHLY ORIGINAL, rather shabby, yet deliciously comfortable' writes our reporter. Be warned: this guest house is not for those that don't get on with dogs (owner Diana Paget has two charming Staffordshire bull terriers) and not for those who expect everything to be spotlessly clean. Diana treats her guests as if they are close friends or relatives: you feel as if her home is your home, indeed to get to the terrace you have to walk through the kitchen where Diana may well be preparing dinner; you help yourself to a drink as you go.

Off the stunning and lushly planted, cobbled courtyard are the bedrooms. They're small, but bursting with character and colour. Antiques are dotted around everywhere, especially in the bedrooms. There are some spectacular views over the Jimena Valley and as far as the Rif mountains of Morocco.

Down a narrow covered walkway are the stables where you can jump on a horse and explore your surroundings, which are rich in flora and fauna, especially birds and wild flowers. Above the pool is the self-contained 'hay loft', perfect for a family or a small group of friends, which is self-catering unless you make special arrangements with Diana, but does include full use of the pool and the horses.

~

NEARBY Rhonda, Marbella, Sotogrande, Malaga.
LOCATION 45 km from Ronda, just before Gaucin, off the A369. Look out for sign to Almuna. La Almuna is just after the tennis courts on the right with limited parking on own grounds
FOOD breakfast, dinner
PRICE €€
ROOMS 4; 3 double, 1 twin, 1 self contained flat, all with bath
FACILITIES dining room, sitting room, bar, garden, swimming pool, tennis court, terrace, horse riding
CREDIT CARDS not accepted **CHILDREN** welcome **DISABLED** one room although access difficult elsewhere **PETS** by arrangement **CLOSED** never
PROPRIETOR Diana Paget

MALAGA

MALAGA

CORTIJO DE LA REINA
~ COUNTRY HOTEL ~

29013 Malaga
TEL 951 014000 FAX: 951 014049
E-MAIL info@hotelcortijolareina WEBSITE www.hotelcortijolareina

A S WE WENT TO press, this Cortijo was small and charming, but there were plans to increase the number of beds from 26 to 40. We don't believe this will spoil its character, but readers' reports will be especially welcome.

Set high up in beautiful countryside near the Montes de Malaga nature reserve, the hotel has spectacular views to the sea from most rooms. Rustic chic is everywhere, from the quaint Andalusian kitchen, serving traditional food, to the beamed, portrait-hung corridors leading to the bedrooms. You feel as if you're in a grand but lived-in country house, except for the piped music. The bedrooms are bright, vibrant and colourful, with fresh flowers and small fireplaces where they actually light fires in the winter.

The gardens are a little too manicured for our taste (especially with the addition of the mini-golf), but the pool has amazing, panoramic views. A more serious drawback is the Cortijo's popularity with wedding parties. The staff are helpful and only too happy to book golf or tell you about the best walking routes.

~

NEARBY Malaga, Nerja, Ronda.
LOCATION leave the C345 between Malaga and Colmenar at the 548.5 km mark. The hotel is down a long dirt track with ample car parking in own grounds
FOOD breakfast, lunch, dinner
PRICE €€€€€
ROOMS 12; 1 suite, 9 doubles, 2 twins, all with bath and shower; all rooms have safe, TV, air conditioning, heating, phone, mini-bar
FACILITIES dining room, sitting room, reading room, garden, swimming pool, tennis court, billiard room, TV room
CREDIT CARDS AE, DC, MC, V
CHILDREN welcome
DISABLED access difficult
PETS by arrangement
CLOSED never
PROPRIETORS German Gemar

MALAGA

MALAGA

PT DE MALAGA-GIBRALFARO
~ HILLTOP PARADOR ~

Monte de Gibralfaro, 29016, Málaga
TEL 952 221902 **FAX** 952 221904
E-MAIL gibralfaro@parador.es **WEBSITE** www.parador.es

IF YOU HAVE TIME to spare in Málaga, spend it at this Parador, set in the peaceful gardens of the Gibralfaro on a hilltop above the city. It is the setting and the spectacular views, rather than the hotel itself, that make it an exceptional place to stay in this drab concrete port. This Parador is often thronged with people who come up here to escape the heat and hassle, and to enjoy the views of the port and Costa del Sol while they dine on the terraces.

The approach road winds through pine and eucalyptus trees, ending up at an stone-arcaded building, just below the remains of the Phoenician/Moorish castle. Throughly renovated and refurbished in 1995, while tripling the number of its bedrooms, the Parador de Málaga-Gibralfaro has all the usual facilities – spacious bedrooms with large balconies, a busy bar serving excellent snacks, and an attractive dining room with tables outside under the arches, and the addition of a new outdoor swimming pool.

Dining up here, with the sea shimmering below you and Gibraltar just visible in the distance, it is hard to believe that you are in the heart of Málaga.

NEARBY gardens of Gibralfaro, Alcazaba; Costa del Sol.
LOCATION on hill above city, next to castle; with gardens and shaded car parking
FOOD breakfast, lunch, dinner
PRICES €€€€
ROOMS 38 double, all with bath; all rooms have central heating, air conditioning, phone, TV, minibar
FACILITIES dining room, sitting room/bar, terrace, swimming pool
CREDIT CARDS AE, DC, MC, V
CHILDREN welcome
DISABLED one specially equipped room
PETS not accepted
CLOSED never
MANAGER Juan Carlos García Alonso

MALAGA

MONDA

EL CASTILLO DE MONDA
~ HILLTOP HOTEL ~

29110 Monda, Malaga
TEL 952 457142 FAX 952 457336
E-MAIL mondas@spa.es WEBSITE www.costadelsol.spa.es/hotel/monda

A SLIGHTLY CONFUSING mixture, but we like it all the same. Outside, you might think you had stumbled across an English castle, renovated and put down in Spain. The entrance is harsh but impressive, and the hall is slightly intimidating. The interior is a tad jumbled, also alternating between Moorish, Andalusian and modern. The dining room is set for tables of five to eight, each decorated differently, with fabulous views over the surrounding countryside. For snacks or drinks, the bar is opposite adorned with Moorish tiles and furniture. Leading off the bar is the jewel in the crown: the terrace and swimming pool. Awash with flowers and shrubbery, it provides plenty of cosy little nooks in which to ferret yourself away and enjoy the tranquil, panoramic views. You get views from the pool, too: it is built on to the side of the castle, looking down on to the ancient town of Monda.

The bedrooms, like the public areas, are somewhat impersonal, but they are also spacious, clean and cool, with large bathrooms. It is a pity that the decoration in the public spaces doesn't mirror the castle's interesting Moorish history, since this would give it the extra character it sometimes needs.

~

NEARBY Marbella, Malaga, Ronda.
LOCATION signposted just off the A355 with ample car parking in own grounds
FOOD breakfast, lunch, dinner
PRICES €€€€
ROOMS 23; all doubles, with bath; all rooms have CD machine, TV, phone, air conditioning, heating (some rooms have Jacuzzis)
FACILITIES restaurant, sitting room, bar, garden, swimming pool
CREDIT CARDS AE, MC, V
CHILDREN welcome
DISABLED access difficult PETS No
CLOSED never
DIRECTOR John Norris

MALAGA

OJÉN

REFUGIO DE JUANAR
~ HUNTING LODGE ~

Sierra Blanca, 29610, Ojén, Málaga
TEL 952 881000 **FAX** 952 881001
E-MAIL juanar@sopde.es **WEBSITE** www.juanar.com

PARADOR SIGNS still point the way from Ojén to the Refugio in the wild foothills of the Sierra Blanca, although it ceased to be a Parador several years ago. Now run (at least as efficiently as it ever was) by the local authorities, it has become a popular mountain retreat from the pressure of the Costa del Sol – for locals and tourists alike.

It was built as a hunting lodge at the turn of the century and still retains its 'hunting' atmosphere. The sitting room is an informal jumble of leather sofas around a log fire – deer antlers and zebra skin hang among old English hunting scenes on the walls. Photographs in the bar show wildlife from around the Refugio – ibex and peacocks on the lawns, birds of prey in action. The bedrooms are comfortably rustic and smell of woodsmoke. The restaurant continues on the hunting theme, specializing in game casseroles and local produce. It opens out on to a terrace overlooking pine trees.

Apart from the neat swimming pool and tennis court, the grounds are wonderfully wild – the perfect place for children of an appropriate age to go exploring. No one with a taste for the outdoors is likely to get bored here.

~

NEARBY National Reserve; Ojén (10 km); Marbella (20 km).
LOCATION in mountains, 10 km from Ojen; follow signs to Refugio; with grounds and car parking in drive
FOOD breakfast, lunch, dinner
PRICES ⓔⓔⓔ-ⓔⓔⓔⓔ
ROOMS 18 double, 1 family room, 1 apartment, 5 suites; all with bath; all rooms have central heating, phone, minibar, TV, safe
FACILITIES dining room, sitting room, TV room, bar; swimming pool, tennis court
CREDIT CARDS AE, DC, MC, V
CHILDREN accepted
DISABLED some ground floor rooms **PETS** not accepted
CLOSED never
MANAGER José Gómez Avila

MALAGA

RONDA

ALAVERA DE LOS BANOS
~ TOWN HOTEL ~

Calle San Miguel E 29400 Ronda, Malaga
TEL and **FAX** 952 879143
E-MAIL alavera@ctv.es **WEBSITE** www.andalucia.com/alavera

BELOW THE MEDIEVAL walls of old Ronda, down a scarily steep cobbled path, lies the little oasis of Alavera de los Banos. It stands side by side with the famous Arab baths, which are regarded as one of the finest of their kind, and date back to the 13th century when Ronda was ruled from Granada by the Nasri Dynasty.

This little hotel is the essence of charming and small, with a twist of eccentricity which you'll notice as you enter the restaurant: an overhead, uncovered walkway that leads to the bedrooms. The hotel is proud of its food: they change the menu regularly and only use the freshest ingredients in the Moorish/Morrocan cuisine.

Reached from the restaurant is a truly delightful garden where little tables nestle amongst the shrubbery for breakfast or drinks. The pool is small but ample enough for a leisurely splash and has fabulous views to the hills. Upstairs are the beautifully decorated bedrooms which are not large, but adorned with Arabesque mirrors, lights and tiles: lively, but cosy. Co-owners Christian and his wife Immaculada have spent a huge amount of time, money and effort on creating something really special.

~

NEARBY Arab baths, Rondan gorge, Marbella.
LOCATION in the old part of Ronda, very difficult to reach by car. Reception will tell you the best places to leave your car, otherwise try the main square, the hotel is perhaps a 5 minute walk downhill
FOOD breakfast, lunch, dinner
PRICES €€€
ROOMS 10; 9 doubles, 1 single, all with shower
FACILITIES restaurant, sitting room, bar, garden, swimming pool, terrace
CREDIT CARDS AE, DC, MC, V
CHILDREN by arrangement
DISABLED not suitable **PETS** no
CLOSED Dec-Jan
PROPRIETORS Christian and Immaculada Reichart

MALAGA

RONDA

EL JUNCAL

~ COUNTRY HOTEL ~

El Juncal 29400 Ronda, Malaga
TEL 952 161170 **FAX** 952 161160
E-MAIL hotel@eljuncal.com **WEBSITE** www.aljuncal.com

EL JUNCAL IS A hotel of contrasts. On the one hand the property dates back to the 18th century and has its own *bodega* to produce wine for its guests and on the other its interior is very modern and minimalistic, which doesn't seem to work too badly in this case. The bedrooms are small but the space has been maximised with clever modern designs and use of fabrics. Although much of the furniture around the hotel is rather hard and stark, fortunately this sentiment does not extend to the beds. The designs on the walls and the rugs in the rooms might be a little try-hard, but the views that you get from the private terraces make up for that. You can dine up in your room or make use of the ultra-chic glass restaurant with its fine organic Spanish food and wine.

During the day you can make full use of the large pool, sauna and Jacuzzi, or for the truly self-indulgent, a massage, either in your room or on your terrace. However, Ronda is tantalisingly close (5 minute drive) for those that cannot resist this ancient hill town. The receptionist can even book you into restaurants overlooking the famous gorge, or organize a guided tour around the Medieval walls, and Arab baths or bullring.

~

NEARBY Ronda, Marbella, Malaga, Gibraltar.
LOCATION on A366 1 km from Ronda in the direction of El Burgo
FOOD breakfast, lunch, dinner
PRICE €€€€-€€€€€
ROOMS 11; 9 doubles or suites, 2 twins, all have bath or shower, some have private patios or terraces
FACILITIES restaurant, sauna room, Jacuzzi, satellite television, gardens, swimming pool, terrace
CREDIT CARDS AE, MC, V
CHILDREN accepted
DISABLED please enquire **PETS** by arrangement **CLOSED** please ring before
PROPRIETORS Dolores Jiménez Moreno

MALAGA

RONDA

HOTEL LA FUENTE DE LA HIGUERA
~ COUNTRY HOTEL ~

Partido de los Frontones E-29400 Ronda, Malaga
TEL 952 114355 **FAX** 952 114356
E-MAIL info@hotellafuente.com **WEBSITE** www.hotellafuente.com

THERE'S JUST ONE (minor) thing wrong with this place: it's very hard to find. But if you follow the directions given below (at Location) you'll be OK. Owners Pom and Tina Piek are charming, with a great sense of humour that infects the whole place. All the rooms are decorated in warm, rich yet light colours: the pictures on the walls are tasteful and the furniture comfortable, especially the beds that seem to mould to your shape. There are fresh flowers in every room, and the bathrooms are large, clean and airy, with a choice of bath or shower. All the bedrooms have a small patio (some larger than others) where you can have breakfast, lunch or dinner enjoying the view over the rolling countryside. If you prefer company, head for the dining room or terrace to try their delicious Spanish/European menu. There's a pleasant swimming pool at the bottom of the garden, with a well-stocked honesty bar.

The famous white town of Ronda makes a great day trip from here: the drive is attractive, and there's plenty to see – Arab baths, bull ring and, of course, the gorge. Alternatively, if sightseeing is not for you, head to the beach for the day, Marbella is less than an hour away by car.

~

NEARBY Ronda, Malaga, Marbella.
LOCATION bypass Ronda on the A376, take the A367 and on the left is the MA 428 for Arriate. Take a left before you reach Arriate to Partido de los Frontones. The hotel is up the track on the left with ample car parking in private grounds
FOOD breakfast, lunch, dinner
PRICE €€€€
ROOMS 11; 3 standard, 1 junior sute, 3 suites, 2 deluxe suites, 1 double suite, 1 artists suite; all rooms have bath or shower and terrace or private garden, suites have open fireplaces
FACILITIES internet connection, library, terrace restuarant, swimming pool
CREDIT CARDS AE, MC, V
CHILDREN accepted **DISABLED** please enquire **PETS** by arrangement
CLOSED mid-Nov to mid-Dec **PROPRIETOR** Christina Piek

MALAGA

RONDA

HOTEL SAN GABRIEL
~ TOWN HOTEL ~

Marques de Moctezuma 19, 2940 Ronda, Malaga
TEL 952 190392 **FAX** 952 190117
E-MAIL info@hotelsangabriel.com **WEBSITE** www.hotelsangabriel.com

WE'VE PREVIOUSLY been unexcited by hotels in the much-visited 'white town' of Ronda, so were pleased to get this unequivocal recommendation from a British teacher with a home in southern Spain. He writes:

'In the middle of the old part of town, it's close to the sites that draw the visitors. It was built in 1736, and the handsome old facade has been preserved; inside, there's been a total rebuild to provide 16 individually decorated rooms. On the ground floor are a large drawing room with log-burning stove; a billiards room; and a bar where you have breakfast in the morning and drinks in the evening. It's spotlessly clean, and Jose Manuel Arnal and his familiy are very welcoming, only too pleased to help. A real gem, which captures the style and atmosphere of Ronda brilliantly – you'll feel at home here.'

The Arnal family, who've lived here for many years, opened in 1998 and have evidently succeeded in preserving the authentic feel of an 18thC Spanish house – while providing all the necessary comforts.

~

NEARBY Ronda's bull ring, ravine and historic sites.
LOCATION in side street of old Ronda; free parking in street
FOOD breakfast
PRICE €€€
ROOMS 16; 6 double, 7 super deluxe, 3 junior suites, all with bath; all rooms have phone, minibar, TV, central heating, air conditioning, hairdrier, safe
FACILITIES 3 sitting rooms, library, billiards, video room, concert room, patio, bar
CREDIT CARDS AE, MC, V
CHILDREN welcome
DISABLED suitable
PETS not accepted
CLOSED never
PROPRIETORS Ilio Perez Giron and José Manuel Arnal

MALAGA

TORREMOLINOS

HOTEL MIAMI
~ TOWN HOUSE HOTEL ~

Calle Aladino 14, 29620, Torremolinos, Málaga
TEL 952 385255 **FAX** 952 053447
E-MAIL hotelmiami@telefonica.net **WEBSITE** www.residenciamiami.com

SOMEWHERE in the ocean of concrete formed by the merger of Málaga and
Torremolinos, a small sign directs you off the main coast road to the
Miami. It is set in its own rounded driveway and is completely walled off
from its surroundings – it feels just like an island. The house was built by
Picasso's cousin as a holiday villa and has made an unusual hotel, set
around a lagoon-like swimming pool. Palms and banana trees overshadow
the pool and give it an exotic, tropical feel – you could be in the Caribbean
rather than in the heart of Torremolinos, only yards away from a crowded
beach and busy sea-front.

Some of the bedrooms are in need of attention; ours was worn and
dusty, but adequate. Most have balconies, and all are cool and airy. One of
the key features of the hotel is the grotto-like sitting room, with its mixture of square and round windows peeping out of pebble-dashed walls and
its curious fireplace of piled stones. It is full of interesting objects – ani-
mal-skin seats, copper pots, pilot lanterns.

There is no restaurant, but the Miami does serve probably the only
'Spanish' breakfast in Torremolinos – on the terrace above the pool.

~

NEARBY beach; Málaga (15 km), Marbella (45 km).
LOCATION on quiet side-street, 50 m from beach; signed from main road through
Torremolinos; with garden and ample car parking in drive
FOOD breakfast
PRICES €€-€€€
ROOMS 23 double, 3 single, all with bath; all rooms have central heating, phone, safe
FACILITIES sitting room, breakfast room, bar/ patio, swimming pool, tropical garden
CREDIT CARDS not accepted
CHILDREN accepted; play area
DISABLED 6 ground floor rooms
PETS accepted (charged €2 per day)
CLOSED never
MANAGER Mercedes Gómez

MALAGA

VELEZ MALAGA

MOLINO DE SANTILLAN

~ COUNTRY HOTEL ~

Velez Malaga, Malaga
TEL 902 120240 **FAX** 952 400950
E-MAIL msantillan@spa.es **WEBSITE** www.hotel-msantillan.net

DOG HATERS BEWARE. Our inspectors were greeted by three huge, very vocal dogs of mysterious breeding. Although they looked scary, they were, in fact, gentle, and give the place a homely feel.

Set high in the hills above Malaga, the hotel has fabulous views of the sea and surrounding countryside. When we visited the garden was being re-landscaped, and a couple of new rooms added, in fact there might eventually be as many as ten rooms. It was hard to visualise the eventual effect of this work, but the old garden looked charming in photographs, so we believe the new one will be too.

The Molino's charm is very much to do with its self-sufficient atmosphere. The garden is worked by traditional methods, providing fruit and vegetables for the table; a hen house ensures fresh eggs for breakfast.

The rooms are beautifully done out, with large flagstones on the floors, gracefully draped mosquito nets and rustic/antique fabrics and furniture. On hand are a range of outdoor activities which the hotel can arrange: riding, tennis and mountain biking; they'll also advise on and arrange trips to local botanical gardens, museums and other cultural events.

~

NEARBY Malaga, Granada, Torremolinos.
LOCATION on the N340 just after Rincon de la Victoria, take the exit sign posted Macharaviaya/Anoreta. Leave this road at the exit by the km 3 mark; hotel is down a dirt track with ample car parking in own grounds
FOOD breakfast, lunch, dinner
PRICES €€€€
ROOMS 12; 2 suites, 3 double, 7 twin, all with bath and shower; all rooms have TV, phone, hairdrier, air conditioning and fans
FACILITIES dining room, sitting room, reading room, garden, swimming pool, Jacuzzi (have to pay extra for)
CREDIT CARDS AE, MC, V
CHILDREN welcome **DISABLED** access difficult **PETS** by arrangement
CLOSED 10th Jan – 1st Mar **PROPRIETOR** Carlo Marchini

HOTELS IN THE ISLANDS

AREA INTRODUCTION

THE *Islas Baleares* consist of four islands. These four islands - Mallorca, Menorca, Ibiza and Formentera - are such an important holiday destination that we produce a seperate guide - *Charming Small Hotel Guides Mallorca and the Balearics* in order to do them justice. In this guide we offer a selection of hotels on all four islands (with many more choices than the last edition) which we hope you will find useful. The largest and most well-known Balearic island is Mallorca, a popular holiday destination comprising beautiful sandy beaches in the south, and towering mountains, sheer cliffs and rocky coves in the north. One of the island's smartest hotels is on its northernmost point, the Cap de Formentor – the luxurious 127-room **Formentor** (Tel 971 899100), splendidly set amidst pine trees on the edge of a beach. It has excellent facilities, especially for children, and comfortable rooms with perfect views of sea and peaks. Deia, close to the rugged north-west coast, has two smart hotels of note; **La Residencia** (page 243) and the **Es Molí**, which is stunningly situated on the edge of the cliff. The gardens are luxurious, 'a dazzling array of trailing flowers, laden fruit trees and immaculate lawns, lovingly tended by an army of gardeners'. For those who want to stay nearer Palma, the 60-room **Punta Negra** (owned by Trusthouse Forte, Tel 971 680762) is in a fabulous position on the Costa de Bendinat, away from the hordes but still reasonably convenient. Further away along the south coast, a simple but popular hotel is the **Cala Santanyi** in the village of the same name. The building is a white arc so that all rooms have a view of one of the most perfect bays imaginable (Tel 971 165505). Further round the coast is the white holiday complex of Cala d'Or.

Menorca, the smaller neighbour of Mallorca, is very different. Unlike Mallorca, it has escaped mass hotel-building and is still a quiet family holiday island with numerous unspoilt beaches. Of the few hotels, the 82-room **Port Mahón** is a comfortable, old-fashioned place overlooking the Mahón harbour, praised for its excellent friendly service (Tel 971 362600); the **Rocamar** at nearby Cala Fonduco is a restaurant with rooms, providing some of the best seafood on the island and good-value accommodation (Tel 971 365601).

Ibiza, smaller though more touristy than Menorca, has a Moorish feel to it – the last vestiges of its 8thC occupation. One of the island's few luxury hotels is the **Hacienda Na Xamena**. The setting is lovely and the facilities are extensive (see page 272). **El Palacio** is especially for film buffs. **Pike's** (Tel 971 342222) is a secluded country house popular with pop stars.

Formentera is a tiny island off the south coast of Ibiza. History and tourism have left it virtually untouched, and it has endless deserted beaches served by a handful of hotels. The choice is mainly between small and simple, such as the 20-room **Sa Volta at Es Pujols** (Tel 971 328125), and big and smart, such as the 330-room **La Mola at Es Arenals**.

Hotels in the Canaries
We don't find much that excites us in the Canaries - except of course the wonderful climate. The islands are full of well-established, conventional hotels catering for the flight-inclusive package market. However, for this edition we have added a few new choices,nearly doubling our coverage. See for example, **Las Calas** on p273, **Relais El Pinar** on p275 and **Hotel Amberes** on p278.

MALLORCA

ALGAIDA

POSSESSIO BINICOMPRAT

~ COUNTRY HOTEL ~

Finca de Binicomprat s/n, 07210 Algaida
TEL 971 125028 **FAX** 971 665773

ALTHOUGH BINICOMPRAT HAS an Algaida address, the land in which it stands is actually much closer to Montuiri, the small hilltop village on the road to Manacor. This is quite heavily forested country, but the estate has its own vineyards, which produce 30,000 bottles of wine a year. Gabriel Moragues takes pride in showing guests his wine cellars and likes to offer a sample bottle; few leave for home without at least one in their suitcase.

Rooms and apartments have a simple, Mediterranean charm. The dominant colour is white; windows are draped in white *voile*; the bedspreads are in subdued natural colours; the deeper colours of pine beams and window frames make a pleasing contrast.

There's a beautiful dining room in which dinner (Mallorcan dishes) is available on request. A large, fully equipped room is available for meetings and conferences, but does not spoil atmosphere. Take a look at the estate's simple old chapel, now no longer used for worship, but a reminder of bygone days when this type of community offered its occupants everything on the spot, for this life and the next.

~

NEARBY Es Trenc's attractive beach (30 km).
LOCATION edge of the village in own grounds; private car parking
FOOD breakfast, dinner on request
PRICE €€-€€€
ROOMS 9; 2 doubles, 1 suite, 6 apartments, all with bath
FACILITIES central heating, telephone, hairdrier, satellite TV, minibar, safe
CREDIT CARDS not accepted
CHILDREN welcome
DISABLED no special facilities
PETS not accepted
CLOSED never
PROPRIETOR Gabriel Oliver Moragues

MALLORCA

ARTA

CA'N MORAGUES

~ TOWN HOTEL ~

Carrer Pou Nou 12, 07570 Artá
Tel 971 829509 **Fax** 971 829530

ARTA HAS RETAINED much of its medieval character: massive walls, a fine church (on the site of an Arab mosque), narrow streets and magnificent views over a lush valley to the sea. Ca'n Moragues was carved some years ago out of the former 19thC town hall in the old part of town. Among all this old and mellow masonry, its minimalist interior makes an intriguing change to the homely, rustic style of so many of the other places to stay on Mallorca.

The heated pool is especially striking, with ultramarine roof, cadmium-yellow walls and yellow-ochre sandstone. Rooms are furnished only with what a guest would find absolutely necessary. The result is a purity which you'll either like or dislike; at least it's not predictable.

Guests can explore the hotel's 130-hectare *finca*, a 10-minute drive away.

~

Nearby Cala Mesquida beach (10 km).
Location in old town, own grounds and private car parking
Food breakfast
Price €€-€€€
Rooms 8; 4 doubles, 4 junior suites, all with bath, central heating, air conditioning, telephone, hairdryer, satellite TV
Facilities sitting room, bar, outdoor swimming pool
Credit cards MC, V
Children welcome
Disabled no special facilities
Pets not accepted
Closed never
Proprietor Concha Morell

MALLORCA

BANYULBUFAR

MAR I VENT
～ COUNTRY HOTEL BY THE SEA ～

Carrer Mayor 49, 07191 Banyulbufar
TEL 971 618000 **FAX** 971 618201
E-MAIL marivent@bitel.es **WEBSITE** www.fehm.es

MAR I VENT IS SPECTACULARLY sited on the coast road next to the village of Banyulbufar. The terrain drops steeply down to the sea to give stunning views, and the Vives family, who have been here for some years, have made the most of their situation: bright, airy rooms have little south-facing terraces to get the most from the heart-stopping sea views. The atmosphere is warm and friendly. In the restaurant, an *à la carte* menu offers Mallorcan country cuisine alongside an unusually interesting selection of Spanish wines. The large, kidney-shaped pool on the cliff is nothing short of an architectonic masterpiece.

Banyulbufar is originally an Arabic name, meaning 'little vineyard by the sea'. It's small, with 500 inhabitants, and perched on vineyard terraces, which have been producing wine since the Moslem occupiers first planted them well over 1,000 years ago. If you're staying at Mar i Vent, a short walk through this idyllic settlement is a must: villagers and holidaymakers alike seem peaceful and content; it's hard to believe you're on the same island as the ever-more-hectic large resorts.

～

NEARBY pebble beach (500 m); Palma (25 km).
LOCATION at entrance to village; own garden and garage car parking
FOOD breakfast, dinner
PRICE ©©©
ROOMS 29; 3 singles, 20 doubles, 6 junior suites, all with bath, central heating, telephone, hairdryer
FACILITIES restaurant, sitting rooms, outdoor swimming pool, tennis court, bicycles
CREDIT CARDS AE, MC, V
CHILDREN welcome
DISABLED no special facilities
PETS not accepted
CLOSED Dec-Jan
PROPRIETORS Vives family

MALLORCA

BINISSALEM

SCOTT'S

~ TOWN HOUSE HOTEL ~

Plaza de la Iglesia 12, 07350, Binissalem, Mallorca
TEL 971 870100 **FAX** 971 870267
E-MAIL reserve@scottshotel.com **WEBSITE** www.scottshotel.com

CALM, SOPHISTICATION and unobtrusive luxury are the hallmarks of the new breed of upmarket 'house' hotels which we find in many fashionable cities: now the unspoilt Mallorcan hinterland can boast one as well. Binissalem is the wine capital of the island, a quiet Medieval town ideally situated just 20 minutes from Palma, 30 minutes from beaches and golf clubs on both coasts and close to the island's beautiful mountains.

In keeping with the genre, a discreet brass plaque is the only sign that the elegant former merchant's house in the town's small main square is a hotel. Inside, nothing disappoints; the interior is as calm, sophisticated and unobtrusively luxurious as you could wish, especial attention having been paid to the 16 bedrooms and suites. Each one is different, although they all display the same high standards, with charming fabrics, furniture and pictures, as well as fresh flowers. The beds are top-quality handmade and feel it, with pure cotton sheets and delicious goose-down pillows (synthetic ones are on offer to those who suffer from allergies). A handful of extra bedrooms have been added since our last edition.

Breakfasts are suitably sumptuous, served in the breakfast room or on the terrace.

~

NEARBY mountains; Palma 12 miles (19 km).
LOCATION in central square; ample parking
FOOD breakfast; dinner available Mon-Sat in Scott's BIstro (300 yds from hotel)
PRICES €€€€
ROOMS 16 double and suites, all with bath; all rooms have central heating, phone, satellite TV/video on request, hairdrier
FACILITIES 2 sitting rooms, breakfast room, bar/bistro, spa pool, terraces
CREDIT CARDS MC, V
CHILDREN welcome over 12
DISABLED access difficult **PETS** not accepted
CLOSED never
PROPRIETORS George Scott and Judy Brabner Scott

MALLORCA

BUÑOLA

FINCA BARCELONA

~ COUNTRY HOTEL ~

Predio Biniforani Nou, 07349 Buñola
TEL 971 180568 **FAX** 971 180568

BUÑOLA IS A STOP ON THE RED LIGHTNING railway line between Palma and
Sóller, and as the hotel is just 1 km away, it's one you can visit without
a car. (The station dates from around 1900, with an amazing façade boast-
ing stuccoed Art Nouveau decoration.)

Barcelona, once a private country estate, lies on a hill with a view over
nearby Buñola in 60 hectares of land studded with pines, olives and
carobs. It is built in typical 19thC local style, the façade enlivened by an
airy *loggia* on the upper level, with arches and slender pillars.

The *finca* is ideal for a large family or a group who will enjoy having the
run of the place; in fact bookings are only taken for groups large enough to
fill the place. Family possessions – beautiful chests, Majorcan rocking
chairs and cosy wooden beds – cared for down the centuries, give it a
homely feel. Paths for exploring the area begin right outside the front
door. No food is served, but if you want to self-cater, there is a dining room
for your use.

~

NEARBY Buñola (1 km); Palma (15 km).
LOCATION on the edge of the village in own grounds; private car parking
FOOD none
PRICE €€€€ for the whole house
ROOMS 5; 1 single, 4 doubles, 3 baths, central heating, telephone, satellite TV
FACILITIES sitting room, outdoor swimming pool
CREDIT CARDS not accepted
CHILDREN welcome
DISABLED no special facilities
PETS not accepted
CLOSED never
PROPRIETOR Maria Franzisca Homar Pons

MALLORCA

CALA RATJADA

HOTEL SES ROTGES

~ TOWN HOTEL ~

Rafael Blanes 21, 07590, Cala Ratjada, Mallorca
TEL 971 563108 **FAX** 971 564345
E-MAIL hotel@sesrotges.com **WEBSITE** www.sesrotges.com

SOME YEARS AGO it might have been a surprise to find a well-established French-run hotel in the middle of this village on Mallorca's east coast. Today it would come as no surprise at all – Cala Ratjada is now a lively cosmopolitan holiday town. The Tétards have kept pace with the local development, cleverly extending their pink-stone hotel in the same style as the original buildings, with arched windows and wrought iron balconies.

The hotel, on the corner of two quiet streets near the beach, overlooks a quiet internal courtyard – a wonderful place to relax among trailing plants, overhanging bougainvillaea and a profusion of colourful flowers. The popular restaurant adjoins the courtyard and is set with red and white tables under a beamed roof. In winter, dinner is served inside in another large, cheerful room. The oldest part of the building, around the original chimney, is now a cosy sitting room. The bedrooms are spacious and airy; they are supposed to be 'individually furnished', but the ones we saw all had the same tiled floors, wooden furniture and bedheads, star-shaped mirrors and modern bathrooms.

Food is a highlight, earning one of the island's very few Michelin stars.

~

NEARBY Artà (10 km); Manacor (30 km).
LOCATION in quiet street 200m from beach; with car parking in street
FOOD breakfast, lunch, dinner
PRICES €€-€€€€
ROOMS 18 double, 2 single, one family room, 3 suites, all with bath; all rooms have central heating, air conditioning, phone, TV, safe, hairdrier, minibar
FACILITIES bar, dining room, sitting room, TV room, patio
CREDIT CARDS AE, DC, MC, V
CHILDREN tolerated
DISABLED access generally difficult; one ground floor room
PETS not accepted
CLOSED beginning Nov - Mid Mar
PROPRIETOR Gérard Charles Tétard

MALLORCA

DEIÀ

ES MOLI

~ COUNTRY HOTEL BY THE SEA ~

Carretera Valldemosa-Deià s/n, 07179 Deià
TEL 971 63 90 00 **FAX** 971 63 93 33
E-MAIL esmoli@fehm.es **WEBSITE** www.ila.chateau.com/es-moli/

D EIÀ'S MANY VISITORS IMMEDIATELY APPRECIATE its distinctive charm. For locals, the reality is not quite so palatable: once it was the haunt of Bohemians and artists, or anyone who cared to live in such a delightful place on a shoestring; now building plots, houses and apartments are barely affordable. Well, you don't have to worry about that if you stay at Es Moli, although you will pay a price that's in keeping. Although the hotel has 87 rooms, they are spread out in three separate buildings, so the feel is of a smaller place. The hotel's principal charm is its dramatic position in a ravine at the foot of a magical, steeply rising mountain. The view over the bay and beyond to the open sea is stupendous.

Bedrooms are generously proportioned. Period furniture, distinctive fabrics and flower pictures work together for a beguiling mood. Bathrooms are roomy, too, and tastefully tiled. Service is friendly and attentive. The huge terraces are elegantly furnished with English Lloyd Loom caneware. Beautiful table linen sets off the food. You'll find it hard to exhaust the many quiet corners for relaxation in the enchanting, 15,000 square-metre garden.

~

NEARBY Valldemosa (15 km); Cala Deià beach. (4 km).
LOCATION at the entrance to the village; large grounds and private car parking
FOOD breakfast, dinner
PRICE €€€€
ROOMS 87; 9 singles, 75 doubles, 1 suite, 2 junior suites, all with bath, central heating, air conditioning, telephone, hairdryer, satellite TV (on request), minibar
FACILITIES restaurant, outdoor swimming pool, private beach, tennis court, hairdresser
CREDIT CARDS AE, MC, V
CHILDREN welcome
DISABLED no special facilities **PETS** not accepted
CLOSED 25 Oct-24 Apr
MANAGER Angel Fernandez

MALLORCA

DEIA

HOTEL LA RESIDENCIA
~ COUNTRY HOTEL ~

Son Canals s/n, 07179, Deia, Mallorca
TEL 971 639011 **FAX** 971 639370
E-mail reservas@hotel-laresidencia.com **WEBSITE** www.hotel-laresidencia.com

ALMOST EVERYTHING about the Residencia is out of the ordinary. Set above the road at the north end of the fashionable village of Deia, it is a cluster of creeper-covered stone buildings in beautiful tiered gardens. The core of the hotel is a 16thC manor house; its original olive mill is now the restaurant. There is also an annexe above the swimming pool behind the main hotel, built in the same pink stone with white shutters.

The interior of the hotel is exquisitely furnished with antique pieces, colourful rugs and fascinating modern art. Bedrooms vary in size – from smallish singles to an enormous suite in a separate building. All have lovely wooden furniture and many have antique or four-poster beds. There are bars and breakfast-rooms in both parts of the hotel, though most people eat out on the terraces overlooking either the swimming pool (surrounded by elegant cypresses and silver birches) or the front lawns.

Another highlight is the hotel's acclaimed restaurant, El Olivo. Its lofty ceiling, dripping candelabra, cane furniture and elegant tables, set among relics of the olive mill, make a romantic setting. On a recent visit, we noticed standardized hotel-style chairs in the bar – a shame.

~

NEARBY Valldemosa (10 km), Sóller (10 km).
LOCATION Signposted from the road from Deia to Soller; with garden and car parking
FOOD breakfast, lunch, dinner
PRICES €€€€
ROOMS 42 double and single, 17 suites, 4 luxury suite (3 with private pool), all with bath; all rooms have central heating, air conditioning, phone, hairdrier, safe
FACILITIES 2 restaurants, 4 sitting rooms, 3 bars, dining room; 2 outdoor swimming pools, 1 indoor swimming pool, 2 tennis courts, rocky cove; beauty salon, gymnasium, sauna, steam room, spa
CREDIT CARDS AE, MC, V **CHILDREN** welcome between 1 to 15 Aug and during Christmas and New Year **DISABLED** no special facilities **PETS** small dogs accepted
CLOSED never **MANAGER** John Rogers

MALLORCA

ESPORLES

LA POSADA DEL MARQUES
~ COUNTRY HOTEL ~

Finca Es Verger, 07190 Esporles
TEL 971 61 12 30 **FAX** 971 61 12 13
WEBSITE www.posadamarques.com

THIS HOTEL HAS A SENSATIONAL POSITION IN Es Verger mountains: it seems like an eagle's nest overlooking the village of Esporles, and is reached, predictably, by a tortuous road. The valley below is a beautiful and typical Mallorcan landscape, with tracts of pine woods and paths winding through wild thyme and rosemary bushes.

The 16thC estate has retained its original appearance, even after extensive renovation: the integrity of the interor remains intact, making you feel as if the place was always like this; yet up-to-date equipment and comforts are everywhere. There are staggering views down to the Bay of Parma.

The rooms and spacious suites exude good taste. Decoration is quite conservative, with period furniture, luxurious silk curtains in unobtrusive colours (such as light pink and yellow stripes); Art Nouveau style lamps give a charming, warm illumination. The bathrooms are luxuriously appointed. The restaurant pampers its guests either in the *tafona*, a restored oil mill, or on the terrace, with its breathtaking views. The light Mediterranean cuisine is the work of José Castoñer, who began his career at El Olivo in Deiá. The wine list is particularly impressive.

NEARBY Esporles (4 km); La Granja estate and national museum (8 km).
LOCATION above village of Es Verger; own grounds and private car parking
FOOD breakfast, lunch, dinner
PRICE €€€€
ROOMS 17; 12 doubles, 5 suites, all with bath, central heating, air conditioning, telephone, hairdryer, satellite TV, minibar
FACILITIES restaurant, sitting rooms, outdoor swimming pool
CREDIT CARDS AE, MC, V
CHILDREN welcome
DISABLED no special facilities **PETS** small dogs allowed
CLOSED never
PROPRIETOR Dietrich Weissenborn

MALLORCA

ESTELLENCS

SA PLANA PETIT HOTEL

~ SEASIDE HOTEL ~

Carrer Eusebi Pascal s/n, 07192 Estellencs
TEL 971 61 86 66 **FAX** 971 61 85 86

As ITS NAME SUGGESTS, this is a modest, small hotel, but it has much charm and offers everything you could expect at the price, which is fair, to say nothing of its superb setting. Every room has its own fireplace. Some of the beds are four-posters, with homely linen bedspreads. Local period furniture is generally of oak or stained pine. The dreamy terrace is a high spot, and so is the Mallorcan food, offered on the daily-changing menu. You will probably be offered the local cabbage soup served with unsalted bread; home-made sausages; or fish simply grilled on an an open fire in the garden. Vegetables are grown in the hotel's garden. There's an interesting local wine list.

Estellencs claims to offer views of the most beautiful sunsets on Mallorca, and its winding hillside streets make for picturesque strolls. The impressive church tower was once a watchtower that protected the village from pirates. There are a couple of charming restaurants that compare very well with those in Andratx or Banyulbufar.

~

NEARBY Banyulbufar (7 km).
LOCATION in village, own grounds and car parking
FOOD breakfast, dinner on request
PRICE ©©
ROOMS 5; 4 doubles, 1 room for 4 people, all with bath
FACILITIES recreation room, dining room
CREDIT CARDS DC, MC, V
CHILDREN welcome
DISABLED no special facilities
PETS not accepted
CLOSED 10 Dec-15 Jan
PROPRIETOR Paquita Bauza

MALLORCA

FELANITX

SA POSADA D'AUMALLIA

~ COUNTRY HOTEL ~

Camino Son Prohens 1027, 07200 Felanitx
TEL 971 58 26 57 **FAX** 971 58 32 69

FELANITX RESEMBLES A LARGE TOWN IN MINIATURE: it boasts a superb church with an imposing outside staircase; a lively market hall; a weekly market that happens every Sunday on the *Rambla;* and many corner shops that sell all manner of things, both practical and useless.

Just 4 km from Felanitx is the lovely Posada d'Aumallia, a perfect example of a classic manor house of the 1900s, decorated with contemporary rural elegance. As you enter the magnificent doorway and step into the main drawing room, you feel as if you've stepped back a hundred years. A fire crackles in the marble fireplace; an opulent, gold-framed mirror hangs above. To the right, an elegant grand piano and cello apparently wait to be played. The bedrooms are in local Mallorcan style, with antique furniture and locally woven fabrics. Bathrooms are a fair size. The half-panelled dining room exudes early 19thC charm.

Meanwhile, in the garden, peacocks shred the air with their strange cries, and the Mallorcan evening meal is announced. The mood could hardly be better. And the sea is just 7 km away from this idyll.

~

NEARBY Felanitx (4 km); Porto Colom beach (7 km).
LOCATION in the countryside; garden; car parking
FOOD breakfast, dinner
PRICE €€-€€€
ROOMS 14 doubles, all with bath, central heating, air conditioning, telephone, hairdryer, satellite TV, minibar, safe
FACILITIES restaurant, sitting room, bar, outdoor swimming pool, tennis court, bicycles
CREDIT CARDS AE, MC, V
CHILDREN welcome
DISABLED no special facilities
PETS not accepted
CLOSED never
MANAGER Maria Antonia Marti

MALLORCA

FORNALUTX

CA'N VERDERA
~ COUNTRY HOTEL ~

Carrer de Toros 1, 07109 Fornalutx
TEL 971 63 82 03 **FAX** 971 63 81 09
E-MAIL canverdera@ctv.es **WEBSITE** www.canverdera.com

C'AN VERDERA IS A GEM OF THE MID-1800S, carefully restored in keeping with the original architecture – arches, oriels and wooden balconies – and now furnished with choice designer furniture. The whitewashed walls help show off the cast-iron beds, the bright chairs upholstered with leather, and of course the curtains; and they are a helpful setting for the hotel's collection of contemporary art, much of it the work of local painters, that fill the walls. The location is in one of the most beautiful valleys on the island, the 'valley of the orange trees'.

If you stay here, take the opportunity to visit Fornalutx's town hall, where trophies, won in competitions for the nation's most beautiful village, fill the shelves. The place has been virtually built into a cliff; stones collected from the fields have been neatly laid into streets and footpaths. Green shutters decorate pretty façades and there are tubs of flowers in front of the doors: the definitive picture-postcard village.

~

NEARBY Sóller (3 km); beach (8 km).
LOCATION above the village, own grounds and private car parking
FOOD breakfast
PRICE €€€€
ROOMS 11; 9 doubles, 1 suite, 1 junior suite, all with bath, central heating, air conditioning, telephone, hairdryer, satellite TV
FACILITIES restaurants, sitting rooms, banqueting room, outdoor swimming pool, tennis court (on request, 5 minutes' walk)
CREDIT CARDS AE, MC, V
CHILDREN by arrangement
DISABLED no special facilities
PETS not accepted
CLOSED Dec-Jan
MANAGER Anna Celma

MALLORCA

LLUC ALCARI

COSTA D'OR

~ COUNTRY HOTEL BY THE SEA ~

07179 Deià
TEL 971 639025 **FAX** 971 639347
E-MAIL costador@arrakis.es **WEBSITE** www.arrakis.es/costador/home.html

MALLORCA'S SOUTH-WESTERN COAST is extremely beautiful: from Andratx to the little harbour town of Sóller, the dreamy coast road winds past the mountain villages of Estellencs, Banyulbufar, Valldemosa, Deià and Lluc Alcari, where a narrow road (but wide enough for cars) snakes its way down through a pine wood to this magical hotel. The view from its terrace and magnificent swimming pool is heart-stopping. The 37 bedrooms are fitted out with imposing mahogany furniture; characteristic Mallorcan blue-and-white fabric decorates windows and beds. The atmosphere is of peace and repose.

The hotel food is perfectly good, local cuisine, but gourmets in search of a change will find many excellent restaurants in the vicinity, either in the former artist's colony of Deiá, or heading towards Sóller.

~

NEARBY Deià (2 km); Sóller (8 km).
LOCATION on the hillside above Lluch Alcari, in own grounds with private car parking
FOOD breakfast, lunch, dinner
PRICE €€€-€€€€
ROOMS 37; 3 singles, 34 doubles, all with bath, central heating, telephone
FACILITIES restaurant, sitting rooms, outdoor swimming pool, tennis court
CREDIT CARDS MC, V
CHILDREN welcome
DISABLED no special facilities
PETS not accepted
CLOSED 29 Oct-31 Mar
PROPRIETORS Magraner family

MALLORCA

MANACOR

SON GENER

~ *FINCA* HOTEL ~

Carretera Son Servera, km 3, 07550 Son Servera
TEL 971 18 36 12 **FAX** 971 18 35 91
E-MAIL songener@todoesp.es

S ON GENER IS A few kilometres beyond Manacor in the direction of Artá, in pleasant countryside. The owner is a creative architect and designer – and this will come as no surprise to those with an eye for details such as artful exposure of architectural structure, and a modern, minimalist interior that accentuates furniture, tasteful fabrics and decorative objects. Sitting rooms, bedrooms and terraces are alive with Mediterranean light: very few other places to stay on Mallorca are as well designed in this respect. It's an ambience that corresponds exactly to many Northern Europeans' idea of what Mediterranean lifestyle is about.

This is the place to stay if you like artificial pearls: just 4 km away is Manacor, Mallorca's second town and the Mecca of the artificial pearl, with dozens of shops selling what claim to be the best quality and most brilliant of their kind.

~

NEARBY Manacor (4 km); Artá monastery (10 km).
LOCATION at the edge of Manacor heading towards Artá, signposted
FOOD breakfast, dinner
PRICE €€€€
ROOMS 10 suites, all with bath, central heating, air conditioning, telephone, satellite TV, minibar
FACILITIES restaurant, wine cellar, swimming pool, bicycles
CREDIT CARDS AE, MC, V
CHILDREN welcome
DISABLED no special facilities
PETS not accepted
CLOSED never
PROPRIETOR Antonio Estevaa Cañellas

MALLORCA

MOSCARI

CA'N CALCO
~ VILLAGE INN ~

Carrer Campanet 1, 07313 Selva-Moscari
TEL 971 51 52 60 **FAX** 971 52 60

TIME STILL PASSES SLOWLY IN THE LITTLE village of Moscari: mass tourism is still at a distance, and the villagers enjoy their peace and quiet. They sit, as their grandparents did, in front of their houses, or at a street café with a *Hierbas*, or sit in the bar playing dice and cards.

This little *finca* hotel, with just five junior suites, is one of a few truly successful examples of pure modern interior design in Mallorca. Dominant colours are restricted to white, sand and black. The walls are whitewashed, and this is combined with the natural sandstone to give a pleasing, warm feel, especially in the restaurant and breakfast room. Delicate black cast-iron furniture, upholstered in natural white completes the effect. Everything is minimalist and tasteful. The kitchen specializes in fresh fish dishes, including the famous *caldereta*, a fine shellfish stew.

The owners have a mission to make Mallorcan art known to their guests and mount regular exhibitions of both painting and sculpture.

~

NEARBY Pollença (25 km).
LOCATION at the exit to the village; in own grounds, private car parking
FOOD breakfast, dinner
PRICE €€€
ROOMS 5 junior suites, all with bath and hydromassage, central heating, air conditioning, telephone, hairdryer, satellite TV, minibar
FACILITIES restaurant, sitting room, outdoor swimming pool
CREDIT CARDS MC, V
CHILDREN welcome
DISABLED one room with large bath, easy access for wheelchairs
PETS small dogs accepted
CLOSED Nov
PROPRIETOR Jaime Vives Mir

MALLORCA

ORIENT

HOTEL L'HERMITAGE

~ COUNTRY HOTEL ~

07349, Orient, Mallorca
TEL 971 180303 **FAX** 971 180411

THE GREAT ATTRACTION of L'Hermitage is its setting – tucked away in a beautiful fruit-growing valley in the mountains, miles from the beaten track (no mean achievement in Mallorca). It consists of a somewhat strange selection of buildings: a narrow 17thC stone manor house (with tower), a two-storey modern block overlooking an orchard and a totally separate cloister with 16 twisted stone pillars enclosing lemon and orange trees. Only four of the bedrooms are in the old house. These have tiny windows peering out of thick walls, making the rooms beautifully cool but also very dim; with polished furniture on old tiled floors, they have much more character than the modern rooms – though these are also cool and comfortable, with palatial bathrooms.

There is a warren of tiny public rooms in the old part of the hotel, including an elegant downstairs sitting room and a cosy upstairs one with an open fire. In contrast, the dining room in the old olive mill is enormous. It still has a sloping, beamed ceiling and the original grinding-stones, which make an admirable table for the generous buffet breakfasts.

New owners, Veit and Barbara Moriggl, from Austria, have not only made the bedrooms and seating more comfortable. They have also heated the terrace so that meals can be enjoyed outside even if the weather is cool. Freshly baked cakes and tarts are available at tea-time.

~

NEARBY Buñola (10 km), Alaró (10 km).
LOCATION in fruit-orchard valley in mountains, 1km E of Orient; with garden and car parking
FOOD buffet breakfast, snacks, lunch, tea, dinner
PRICES €€€€
ROOMS 24 double, all with bath; all rooms have central heating, phone, minibar; some rooms have TV, safe, hairdrier
FACILITIES dining room, 2 sitting rooms, bar, terrace; sauna, 2 tennis court, heated swimming pool **CREDIT CARDS** AE, DC, MC, V **CHILDREN** accepted **DISABLED** no special facilities **PETS** not accepted **CLOSED** Nov to Feb **MANAGERS** Veit & Barbara Moriggl

MALLORCA

HOTEL BORN

~ HISTORIC TOWN HOTEL ~

Carrer Sant Jaume 3, 07012 Palma
Tel 971 712942 **Fax** 971 718618

CARRER SANT JAUME, an important conduit between the Plaça Espana and the Plaça Joan Carles, is in Palma's *Casco antiguo* (old town), and on it is the Hotel Born. The district is designated a national treasure, part of the Monumento Nacional de España. One fine façade succeeds another; playful oriels jut out from the fronts of houses; behind wooden slatted windows hang heavy fabrics of brocade, velvet and silk. Over the centuries, pedestrians have polished the cobbles to a high gloss.

Inside the hotel, great marble pillars support the Gothic arches of the entrance hall. This opens on to the patio, lush with palm trees, where in summer they serve a Mallorcan breakfast with authentic local *ensaimada* (pastries). A stone staircase sweeps in a broad and elegant arc up to the first floor. Bedrooms are comfortable and charmingly furnished; suites are considerably more spacious.

Just around the corner from the hotel is the famous Avenida Jaime III, with its elegant shops.

~

Nearby old town; beach (2 km).
Location in town centre; own car parking
Food breakfast
Price €€-€€€
Rooms 35; 26 doubles, 6 singles, 3 suites, all with bath, central heating, air conditioning, telephone, satellite TV, minibar only in the suites
Facilities patio
Credit cards AE, MC, V
Children welcome
Disabled no special facilities
Pets not accepted
Closed never
Manager Miguel Angel Frontera

MALLORCA

PALMA

SAN LORENZO
~ TOWN HOTEL ~

Carrer San Llorenc 14, 07012 Palma
TEL 971 72 82 00 **FAX** 971 71 19 01
E-MAIL sanlorenzo@fehm.es **WEBSITE** www.fehm.es/pmi/sanlorenzo

THE NARROW CARRER SAN LLORENC, with its hotel of the same name, lies in the heart of Palma's old town, only a few metres from the harbour area with its picturesque streets and the Plaça Drassana, where in times gone by, ship's ropes were manufactured, hence the name. The area comes alive at night – it's a meeting place both for locals and newcomers from all over Europe.

A glimpse through the wrought-iron gate reveals the San Lorenzo's welcoming character. At the end of the 1980s, it was one of the first Mallorcan hotels to have new life breathed into its ancient walls by modern style. When it opened, it caused quite a stir: the owners' courage in opening such a hotel in the heart of Palma was much admired – conventional wisdom had it that most visitors to Mallorca prefer the beach and the sea. The (few) rooms are decorated in Provençal style. Beautiful design features, paintings by native artists and *objets d'art* reveal the originality of the owners' taste. The two rooms on the street can be rather noisy at night, so be sure to ask for a room at the back.

~

NEARBY harbour (500 m).
LOCATION in the old town
FOOD breakfast
PRICE €€€€
ROOMS 6; 4 doubles, 2 junior suites, all with bath, central heating, air conditioning, telephone, hairdryer, satellite TV, minibar
FACILITIES bar, sitting room, outdoor swimming pool
CREDIT CARDS AE, MC, V
CHILDREN welcome
DISABLED no special facilities
PETS by arrangement
CLOSED never
MANAGER Rudolf Schmid

MALLORCA

POLLENÇA

CALA SANT VICENÇ

~ SEASIDE HOTEL ~

Carrer Maressers 2, 07469 Cala Sant Vicenç/Pollença
TEL 971 53 02 50 **FAX** 0971 53 20 84
E-MAIL cala@pobox.com **WEBSITE** www.pobox.com/hotel.cala.sant.vicenç

EN ROUTE TO PUERTO POLLENÇA, few drivers notice the country road sign-posted to Cala Sant Vicenç. Follow it, and you will come upon a small, enchanted bay that has remained unspoiled by mass tourism. The road leads past a complex of holiday and weekend homes with lovely gardens, owned mainly by Mallorquins, to this fabulous spot.

There is no problem finding the hotel among the palm trees. It is painted a strong terracotta colour, and has an isolated position on a promontory. As soon as you arrive, you will notice the friendly, attentive mood radiated by the Suau family. You get views to the bay, with its surrounding cliffs, from the terraces, the rooms and the outdoor swimming pool; and it's a 300-m walk to the sea. Decoration is simple and traditional: mahogany furniture, heavy fabrics and vividly coloured bedspreads are smart and acceptable, if not very imaginative. British companies such as Hogg Robinson Travel have singled it out as a 'Best small hotel'. There are two restaurants, the Cavall Bernat (classic Mediterranean fare) and the Trattoria (Italian cuisine); in both, the food reaches a high standard.

~

NEARBY Pollença (7 km).
LOCATION off the Puerto Pollença road, on remote bay; own grounds and private car parking
FOOD breakfast, lunch, dinner
PRICE €€€-€€€€
ROOMS 38; 4 singles, 19 doubles, 15 suites, all with bath, central heating, air conditioning, telephone, hairdryer, satellite TV, minibar
FACILITIES 2 restaurants, sitting rooms, outdoor swimming pool, gym, sauna
CREDIT CARDS AE, MC, V
CHILDREN welcome
DISABLED no special facilities
PETS not accepted
CLOSED Dec and Jan
PROPRIETORS Suau family

MALLORCA

PORRERAS

SA BASSA ROTJA
~ COUNTRY HOTEL ~

Camino Sa Pedrera `Finca Son Orell', 07260 Porreras
TEL 971 168225 **FAX** 971 166563

SA BASSA ROTJA IS ON A LOVINGLY RESTORED ESTATE surrounded by vineyards and vegetable plantations, just 3 km from the typically Mallorcan village of Porreras, in the heart of the island. Plants are gradually colonizing the barren agricultural land around the hotel.

All the rooms are individually furnished and very comfortable. A fine library and delightful sitting rooms make charming places in which to while away the hours, but the hotel's high spots are definitely the recreational and therapeutic facilities. There is a large outdoor pool and a heated covered pool, as well as bicycles. As for health and well-being, put yourself in the expert, caring hands of Angela Jung, who offers Ayurvedic treatments, aromatherapy and massage.

The excellent restaurant offers Mallorcan and international dishes.

~

NEARBY Campos (10 km); Es Trenc beach nature reserve (18 km).
LOCATION 3 km from the town centre
FOOD breakfast, lunch, dinner
PRICE €€-€€€€
ROOMS 25; 10 doubles, 3 singles, 12 suites, all with bath, central heating, air conditioning, telephone, hairdryer, satellite TV, minibar, sound system
FACILITIES 2 tennis courts, heated indoor swimming pool, outdoor swimming pool, gym, therapy centre, sauna, Turkish bath, Jacuzzi, beauty salon, *boccia* playing field, archery, bicycles
CREDIT CARDS AE, MC, V
CHILDREN welcome
DISABLED good access
PETS not accepted
CLOSED never
MANAGER Guillermo Rosselló

MALLORCA

PORTALS NOUS

HOTEL BENDINAT

〜 SEASIDE HOTEL 〜

Avenida Bendinat 58, 07015 Portals Nous
TEL 971 67 57 25 **FAX** 971 67 72 76

THIS CAN CLAIM TO BE one of Mallorca's most beautiful country hotels that also has a sea view. Just before reaching it, you pass through an upmarket area of luxury villas, where prosperous Mallorcans from Palma have their summer residences. This sets the scene for the hotel's exclusive feature – its spectacular position. Built in the 1950s, it has lost none of its original charm, even after comprehensive (but careful) restoration in 1993. Plants are gradually colonizing the barren agricultural land around the hotel.

Especially good views are to be had over the sea and bay of Palma Nova from the upper storey of the main building, in which some of the 46 rooms are to be found. The original Edwardian English furnishings have been retained in the rooms; they suit the house and create an elegant ambience. Magnificent pines cast the necessary shade on the terrace, where lunch and dinner are served from May to October. Tasteful cane furniture and immaculate table linen are what you'd expect, and what you get, together with attentive service. Many Mallorcan regulars come here at the weekend for the good food.

〜

NEARBY Portals Nous; marina (2 km).
LOCATION 9 km SW of Palma; close to the sea, signposted Hotel Bendinat
FOOD breakfast, lunch, dinner
PRICE ©©©©
ROOMS 46; 38 doubles, 2 singles, 6 junior suites, all with bath, central heating, air conditioning, telephone, hairdryer, satellite TV, minibar, safe
FACILITIES restaurant, sitting rooms, outdoor swimming pool
CREDIT CARDS AE, MC, V
CHILDREN welcome
DISABLED no special facilities
PETS not accepted
CLOSED 1 Nov-1 Feb
MANAGER Bertram von Ondarza

MALLORCA

PORT D'ANDRATX

VILLA ITALIA
∾ SEASIDE HOTEL ∾

Camino de San Carlos, 13, 07157, Port d'Andratx, Mallorca
TEL 971 674011 **FAX** 971 673350
E-MAIL info@hotelvillaitalia.com **WEBSITE** www.hotelvillaitalia.com

FROM THE FAR SIDE of the bay, the hotel looks very much like a Florentine villa. It was built in the heady 1920s at the whim of an eccentric Italian multimillionaire who wanted to give his lover something more than a string of pearls.

Today Villa Italia is arguably the closest thing to Beverly Hills-on-sea. Politicians, actresses and pop stars have enjoyed a glass of champagne in its swimming pool and a stroll among the oleanders and palm trees in the gardens.

With its stucco ceilings, Portuguese marble floors, Cretonne curtains, Roman capitals and plinths, mirrors, alabaster chalices, round baths, linen sheets, lace pillows and other hand-made details it is indulgence all the way. For something extra special, if money is no object, book the royal suite.

Service is personal – everything you would expect. An elevator and a small funicular railway transport the luggage to the rooms above.

The area around Andratx (a small, low-key town) is one of the less-developed parts of the Mallorcan coast with some fine cliff-top walks, where Northern Europeans, in particular, will enjoy the specialized and varied wild flowers.

∾

NEARBY Dragonera Isle (by boat); Palma de Mallorca (22 km).
LOCATION on a slope on the south of the bay, badly signposted; garden and car parking
FOOD breakfast, lunch, dinner
PRICES €€€€
ROOMS 10 double, 6 suites, all with bath; all rooms have air conditioning, telephone, minibar, TV (satellite)
FACILITIES restaurant; terraces, swimming pool, sauna
CREDIT CARDS AE, MC, V
CHILDREN welcome
DISABLED access difficult **PETS** not accepted
CLOSED never
MANAGER Antonio Martín

MALLORCA

SON SUREDA

SON SUREDA
~ COUNTRY HOTEL ~

Carretera Manacor–Colonia de Sant Pere, 5.6km, 07500 Manacor
TEL 971 183105 **FAX** 971 183105

ABOUT SIX KILOMETRES FROM MANACOR, town of pearls, lies the 16thC *finca* of Son Sureda in the gently rolling countryside that is typical of the east of the island. It stands in grounds of some 200 hectares, surrounded by carob and almond trees, a Mediterranean forest and a botanic garden.

After extensive renovation, the rooms, some with open fireplace, have a homely, earthy character, and are ideal for families or small groups. Reclaimed olive wood has been used effectively for work surfaces in the apartments' kitchens. Walls are painted a sunny yellow and make a brilliant contrast to the rustic wooden furniture.

There are two fine swimming pools in the garden, so you won't be overcrowded as you cool off. If you like riding, this is the place for you: Spanish racehorses are bred on the estate and the owners will be pleased to tell you all about it.

~

NEARBY Manacor (6 km); Colonia Sant Pere beach (10 km).
LOCATION in own extensive grounds; ample private car parking
FOOD breakfast
PRICE €€-€€€
ROOMS 9; 5 apartments, 4 studios, all with bath, central heating, minibar
FACILITIES 2 outdoor swimming pools
CREDIT CARDS not accepted
CHILDREN welcome
DISABLED no special facilities
PETS not accepted
CLOSED never
PROPRIETOR Fernando Dameto

MALLORCA

SON TERMES

LOS NARANJOS
~ COUNTRY HOTEL ~

Cami Destre 61, 07120 Palma-Son Sardina
TEL 971 439000 **FAX** 971 438483
E-MAIL hotel-naranjos@jet.es **WEBSITE** www.hotellosnaranjos.com

YOU CAN SEE THE TERRACOTTA-COLOURED tower of the Los Naranjos estate from quite a distance – a significant landmark in its own right, and because it houses the hotel's finest set of rooms: a suite with a magnificent panorama over the valley, full of lusciously green orange trees.

This place is the dream of a German owner who has achieved a major transformation over several years. You enter through a heavy iron gate, along a narrow tree-lined road, to find an elegant, intimate country hotel, with just eight rooms, fitted out with every conceivable comfort. The interior design is Provençal rather than Mallorcan: cream-coloured sofas, armchairs, opulent fabrics, cherrywood furniture, elegant teak sunloungers with white upholstery, all bearing witness to a sophisticated design sense. The four-metre-long wooden table used for communal breakfasts and evening meals is a focal point, suiting best those guests who like a houseparty atmosphere. The food is outstanding.

~

NEARBY Palma (5 km); mountain village of Orient (15 km).
LOCATION on the Palma-Sóller country road; garden and private car parking
FOOD breakfast, picnic baskets, dinner
PRICE €€€€
ROOMS 8; 5 doubles, 3 suites, all with bath, central heating, air conditioning, telephone, hairdryer, satellite TV, CD player, minibar
FACILITIES sitting room, library, terraces, heated outdoor swimming pool, health farm, sauna, gym, solarium, massage, off-road vehicles, mountain bikes
CREDIT CARDS AE, MC, V
CHILDREN over 12 years welcome
DISABLED no special facilities
PETS not accepted
CLOSED Nov
MANAGER Danielle van Dongen

MALLORCA

VISTAMAR DE VALLDEMOSA

~ COUNTRY HOTEL ~

Carretera Andraitx km2 07170, Valldemosa, Mallorca
TEL 971 612300 **FAX** 971 612583
E-MAIL info@vistamarhotel.es **WEBSITE** www.vistamarhotel.es

VISTAMAR IS AN appropriate name for this lovely old villa set in countryside on rocky cliffs – you get tantalizing glimpses of the sea through the tangle of pines and olives in front of the hotel. Paths go some way down the cliffs; you cannot get right down to the cove from here, but then you don't really need to – the hotel has its own spectacularly positioned swimming pool, and is only minutes away from the delightful port of Valldemosa.

A stone archway leads under a balustraded balcony (impressively lit at night) into a cobbled courtyard, with the rooms of the hotel set around three sides. The atmosphere inside is of absolute calm. Rooms are beamed and have heavy wooden doors and antique furniture. Comfortable green and white sofas and chairs are dotted around the two white-walled sitting-rooms, and interesting modern art adds a splash of colour. Dinner is served either inside, or in the partly glassed-in terrace overlooking the gardens.

Bedrooms, some of which have large sun terraces, are cool and comfortable, with spotless white bathrooms, linen bedcovers and massive wooden cupboards. There are further examples of modern art along the walls of the tall corridors.

~

NEARBY Valldemosa; Bañalbufar (15 km); Deia (15 km).
LOCATION on flat olive plain, 2.5km W of Valldemosa; with garden and car parking
FOOD breakfast, lunch, dinner
PRICES €€€€
ROOMS 19 double, all with bath; all rooms have central heating, phone, TV, minibar; a few rooms have Jacuzzi
FACILITIES dining rooms, sitting rooms, bar, terrace; swimming pool
CREDIT CARDS AE, DC, MC, V
CHILDREN accepted
DISABLED access difficult
PETS not accepted
CLOSED Nov to Jan
PROPRIETOR Pedro Coll

MENORCA

CALA MORELL

BINIATRAM

~ COUNTRY HOTEL ~

Carretera Cala Morell, 07760 Ciutadella
TEL 971 383113 **FAX** 971 383113
E-MAIL biniatram@infotelecom.es **WEBSITE** www.infotelecom.es

THE *FINCA* OF BINIATRAM ALREADY HAS 500 years of history under its belt. Like many villages and farms on the island beginning with 'Bini' (meaning 'sister of'), its name has its origins in Arabic and, therefore, of the Moorish occupation of southern Spain in the early Middle Ages – of which there are plenty of traces on all the Balearic islands.

This is a small 'farm' hotel, only a kilometre from the beautiful but crowded bay of Cala Morell, and it makes a pleasant, cool spot at the height of summer. The few rooms are simply decorated in country style, with a minimum of fuss and certainly no superfluous ornaments – which would not suit the style of the owners, who still farm the land, and are proud to do so. As a result, the atmosphere is homely, welcoming and relaxed. In the annexe, a fine room has been converted for celebrations, seminars and other events, also decorated in rustic style. The large kidney-shaped pool in the grounds is a refreshing oasis.

~

NEARBY Cala Morell (1 km); Ciutadella (4 km).
LOCATION on the country road to Cala Morell; garden and private car parking
FOOD breakfast
PRICE ⓔⓔ
ROOMS 6; 4 doubles, 1 apartment with bedroom, 1 apartment with 2 bedrooms, all with bath, hairdryer
FACILITIES outdoor swimming pool, tennis court
CREDIT CARDS MC, V
CHILDREN welcome
DISABLED no special facilities
PETS by agreement
CLOSED one week in winter (enquire when booking)
PROPRIETORS Esperança Juaneda Benejam and Joan Tomás Bagur

MENORCA

SANT IGNASI

~ COUNTRY HOTEL ~

Carretera Cala Morell, 07760 Ciutadella
TEL 971 385575 **FAX** 971 480537
WEBSITE www.santignasi.com

THE ROAD TO THIS FORMER *FINCA*, dating from 1777, leads past cultivated farmland and stables; it's a flat, sparse landscape, but in it is an oasis of evergreen oaks and palm trees, among which is hidden Sant Ignasi's ochre-yellow building, with its 20 rooms. The ten rooms on the *finca's* ground floor have access to a small private garden, where guests can breakfast in peace and enjoy a relaxed start to the day. Decoration of the public rooms, and the cosy bedrooms, is stylish and traditional. The restaurant spoils you with delicious Mediterranean food. An annexe close by offers a sauna, spacious terraces and a fine swimming pool.

The pretty harbour town of Ciutadella, only three kilometres away, has great shopping, cute little alleyways and the imposing Plaça Conquistador. Ferries leave the harbour for Mallorca (Cala Rajada, 90 minutes) and other destinations.

~

NEARBY Ciutadella (3 km); Cala Morell beach (3 km).
LOCATION northern outskirts of Ciutadella
FOOD breakfast, lunch, dinner
PRICE ©©©©-©©©©
ROOMS 20; 18 doubles, 2 junior suites, all with bath, central heating, air conditioning, telephone, hairdryer, satellite TV, minibar
FACILITIES restaurant, sitting room, bar, outdoor swimming pool, sauna
CREDIT CARDS MC, V
CHILDREN welcome
DISABLED no special facilities
PETS not accepted
CLOSED early Dec-early Jan
PROPRIETOR Pedro Mayans

MENORCA

SON TRIAY NOU
~ COUNTRY HOTEL ~

Carretera Cala Galdana 3, 07750 Ferreries
TEL 971 155078 **FAX** 971 360446

THE ROAD TO THE SON TRIAY NOU ESTATE is littered with sticks and stones, and runs past an endless dry-stone wall; but your journey will be brightened by the intense terracotta colour of the building, which comes into view from quite a distance.

There are just three guest rooms in the house, and a generously sized apartment in the annexe; so this really is a small hotel and an informal stay is guaranteed. The owners don't want to increase the accommodation with further conversions of estate buildings.

The elegant house looks more like a town villa than a farm, but farming is still practised here with all that that entails, including pigs and poultry. You'll have to get used to the strong country smells, but by the end of the first night we believe that you will have learned to cherish the special atmosphere of these simply furnished rooms. Enjoy the unique peace and quiet of the *finca* by the poolside or on a sunlounger: a real Menorcan idyll.

~

NEARBY Ferreries (3 km).
LOCATION open country; own grounds and car parking
FOOD breakfast, lunch, dinner
PRICE €€€-€€€€
ROOMS 4; 3 doubles, 1 apartment, all with bath, central heating, satellite TV
FACILITIES sitting room, outdoor swimming pool
CREDIT CARDS not accepted
CHILDREN welcome
DISABLED no special facilities
PETS not accepted
CLOSED never
PROPRIETOR Socorro Moisy

MENORCA

ALCAUFAR VELL

~ COUNTRY HOTEL ~

Carretera Cala Alcaufar, km 7.3, 07710 Sant Lluis
TEL 971 151874 **FAX** 971 151492
E-MAIL info@alcaufarvell.com **WEBSITE** www.alcaufarvell.com

THE MAGNIFICENT ALCAUFAR ESTATE, near Sant Lluis in the south-east of Menorca, is mentioned in local records as early as the 15th century. The changes that have affected other Balearic properties over the past few decades have to some extent passed Alcaufar by: agriculture and dairy farming still go on here, making it a great place for an authentic farm holiday.

Guests are lodged in the four rooms of the main house, where old family photos cover the walls. These, and tarnished mirrors, along with antique furniture (including wonderful *chaises longues* and fine mahogany beds) provide a glimpse into domestic life gone by on a Menorcan farming estate.

At 150 hectares, this is one of Menorca's largest estates. There's good walking and cycling on tracks through fields bounded by dry-stone walls, and the *finca* also owns a kilometre of coast, with one of the most beautiful sandy beaches on Menorca and crystal clear water. You can hire windsurfers (with tuition) or ride the horses.

~

NEARBY Mahó (6 km); Punta Prima beach (3 km).
LOCATION in open country; own grounds and car parking
FOOD breakfast; lunch and dinneron request
PRICE €€-€€€
ROOMS 4; 2 doubles, 2 junior suites, all with bath, hairdryer, satellite TV
FACILITIES room with open hearth
CREDIT CARDS MC, V
CHILDREN welcome
DISABLED no special facilities
PETS not accepted
CLOSED never
PROPRIETORS Maria Angeles and son Jaume de Olives

MENORCA

SANT LLUIS

BINIDALI
∼ COUNTRY HOTEL ∼

Carrer Suestra 50, 07710 Sant Lluis-Biniali
TEL 971 151724; 971 354128 **FAX** 971 150352

YOU APPROACH THIS HOTEL from Mahó via Sant Lluis along a charmingly Menorcan country road lined with an old dry-stone wall. (Sant Lluis is one of only seven villages on Menorca: only Ciutadella and Mahó count as towns.) The pretty building, surrounded by imposing palm trees, is in delightful countryside, but if you are expecting local design flair, think again. The owners, originally from Greece and Holland, can't do enough for their guests and have skilfully blended their own lifestyle with the layout of the house and the needs of guests. (Besides Greek and Dutch, English, Spanish and German are spoken here.)

Bedrooms are simply and tastefully furnished and decorated, and all have a bathroom. Some of the rooms have a generous terrace. From the large swimming pool you have a view to the sea. The cooking focuses on good, but plain and simple fare, and they'll prepare you a special dinner (or in summer a barbecue) on request. Both half and full-board are available.

∼

NEARBY Cap de Font beach/bay (4 km).
LOCATION on the country road 2 km from Sant Lluis in direction of Climent; garden and car parking
FOOD breakfast, lunch, dinner
PRICE €€-€€€
ROOMS 11 doubles, all with bath, telephone
FACILITIES sitting room, outdoor swimming pool
CREDIT CARDS AE. MC, V
CHILDREN welcome
DISABLED no special facilities
PETS not accepted
CLOSED 1 Nov-28 Feb
PROPRIETOR Konstantinos Costas

MENORCA

SANT LLUIS

BINIARROCA

~ COUNTRY HOTEL ~

Carretera Es Castell-Sant Lluis, 07710 Sant Lluis
TEL 971 150059 **FAX** 971 151250
E-MAIL hotel@biniarroca.com

THIS ROMANTIC COUNTRY HOTEL, a former 16thC estate comprising several buildings, lies in the triangle formed by the capital, Mahó, and the villages of Es Castell and Sant Lluis to its south. It's a typically Menorcan landscape, with dry-stone walls snaking their way through gently rolling countryside and edging the narrow lanes; the technique used for the walls' construction was brought to the Balearics by the Moors.

The property glistens like snow in the sun, its window frames and doors lacquered an aristocratic green. The entrance hall is decorated with opulent hangings, and on the walls there are flower paintings in oils by Lindsay Mullen that recall the French Impressionists, and which communicate the spiritual quality of the landscape. Rooms vary in size and decoration, but all have been individually and lovingly designed in a style reflecting the English charm of the owner, Sheila Ratliff. She creates an easy-going atmosphere that should enhance your time here.

The large pool and the sheltered pergola on the surrounding terrace are ideal for relaxation.

~

NEARBY Sant Lluis (3 km).
LOCATION well signposted on the Es Castell-Sant Lluis country road; own grounds and car parking
FOOD breakfast; lunch and dinner on request
PRICE €€€-€€€€
ROOMS 15 doubles and suites, all with bath, central heating, air conditioning, telephone, hairdryer, satellite TV
FACILITIES restaurant, sitting rooms, library, bar, 2 pools
CREDIT CARDS AE, MC, V
CHILDREN welcome
DISABLED no special facilities **PETS** not accepted
CLOSED Nov-Feb
PROPRIETOR Sheila Ratliff

IBIZA

IBIZA TOWN

LA TORRE DEL CANONIGO

~ TOWN HOTEL ~

Calle Mayor 8, Dalt Vila, 078001 Ibiza
TEL 971 303884 **FAX** 971 307843
WEBSITE www.elcanonigo.com

THIS HOTEL HAS BEEN CARVED OUT OF A 14TH-CENTURY tower in Ibiza's upper town, but the harbour and the old town, the *Casco Antiguo*, with its many boutiques, bars and restaurants, are still accessible from here. The climb back up at night may not be for everyone; however, hotel guests are given a key to open the barrier that protects the old town from excessive traffic – so you can take your car up.

It's a charming place, with impressive old masonry everywhere, and well maintained. The eight suites come in various sizes, hence the wide range of prices. Some have the advantage of a terrace with a view over the old town, others overlook the courtyard. The largest are big enough for four and have a separate kitchen. The furnishings are rustic-influenced: lacquered iron beds with canopy and fine bed linen, and pretty decorative objects. There's a bar and a sitting room where drinks are served. Perhaps the most remarkable feature is the peace and quiet. Staff are attentive.

~

NEARBY centre and harbour (1 km).
LOCATION Ibiza's old town; street parking nearby
FOOD breakfast
PRICE €€€
ROOMS 8 suites, all with bath, central heating, air conditioning, telephone, satellite TV, minibar
FACILITIES sitting rooms, gym, sauna
CREDIT CARDS AE, MC, DC, V
CHILDREN welcome
DISABLED no special facilities
PETS accepted
CLOSED never
PROPRIETOR Javier Barcalzar

IBIZA

SANTA EULALIA DEL RIO

LES TERRASSES

~ COUNTRY HOTEL ~

Apartado 1235, Carretera de S. Eulàlia – km 1, 07800 Santa Eulàlia del Río, Ibiza
TEL 971 332643 **FAX** 971 338978
E-MAIL lesterrasses@internetou.com **WEBSITE** lesterrasses.net

A VIVID COBALT BLUE ROCK 1 km south of Santa Eulàlia, marks the country track which leads up to this enchanting *finca*. Without losing the simplicity of its farmhouse origins, Françoise Pialoux, who is French, has embellished Les Terrasses with great panache. Everyday items, such as a jar of preserved fruit, a plant pot or an ironwork chair are perfectly placed, wall colours are exquisite. As the name suggests, the main house, bedrooms (in a separate building) and gardens are on different terraced levels. So are the two secluded swimming pools. Crisp, white bedlinen in the plainly furnished bedrooms is offset by walls painted in hues of ochre, blue or pink; recessed baths and tiled shower areas, which form an integral part of the rooms, suggest an exotic, North African influence. Meals are taken outside on the main terrace, or in the yellow dining room. On some evenings couscous dishes are served.

Hammocks, padded benches, sofas, tables and chairs adorn the many unexpected little patios, shady nooks and peaceful courtyards. They make enticing spots in which to while away a lazy afternoon; more than anything they endorse the private villa atmosphere.

~

NEARBY Santa Eulàlia del Río (3 km), Ibitha Town (Eivissa) (9 km).
LOCATION between Ibitha Town (Eivissa) and Santa Eulàlia; large gardens, ample car parking
FOOD breakfast, lunch, dinner
PRICES €€€€
ROOMS 9 double, all with bath, phone, minibar, air conditioning
FACILITIES sitting room, dining room, breakfast room, garden; two swimming pools, tennis
CREDIT CARDS V
CHILDREN welcome
DISABLED not suitable **PETS** accepted
CLOSED 15 Nov to 20 Dec
PROPRIETOR Françoise Pialoux

IBIZA

SANTA EULARIA

CA'N CURREU
~ COUNTRY HOTEL ~

Carretera Sant Carles, km 12, 07850 Santa Eularia
TEL 971 335280 **FAX** 971 335280
E-MAIL hotel@cancurreu.com **WEBSITE** www.cancurreu.com

T HIS TYPICALLY IBIZAN *FINCA* lies in the heart of the island, surrounded by fig and orange trees, a mere 20-minute drive from Ibiza Town and a kilometre outside the picturesque little village of Sant Carles. Gleaming, whitewashed exterior walls are clothed in bougainvillea.

Inside, there are just five suites and two double rooms, all luxuriously fitted out, even with a kitchen. The design is typically 'Ibizan minimalist' – warm terracotta floor tiles, old wooden beams, white walls and bed linen – which exposes and emphasizes the building's structure instead of covering it up with kitsch. You probably won't use your kitchen much: the restaurant is the domain of one the finest chefs on the island, Carlos Posadas, highly regarded for his elegant, international dishes. The wine list is superb, too. A wonderful haven of peace and quiet on an otherwise busy holiday island.

~

NEARBY Cala Boix beach (2 km).
LOCATION on country road between Ibiza Town and Sant Carles; in garden with private car parking
FOOD breakfast; lunch and dinner on request
PRICE €€€€
ROOMS 7; 2 doubles, 5 suites, all with bath, central heating, air conditioning, telephone, hairdryer, satellite TV, minibar, safe
FACILITIES restaurant, sitting room, outdoor swimming pool, sauna, Jacuzzi, gym, solarium, horse riding
CREDIT CARDS MC, V
CHILDREN welcome
DISABLED no special facilities
PETS not accepted
CLOSED never
PROPRIETOR Vicente Mari Tur

IBIZA

SANTA GERTRUDIS

CA'S GASI
~ COUNTRY HOTEL ~

Cami Vell a Sant Mateu, 07814 Santa Gertrudis
TEL 971 197700 **FAX** 971 197899
E-MAIL casgasi@steinweb.net **WEBSITE** www.casgasi.com

A S SOON AS YOU SET FOOT IN CA'S GASI, you'll be bewitched by the scents wafting in from the surrounding land. The hotel is run by Margarete Martin von Korff, born in Barcelona but a citizen of the world - she worked for Lufthansa and spent four years going round the world on a boat. She puts a very personal stamp on it all, but it was never her ambition to run a hotel – opening up just seemed the obvious thing to do because the estate is so large. Guests get all the freedom and space they could need. There is no pressure, but whoever feels like it is welcome to participate in the preparation of meals and the everday running of the hotel.

The elegant rooms are discretely furnished in a blend of country-house and oriental style. Shrimp-pink Venetian stucco gleams on the bathroom walls and Moroccan tiles decorate the fittings. Guests gather in a wonderful sitting room with an open fire for unforced get-togethers. Vegetables for the exquisite food are grown organically in the *finca's* garden. Another oasis of peace on this busy island.

~

NEARBY Santa Gertrudis (3 km).
LOCATION in open country; garden and own car parking
FOOD breakfast, lunch, dinner
PRICE ©©©©
ROOMS 11; 9 doubles, 2 suites, all with bath, central heating, air conditioning, telephone, hairdryer, satellite TV, minibar
FACILITIES restaurant, sitting rooms, outdoor swimming pool
CREDIT CARDS AE, MC, V
CHILDREN welcome
DISABLED no special facilities
PETS not accepted
CLOSED never
PROPRIETOR Margarete Martin von Korff

IBIZA

SANT MIGUEL

CA'S PLA
~ COUNTRY HOTEL ~

Apartado 777, Sant Miguel, 07800 Ibiza
TEL 971 334587 **FAX** 971 334603
E-MAIL hotel@caspla-ibiza.com

IBIZA TOWN IS ONE OF THE liveliest centres of the Balearic Islands; the old town in particular is a Mecca for nightbirds, voyeurs and tourists. Staying up until dawn and spending the day asleep on the beach is many people's object here, but for those who want to do exactly the opposite, there are a few hidden havens of peace and quiet; Ca's Pla is one of them.

It's a real gem: a former *finca* standing on a hill only a few metres from the beach and harbour of Sant Miguel, and surrounded by gnarled old pines, olives and carob trees. The Spanish style of decoration of the generous rooms is discretely highlighted with antiques, pictures and *objets d'art*. The bedrooms are painted in light colours and have a Mediterranean feel. There's a huge pool, surrounded by palm trees.

~

NEARBY Sant Miguel harbour (2 km).
LOCATION on country road heading towards Sant Miguel from Ibiza Town; garden and own car parking
FOOD breakfast; lunch and dinner on request
PRICE €€€-€€€€
ROOMS 16; 4 doubles, 9 junior suites, 3 suites, all with bath, central heating, air conditioning, telephone, hairdryer, satellite TV, safe
FACILITIES restaurant, sitting room, bar, outdoor swimming pool, tennis court, bicycles, riding
CREDIT CARDS MC, V
CHILDREN welcome
DISABLED no special facilities
PETS small dogs by arrangement
CLOSED 1 Nov-1 Mar
PROPRIETOR Rosa Maria Natalia Sanchez

IBIZA

HOTEL HACIENDA NA XAMENA
~ CLIFFTOP HOTEL ~

Na Xamena, San Miguel, Ibiza 07800
TEL 971 334605 **FAX** 971 334606
WEBSITE www.hotelhacienda-ibiza.com

REACHED BY ONE of the prettiest lanes on Ibiza, Hotel Hacienda also enjoys one of the most fortunate locations on the island, and is surrounded by crags and pine woods. The terrace around a large, curvacious swimming pool hangs over a spectacular, rocky cove which is accessible only by a scramble. (There are two others – one, indoor and heated.) The hotel is built in bright, white Ibizenco style, complemented by natural materials such as rocks and shady palm fronds, with many arches and rounded corners, and is arranged around a central patio. Solid chunks of wood and massive wooden beams create an impressive effect in the bar area. Bedrooms are downstairs, and each has a terrace or balcony (except for single rooms) and magnificent views. Some have whirlpool baths situated beside enormous windows which directly overlook the sea. The poolside restaurant, Las Cascadas, is ideal for watching the sun go down while dining, and has an enviable local reputation. El Sueno de Estrellas, the other restaurant, is more intimate, and decorated in Arab style.

A luxurious and secluded place in which to take refuge from the tourist traps of Ibiza. The native flora and fauna can be discovered through guided hiking tours into the surrounding hills.

~

NEARBY Can Marça cave; Ibiza (23 km).
LOCATION a left turning before the port of San Miguel; car parking
FOOD breakfast, lunch, dinner
PRICES €€€€
ROOMS 37 double, 5 single, 10 suites; all rooms have central heating, air conditioning, telephone, minibar, TV
FACILITIES 2 restaurants, bar; discotheque; 3 swimming pools (one heated), steam room, sauna, tennis court, mountain bikes, spa
CREDIT CARDS AE, DC, MC, V
CHILDREN welcome **DISABLED** access possible **PETS** not accepted
CLOSED end Oct-Apr
MANAGER Sabine Lipszyc

GRAN CANARIA

SAN MATEO

LAS CALAS
∼ COUNTRY HOTEL ∼

Elarenal 36, La Lechuza 35320 San Mateo, Gran Canaria
TEL 928 661436 **FAX** 928 660753
E-MAIL Informacion@lascalas.net **WEBSITE** www.lascalas.net

REMEMBERING THIS guesthouse a few days after leaving, several things had particularly stuck in the mind: the dusty pink dining room; the spray of flowers around the tables outside; the high ceilings and the dark wooden beams. It may not have the most stylish interior decoration and the building is low and square; but it has a wonderful traditional atmosphere, warm hosts and offers excellent value – even for the suite with its spa bath. The gastronomic weekends can be fun: you'll discover dishes such as *escudella i carn d'olla* (stew made with vegetables, rice, noodles and potatoes), or the delicious *postre del musico* (dessert with pine-kernels and raisins). Furniture is nicely worn and eclectically chosen, and there is a large collection of traditional blue and white pottery on the walls of the main salon. It's located in a tiny, peaceful hamlet, far away from the hustle of Gran Canaria's beaches. Walking and riding opportunities abound.

∼

NEARBY San Mateo, Tejeda.
LOCATION just outside hamlet of La Lechuza in own grounds with limited private car parking
ROOMS 7; 6 doubles, 1 suite; all rooms have bath, phone, TV, hairdrier
PRICES €€
CREDIT CARDS AE, DC, MC, V
FACILITIES sitting room, dining room, bar, solarium, garden
CHILDREN welcome
PETS accepted
DISABLED no specially adapted rooms
CLOSED never
PROPRIETOR Magüi Carratalá

GRAN CANARIA

HACIENDA DEANZO

~ COUNTRY GUESTHOUSE ~

Prolongación Pablo Díaz 37 35460, Gáldar, Gran Canaria
TEL 928 551655 **FAX** 928 551244
E-MAIL haciendadeanzo@haciendadeanzo.com **WEBSITE** www.haciendadeanzo.com

THEIR CHARMINGLY homespun website should give you some idea of the welcome you will receive at this guesthouse – genuine, down-to-earth, nothing too much trouble. The bright, modern-looking building seemed a little off-putting on arrival, but once inside we found a cheerful home, renovated by artist Facundo Fierro, with beautiful gardens. The food is hearty Spanish fare. Try their *cocido con judias blancas* (a regional sausage) or *zarzuela* (cuttlefish, mussels and prawns). Bedrooms are well sized, if a little too sterile – those white wall-mounted hairdryers in the bathrooms always make us feel we are getting mass-produced hospitality, but do not put off their many regular visitors, who are drawn by the views, the peaceful surroundings and the hospitality. The hotel is remote, and on an island where many visitors are drawn to the coastline, which is no doubt why the owners also need to attract conferences. These are held in their cave at the *hacienda* (a remarkable space literally hewn out of the rock face) so you may want to check any big group bookings before you arrive.

~

NEARBY Galdar, Sardina Beach, Las Palmas de Gran Canaria.
LOCATION North Gran Canaria, in valley of Anzo de Galdar; in own grounds with ample car parking
FOOD breakfast, lunch, dinner
PRICE €
ROOMS 8 doubles; all have bath, phone, TV, hairdryer, safe
CREDIT CARDS MC, V
FACILITIES bar, summer sitting room, garden, swimming pool
CHILDREN welcome
DISABLED no specially adapted rooms
PETS accepted
CLOSED never
PROPRIETOR Facundo Fierro

GRAN CANARIA

TENTENIGUADA

RELAIS EL PINAR

～ COUNTRY GUESTHOUSE ～

Carretera General s/n. Tenteniguada 352117 Valsequillo
TEL 928 705239 **FAX** 928 570946
WEBSITE www.hotelruralelpinar.com

A N UNUSUAL BLACK and white exterior makes this guesthouse seem curiously un-Spanish; in fact it's the reverse. Surrounded on all sides by pine trees, this was the (very large) home of the Carmen family until a few years ago, when they decided to open up nine rooms and take in guests. A beautiful corridor with arched windows runs alongside the bedrooms, giving the place a romantic, Moorish atmosphere. Things can get a little clunky and old-fashioned at times - the black and white walls in the dining room may be somewhat disconcerting - and solid wooden beams in the bedrooms are complemented by equally heavy wooden bedsteads. But the house has a charm and character all its own, and if you fall in love with its idiosyncrasies, you may well want to return. Surrounding the pool and lovely gardens are a further 100 acres of private land in the beautiful Tenteniguada valley, full of butterflies and birds, so take your walking boots.

～

NEARBY Las Palmas, Agaete.
LOCATION in the Tenteniguada valley in own large grounds with private car parking
ROOMS 9 doubles; all rooms have bath, phone, TV, hairdrier
PRICE €€
FACILITIES dining room, garden, swimming pool
CHILDREN welcome
DISABLED no specially adapted rooms
PETS accepted
CLOSED mid Jun to mid Jul
PROPRIETOR Carmen family

LANZAROTE

MOZAGA

CASERIO DE MOZAGA

~ VILLAGE HOTEL ~

Mozaga, 8, 35562 San Bartolomé, Lanzarote
TEL 928 520060 **FAX** 928 522029
E-MAIL reservas@caseriodemozaga.com **WEBSITE** www.caseriodemozaga.com

GONZALO BETHENCOURT'S 200-year-old *finca* is just the place to savour some of the oddities that make Lanzarote an island like no other. The farmhouse – painted the island's regulation white and green – sits in a scruffy, windswept, inland village, a world away from the seaside resorts. In an adjacent field, Gonzalo grows palms and drago plants in soil covered in picûn, a grey volcanic gravel used by locals to keep the earth underneath moist. More ancient methods of dealing with the island's scarcity of water are evident in a rock terrace incised with rivulets to catch the infrequent rain, and a traditional water purifier in the form of a chunk of lava rock set over an old urn.

Most bedrooms are set around a pretty geranium-decorated courtyard centred on an old well. Rugs on wooden floors, shutters and country antiques such as a chunky washstand or potty cabinet imbue them with lots of character. This is very much a place where you feel part of a home. Breakfasts (generous buffets) and dinners (set meals featuring local vegetables and fresh fish) are eaten at one large table, together with other guests and maybe Gonzalo – who speaks good English – and his sister Maria Luisa.

~

NEARBY La Casa Museo del Campesino (1 km); Teguise (8 km); Fundaciûn Cèsar Manrique (11 km).
LOCATION on the edge of the village; ample parking
FOOD breakfast,lunch, dinner
PRICES €€€€-€€€€€
ROOMS 5 double, 1 single, 2 suites, all with bath; all rooms have TV, phone, minibar
FACILITIES sitting room, dining room, hairdrier, modem point
CREDIT CARDS AE, DC, M, V
CHILDREN welcome
DISABLED most rooms on ground floor **PETS** not accepted
CLOSED never
PROPRIETOR Gonzalo Rodrigues Bèthencourt

LANZAROTE

YAIZA

FINCA DE LAS SALINAS
~ VILLAGE HOTEL ~

Calle La Cuesta, 17, 35570, Yaiza, Lanzarote
TEL 928 830325 **FAX** 928 830329
E-MAIL fincasalinas@hotmail.com **WEBSITE** www.fincasalinas.com

CESAR MANRIQUE, the artist/architect who ensured that Lanzarote should be largely spared from ugly tourist development, would surely have approved of the bold, classy conversion of this 18thC *finca*. Public areas are ranged around the little mansion – a Moorish folly of a building, with low, castellated turrets. Its two patios – one still open to the elements with palms sprouting skywards – have been turned into stylish sitting areas, decked out with modern art and white-cushioned wicker armchairs. Appropriately, the room where grapes were once crushed (the old machinery has been retained) now serves as the bar. Most bedrooms lie in the former stable block. They are modern rustic in design, with washed blue, yellow or lime green walls, wrought-iron beds, wacky bedside lamps and stainless steel bathroom sinks set into glass tops. Each has a private terrace, enclosed by lava walls, and overlooks a slick swimming pool surrounded by a boarded deck.

The pretty village of Yaiza stands right on the edge of Lanzarote's malpais or volcanic badlands. The island's most charming restaurant, La Era, converted (by Manrique) from another old farmhouse, is a short walk down the road from the hotel.

~

NEARBY Parque Nacional de Timanfaya (19 km); resorts of Puerto del Carmen and Playa Blanca (15 km).
LOCATION on the edge of the village; ample parking
FOOD breakfast, dinner
PRICES €€€€-€€€€€
ROOMS 17 double, 2 suites, all with bath; all rooms have central heating, TV (satellite), radio, phone, air conditioning, minibar
FACILITIES bar, sitting room, dining room, swimming pool, games room, tennis, gym, sauna
CREDIT CARDS AE, DC, M, V **CHILDREN** accepted, but no child discounts
DISABLED all bedrooms on ground floor, but none adapted **PETS** not accepted
CLOSED never **PROPRIETOR** Maria Carmen Lleo

LA PALMA

HOTEL AMBERES

~ TOWN HOTEL ~

General Street Franco 13 38760, Level 1 Aridane, La Palma
TEL 922 401040 **FAX** 922 402441
WEBSITE www.hotelesconsecreto.com

THIS CORNER OF THE CANARIES is steeped in history, and the village of Llanos, in the Aridane Valley, has plenty of fine old squares, buildings and churches. The hotel is a perfectly restored 17thC patrician house, and the husband and wife team who run it have filled it with paintings and a host of items from their travels. The cooking draws heavily on fresh local produce, and, as the Valle de Aridane forms the largest cultivated area of banana and avocado on the islands, expect some pretty incredible salads and sauces. Breakfasts are served outside, in the patio courtyard. You will also find a lovely fountain and walled garden – be sure to ask for a bedroom with one of the traditional dark wood and tile balconies that look out on to this peaceful space. We think that the food slightly outweighs the accommodation. Not an expensive place, but well run, offering charm and value for money.

~

NEARBY Santa Cruz.
LOCATION in village centre; free car parking 5 minutes from hotel
ROOMS 7; 3 doubles, 1 single, 3 suites; all rooms have bath, TV, phone, hairdryer
FOOD breakfast, lunch, dinner
PRICES €€-€€€
CREDIT CARDS MC, V
FACILITIES garden, sauna
CHILDREN welcomed
PETS accepted
DISABLED no specially adapted rooms
CLOSED never
PROPRIETOR Engelina and Joseph Van Den Bogaert

TENERIFE

SAN ROQUE

~ SEASIDE VILLAGE HOTEL ~

Calle Esteban de Ponte, 32, 38450, Garachico, Tenerife
TEL 922 133435 **FAX** 922 133406
E-MAIL info@hotelsanroque.com **WEBSITE** www.hotelsanroque.com

HANDS-ON OWNERS Dominique Carayon, a Frenchman, and his Spanish wife Laly have created nothing less than a *tour de force* of modernist elegance, wrapped up in a grand 17thC mansion. Set around two wooden-galleried patios (one containing the swimming pool), the building itself is a treat, with walls painted a rich russet, and floors of honey-coloured Canarian pine. But the eye is drawn to the startling modern art – say the giant steel sculpture of a grasshopper in the main patio – and the many pieces of original Bauhaus furniture, copied under licence. With their pitched roofs, more beautiful wood floors, interesting art and furniture, bedrooms are as stylish as the rest of the enterprise. They also come with indulgent mod-cons, such as CD and video players. Don't be put off if it all sounds intimidatingly swanky: the Carayons ensure that the atmosphere is thoroughly easy-going.

In the evening, modern jazz wafts through the candlelit patios, and Laly's set dinners are served at the poolside (if breakfasts are anything to go by, they should be top-notch). But there is no pressure to eat in. Little Garachico – a beguiling, ancient seaside backwater that was once Tenerife's most important port – has half-a-dozen fish restaurants to choose from.

~

NEARBY Puerto de la Cruz (26km); Parque Nacional del Tiede (57km).
LOCATION on quiet back street near the village centre; easy street parking
FOOD breakfast, lunch, dinner
PRICES €€€€,
ROOMS 16 double, 4 suites, all with bath; all have central heating, TV (satellite), phone, air conditioning, minibar, Jacuzzis
FACILITIES sitting room, swimming pool, sauna, fishing rods and mountain bikes for hire, tennis courts (100m), golf
CREDIT CARDS AE, DC, M, V
CHILDREN welcome **DISABLED** no special facilities **PETS** accepted
CLOSED never **PROPRIETORS** Laly and Dominique Carayon

TENERIFE

PT CANADAS DEL TEIDE
~ MODERN PARADOR ~

Las Cañadas del Tiede, 38300 La Orotava, Tenerife
TEL 922 386415 **FAX** 922 382352
E-MAIL canadasdelteide@parador.es **WEBSITE** www.parador.es

THIS PARADOR has arguably the most extraordinary location of any hotel in Spain. The only proper building for miles around, it stands within an enormous volcanic crater – a bizarre jumble of chocolate-brown and red rubble and weirdly-shaped rocks – and towering over it is the cone of Mount Tiede, Spain's highest peak. The hotel is most enjoyable when the day-trippers who descend on its cafeteria and park information centre have departed. Come evening, the setting sun turns the landscape a deep orange, and at night the clear air reveals a firmament of a thousand stars.

Styled as a plush mountain chalet, the parador has recently undergone a much-needed revamp. Bedrooms (try to bag one with a view of Mount Tiede) are very comfortable and understated, with Canarian pine floors, dark wood furniture, and swish marble bathrooms. Spacious, open-plan public areas capitalise on the views, and feature a large selection of prints showing Tenerife's stunning scenery. Expect good food, in the form of mammoth buffet breakfasts, and hearty dinners that concentrate on Canarian specialities such as rabbit and goat stews. To work up an appetite, you can follow two circular walks through the crater that start from the hotel's front door.

~

NEARBY cable car up Mount Tiede (3 km); La Orotava (42 km).
LOCATION in heart of national park; with car park
FOOD breakfast, lunch, dinner
PRICES €€€€
ROOMS 34 double, 1 single, 2 suites, all with bath; all rooms have central heating, TV (satellite), phone, minibar
FACILITIES bar, sitting room, dining room, cafeteria, heated indoor swimming pool, gym, sauna
CREDIT CARDS AE, DC, M, V
CHILDREN welcome
DISABLED lift/elevator; one bedroom adapted **PETS** not accepted
CLOSED never **MANAGER** Jesus Garrido Pozo

La Palma/Ibiza

La Palma Romantica

SEASIDE HOTEL

Las Llanadas s/n, 38726
Barlovento,
La Palma
TEL 922 186221 FAX 922 186400
E-MAIL *reservas@hotellpalma*
romantica.com
FOOD breakfast, lunch, dinner
PRICES €€
CLOSED please enquire
PROPRIETORS Juan and Erika Rodríguez

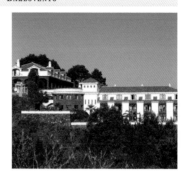

GREAT SEA VIEWS from the northern tip of La Palma is perhaps the main selling point of this reliable but conventional place.

The handsome building has around 40 rooms, outside our usual size limit, but there's peace, dedicated husband and wife owners, and plenty of facilities including gym, tennis court, bowling, indoor and outdoor pools, and play area for small children. Useful choice for a family holiday.

El Palacio

TOWN HOTEL

Calle de la Conquista, 2, Ibiza,
Baleares
TEL 971 301478 FAX 971 391581
FOOD breakfast, snacks
PRICES €€
CLOSED Sep-April
PROPRIETOR Mme Marlise Etienne

THE HOTEL OF THE Movie Stars', El Palacio is a Mecca for film buffs. Every room is named after a legendary Hollywood star. A recent reporter noted superb bedroom views, white leather sofas and antique furniture. It is a converted mansion in the city's old quarter (peaceful, but five minutes' walk from the nightlife), decorated throughout with posters, photographs and movie memorabilia, including the only award James Dean received in his lifetime. The hotel's brochure describes not only every room, but also gives the biographies of the eponymous stars and the history of the objects on display. A small pond and a trickling fountain create a tranquil atmosphere in the courtyard garden.

HOTEL NAMES

Hotels are arranged in order of the most distinctive part of their name; other parts of the name are also given, except that very common prefixes such as 'Hotel' and 'La' are omitted. The abbreviation PT is used for Parador de Turismo de España (see Introduction for further explanation). Hotels covered in the several Area introductions, and in the feature boxes on Paradores, are not indexed.

HOTEL NAMES

HOTEL NAMES

HOTEL NAMES

D

E

Hotel Names

HOTEL NAMES

HOTEL NAMES

N

O

P

Hotel Names

HOTEL NAMES

R

S

HOTEL NAMES

HOTEL LOCATIONS

In this index, hotels are arranged by the name of the city, town or village they are in or near. Where a hotel is located in a very small place, it may be indexed under a nearby place which is more easily found on maps. The abbreviation PT is used for Parador de Turismo de España (see Introduction for further explanation).

A

Hotel Locations

B

C

HOTEL LOCATIONS

D

E

Hotel Locations

HOTEL LOCATIONS

H

I

J

L

Hotel Locations

M

N

O

HOTEL LOCATIONS

Hotel Locations

S

HOTEL LOCATIONS

HOTEL LOCATIONS

HOTEL LOCATIONS

X

Y

Z